# LAST IN LINE

On the road and out of work...a desperate
journey with Canada's unemployed ■

## BY ALAN METTRICK

KEY PORTER·BOOKS

**Canadian Cataloguing in Publication Data**

Mettrick, Alan.
  Last in line

ISBN 0-919493-72-6

1. Poor - Canada.  2. Unemployed - Canada.
3. Canada - Social conditions - 1971-
I. Title.

HC120.P6M48   1985        305.5'69'0971        C85-099455-1

Key Porter Books Limited
70 The Esplanade
Toronto, Ontario
Canada M5E 1R2

Cover Photograph: Brian Smale
Cover Design: Atlanta
Design: Joanna Gertler
Typesetting: Compeer Typographic Services Limited
Printing and Binding: Imprimerie Gagné Ltée.
Printed and bound in Canada

85 86 87 88  6 5 4 3 2 1

# LAST IN LINE

for
TIM and PAIGE

# Prologue

He didn't recognize me when I first stood in the door to his hotel room. He wouldn't have recognized his mother. He lay on top of the bedsheets, looking at me, but stupefied from booze and God knows what drugs. A real death glaze. He'd been paid off three days earlier. He'd spent six hundred dollars in one tavern his first night out, I knew that much. Since then I hadn't seen him. The room was warm and sour-smelling even though the door had been wide open, and it was full of empties. Terry's chest and feet were bare, but he had on a pair of grey rugby pants. There was no light in his eyes at all. He looked like some poor purblind beggar in a holding cell waiting to be hanged.

I said something. There was a delay while some tripwire went in his head, and then he lunged and stumbled off the bed, his face working in a spastic way. He embraced me clumsily, and we hung in the doorway with his boozy face up against mine, sagging down onto my shoulder. I felt the bristles on his cheek, extraordinarily rough. He held onto me like a drowning man while I looked at the room and listened to his babbling. The sunlight came in through the door behind me. His room opened onto a veranda. Beyond that were a few yards of dirt, a ditch, and then the Alaska Highway.

"God damn, I've been waiting so long," he said. "I'm sick of that bar."

He sat down on the end of the bed. "I phoned my mother, my son . . ."

He looked up. He was crying.

"Help me. I'm sorry."

We'd met in Whitehorse less than six weeks before, in a laundromat. He'd come down from Alaska, and I'd come up from the south. They'd seized his camper at the border for various transgressions, jailed him, and then deported him. I'd eaten gravel hitchhiking up the Cassiar. We were both dirty and busted. We'd camped on the Yukon River and talked about getting a stake. And we'd got it too. I had around $2,700 on me when I walked into that hotel room not much more than a month later. In the middle of a depression! (If you called it a recession up north at that time they'd have spit between your boots. It was a depression.)

I figured my money would follow Terry's, though, if I didn't get us both out of there. A two-tavern town way up the Alaska Highway with winter coming on is no Shangri-La.

I spent a couple of days trying to straighten Terry out, and then I left him with yet another bottle of Bailey's Irish, which was all he wanted, took his machete so he wouldn't kill anybody, and caught a bus south.

Passing mile after mile of roadside desolated as far as the eye could see by the forest fire we had worked on, I considered it. The drunken emotionalism, the debauched confession; how many men I'd seen succumb to it in the past couple of years. Terry was no cry-baby. I'd seen him fist-fight, light a fire in a swamp amid a rainstorm, play classical guitar, quote Montaigne. . . . He was a descendant of wild Gaels, an iron man made for a time of wooden ships, a heavy hitter blasted by too many ups and downs. He was lost.

I looked out at the charcoal landscape and then across the aisle of the bus at a young man I'd worked with the last few days of the fire. He'd been at base camp; not on the fireline, but we had done some clean-up together at the end. A girl used to come and see him every day while he worked, a pretty native girl with whom he had been living. She'd been there to see him off on the bus today, clinging to him, trying to persuade him to stay. He had told me that he cared for the girl and that he would go back to her. Why, then, was he leaving? He would not likely be better off elsewhere the way things were for jobs. He didn't even know where he was going.

Once I read about a word the Indians used which, roughly translated, means "passer", or a man who belongs to no tribe. It is a fine word to describe many of the men I met on the road.

I looked at the kid and wondered if he, too, would end up going crazy in some hotel room, alone. I tried to think of all the people I had met, young and old, in the past two years or so, but all I could get was a depressing sense of their pain, the way you always come to think of surf when you try to imagine the ocean. And it was hard to forget the girl, standing there alone as the bus pulled away. On the other hand it was Don Juan who said, "Our lot is to learn, and to be hurled into inconceivable new worlds." Maybe the kid would take one look at the world I had seen and go back to her. He grinned at me and I passed him a beer.

This business of putting on old clothing and venturing into the underworld, so to speak, is a literary tradition that goes back at least as far as the Arabian Nights. Originally, I had not planned anything so melodramatic. I had been reflecting for some time on those stuffed figures in old pictures: logging bums, goldrushers, furmen, cowhands, blanket stiffs. Drifters. And how much we seemed to despise their wandering counterparts now. I saw more and more men and women displaced from waning traditional industries, and I wondered how it would be to have no roots now that the tall buildings are everywhere and the wild horses are gone. I took one tentative step and then another, and ultimately was overwhelmed, not only by the horror of the sub-world in which I found myself, but also by the tragedy of a recession.

I was on the road, with few breaks, from the early summer of 1980 to the beginning of 1983. The geography through which I travelled was in the West because that is where the transients head, in their thousands, to escape the prospect of freezing winters. Nearly 80 per cent of Canada's food banks are in the three most westerly provinces. But *Last in Line* is a national story. The jobless, homeless men and women I travelled with were from all parts of the country. The number of homeless people in Toronto alone has been estimated at forty thousand.

I wrote the book because I believe this displacement of people, this upheaval in society, is the biggest story in North America. Even as the economy in the United States took an upturn, the demand on soup kitchens and charity agencies increased last year by 20 per cent. In British Columbia, a quarter of the population is on some sort of government assistance. It is a phenomenal story. Men rummage like rats in garbage cans. The power over the lives of these people and the responsibility for their misfortune are so dispersed they can't figure it out and neither can anybody else. Most of the people I write about are not tramps and bums but men whose skills we no longer think we need. When a man steps outside the world he knows, as I did, or is forced out, as most of my fellow travellers were, it is as if he has dropped off the world. It is happening to men and women from many walks of life.

What follows is what happened to me. It is in chronological order and is completely true.

I have tried to be objective in my narrative. It should be said at the outset, though, that this was a terrible journey, fraught with fear. I was attacked; I lost possessions; I tried to sleep, too many times to count, under dripping trees or in cracks in a cliff. I went hungry for days on end. None of these things are enumerated in what follows because they are as routine as clouds in winter. Normalcy, where I went, is a state of siege. The abyss where men and women with no homes or steady jobs find themselves is nothing less than a slaughterhouse. It is very wrong indeed.

# LAST IN LINE

# 1

*Without doubt many men
begin the wandering life in revolt
against the monotony of modern industry.
It can hardly be expected that the
descendants of the most daring and
adventurous of nations of the earth
should be willing to submit to humdrum,
unchanging toil.*
— Rev. Frank Charles Laubach
Why There Are Vagrants. A Study, 1916

The chemical plant was in an industrial park in Regina, a rumbling dustbowl during the day, a forlorn plague of concrete at night.

A forklift was careening around outside with a scrawny coloured boy stranded way up high, spread-eagled on the hoisted forks, one foot on each, trying to control his lurching frame.

"Somebody shoot the fucker," the forklift operator screamed, jamming the machine this way and that, spinning it, kicking the shit out of it, trying to dislodge his precarious passenger.

I walked out of the sun into the dark trailer that served as an office. The plant itself was behind the trailer, a long shed running alongside a railway spur where a single boxcar sat. From the office window I could see the madman on the forklift. The black kid was still hanging in there.

"No, you don't have to work with him," chuckled the man in the office in response to my question. A dark girl looked up from a typewriter, but she didn't smile. "You go on up to the warehouse, help out there." He was still laughing when I left.

I walked to the warehouse, which was way over the other side of the industrial sprawl. Time to think. Of all the stupid ideas, is what I thought. You're too old for this.

There was just one young fellow at the warehouse, well built, clean-cut, and bright looking. "Oh, yes," he said. "You're just in time. We've got some stuff to unload."

Out back was a huge container car. The rear doors were open and there was a bunch of big drums in there, like oil drums. They weren't on pallets, but were piled two high with cardboard between the bottom row and the top.

"I'd better show you how to do this," the youngster said. With a forklift he manoeuvred a pallet within an inch or so of the topmost drums. He jumped onto the truck and, bracing his foot sideways on the bottoms of the first drum, gripped the rim with his hands and pulled it over toward him, holding it with his body and then rolling it smoothly on its edge onto the pallet. He rolled a couple more on, to make some room for me in the car. The drums made a crushing sound as they hit the edge of the wooden pallet, as if the wood was nothing more than shell ice. He indicated I should try it, showing me how to place my hands and feet to get leverage. I stepped up so that my right leg was alongside the drum to hold it when it fell toward me and pulled with my arms. I pulled again. I couldn't move it. Not an inch. I was pulling hard. I could feel the strain on my chest. For a moment I suffered the twisting dizziness that is close to blackout. I straightened up for a moment and looked way back into the dusty gloom of the car. There must have been a hundred of the green metal drums in there.

The youngster, who had got back on the forklift in anticipation of a full pallet he could run into the warehouse, got off again.

"They weigh close to six hundred pounds each," he said.

"Six hundred pounds?"

"No problem," he said. "I've emptied one of these on my own in a couple of hours. And there's lots more coming in. You gotta learn. It's the way you do it. You gotta do it right or you'll hurt yourself bad."

Eventually I found I could create a rocking motion with the huge drums full of chemicals that inched them toward the pallet.

"You'll kill yourself," the boy said soberly.

Anyway, it was much too slow, and finally another worker had to be summoned from the plant to help out. This turned out to be the crazy forklift operator, a Newfie, and his presence probably kept me from walking away. He joked constantly, but never at my expense, in great screeds of blasphemy and rebellion. He and my other companion re-

2

called, with complete humility, how long it had taken them to master the various techniques of their meaty trade. I had no right, God knows, but finally I felt part of a team, sweating in and out of the rapidly emptying innards of that first car and a second one that subsequently arrived. And by the end of the day I could move the massive cargo fairly effectively.

For the next few days, in a near heat wave, I unloaded trucks. Some held more of the drums of chemical; others contained bags of powder, pesticides, weighing fifty or a hundred pounds.

Then things slowed down at the warehouse, and I was moved back to the plant, on the line. My job was to fill one-gallon pails with chemical from a tap, squeeze on the lids with a device powered by compressed air, and slide them down an arrangement of metal rollers to a second man who would insert spouts and caps and stack the pails on pallets. We worked face to face with another crew doing the same thing. Everybody agreed that this was far worse than being on the trucks. We could scarcely breathe for the stench of chemical we were forced to inhale as we bent over the pails. Any spillover slopped onto the floor until it ran over the soles of our boots. No protective clothing was provided. When the chemical splashed into an eye, the victim would stagger to a water tap to wash it out. One of the workers, a teenage lad, spilled some chemical over his running shoes. His feet began to burn, so that he was forced to take off his shoes and socks. His feet had turned black, and the skin was already starting to peel off. He had to be taken to hospital.

Government inspectors descended on the place in the days that followed. The floors were supposed to be cleaned and kept clean. Respirators, goggles, coveralls, and gloves were issued. Yellow warning notices were posted throughout the plant listing health violations. The activity was sudden and stern. It was also farcical. The day after the inspectors left, most of the protective clothing was discarded. It was just too hot to wear that stuff without any type of air conditioning. The yellow notices began to disappear, the floor backed up with oily, foul-smelling, and highly toxic chemicals. Management stayed inside the trailer and out of harm's way.

The physical danger came not just from the liquid chemicals but from the bags full of powdered pesticides that were stacked inside both the warehouse and the plant. In the process of handling, many had been split, and a dust of pesticides filled the air. The government inspectors said the spillage was deadly and ordered the broken bags removed. This, of course, brought the workers directly in contact with the pesticides. I spent several days loading by hand a boxcar full of one particular brand of split bags full of a foul-smelling pink stuff. It took so long because in the confined, airless space of the boxcar the loose powder constantly disturbed, choked, and blinded me. I would have to stumble to the doors of the container for relief. I could actually feel the powder settling on my lungs, and at night for some time to come my breathing was impaired. It was not until later, though, that I learned the material I had handled was so dangerous it was expressly prohibited, banned even to farmers. What it was doing at the plant, or where the boxcar took it, I don't know. I felt, though, for the men who would have to unload it.

The chemical company was owned by a large multinational corporation and, though I don't consider myself naive, I was shocked by this initial exposure to the shabby industrial world behind the numbers on the big boards of Wall Street and Bay Street. Was this where the share prices came from – a hundred thousand shoddy, death-trap subsidiaries like this one? Would it cost so much to clean up the operation, make it safe for people who work there?

And the men, the workers. Why would they remain, humping incredible loads, swallowing poison, all for five bucks an hour or less?

The answer to that was a simple one. The employees dared not quit or even complain. The company had entered into an agreement with local corrections officials to provide work for a certain number of prisoners who were completing the balance of their sentences at a halfway house. The bulk of the company's work force at the busiest time of year, when pesticides had to be shipped to farmers, came from this halfway house. Most of my workmates were cons. For the rest, the company relied on transients, who didn't know what they were getting into.

The prisoners, mostly native people, were not even paid five dollars an hour, but received simply the minimum legal wage. Any reluctance to perform a task, any absenteeism, and they could expect to be shipped back not to the halfway house but directly to prison, where they would have to complete the balance of their sentence – with extra time added on.

However bad conditions got at the plant, the company had a guaranteed source of labour.

The transients, there because they could not find temporary work anywhere else, were less docile. The Newfie was one, and his brother worked there too. They hated the work and would dump any debris they could find into the pails of chemical – scale weights, spouts, nuts, bolts, tools. They sprayed paint over the face of the weigh scales, obscuring the numbers. They urinated into the pails.

Because of the dank, poisoned surroundings and the hostility of the men, the supervisors hated to set foot in the plant, preferring the comfort of the trailer or of a small office adjoining the plant, and so the work force was left largely unsupervised.

It was as if the men were gripped by some delirium caused by the chemicals. They would sabotage machinery – even the prisoners would do this if they thought they could get away with it – hold water fights with the clean-up hoses, and race the forklift trucks until they broke down. It was like the boiler room of a death ship in that plant.

I began to feel the lawlessness creep into my own spirit. There was a camaraderie of shared suffering and rebellion among us. We went around with a kind of senile glee in our eyes. Maybe the weather had something to do with it, too – the sun was a frenzy, day after day.

Nobody had any money, but several had managed to get credit with the catering truck that came by the plant twice a day. They would take sandwiches and drinks and charge them, and the poor dumb vendor, presumably new to the job, would write their accounts down on a piece of paper. Some of the accounts were up over the hundred-dollar mark when the guys walked out. "I'll pay you when I get paid," they kept telling the vendor, but they never did. It was a matter of honour. They much preferred to quit the job and move on rather than capitulate. For them it was like war.

Once I loaned fifty dollars to the Newfie, and the foreman, hearing about it, told me to forget it, that I'd never get it back. I didn't get the fifty, but the Newfie rode to work one day on a beautiful new ten-speed bike worth four times that much and offered it to me. The bike, of course, was stolen.

A morbid fascination held me there. To be among plundering, cursing, stealing, hating men acting without reservations or moral brakes was a sort of therapy; it had its own perfect logic. The company was

5

getting exactly what it deserved. And it was a beautiful prairie summer. Even in the city you could smell that prairie, that gumbo earth.

The city itself was a dead place. In the beginning there had been a creek just big enough to wash a sheep in, and around it a prairie full of picked bones and wolves. The railway made it, such as it is. And wheat. A drought made a dustbowl of it in the thirties. The wind blew like a black snowstorm. The land went up in clouds. There's the story about the baseball player who lost his way running the bases and was found three miles out on the baldheaded prairie. And other stories, not at all funny. The Depression. Relief-camp strikers on their way east to complain about camp conditions, to demand work, not welfare; sixteen hundred of them rolled into town on a freight train; and police, ordered by the government to turn them back, provoked one of the worst street battles in Canadian history. The Depression had been a haunting spectre here ever since, but with a saving grace – the old ones remembered how stupid and impotent government had been. Now they rarely expected anything better from their elected representatives.

There wasn't any real sign of new suffering that summer. Just muttering about maybe some belt-tightening in the future. I took great delight in every new thing I learned, basic as it was. I could now unload a truckload of six-hundred-pound drums without any help, a thing I had initially thought would be impossible and that, when I thought about it, seemed like some kind of miracle. I could run the forklift and retool the conveyor belt when we switched product. I was fitter physically than I had been in a long time, and was feeling the moral affirmation of hard labour.

Amid the contradictions of well-being and repugnance the job provoked, I had arbitrarily decided to quit when one of the prisoners, Ray, was released from the halfway house. We had become friends, and it seemed as good a time as any.

Ray was a Stoney Indian from the north. He had saved his money, largely because he was not allowed to drink at the halfway house, and he hadn't had a drink for three months. If he or any of the others had got drunk they would have been shipped back to prison. Another bonus for the chemical company: they had little need to worry that absenteeism or hangovers would interfere with productivity.

Ray and I had often squatted together in the shade of a boxcar or a pile of empty drums outside the plant during breaks. He was quiet and direct. His face was scarred by some childhood disease. He was squat and strong and a leader because he went his own way, swayed less than any of us by the madnesses around him. He wanted to do his time, take his money, and go back to the lake where his brother was chief, and where he was assured of his share of various swindles and boondoggles that relieved the government treasury of funds. The white man was a joke to Ray.

On the night he was released we went for a drink in a rundown tavern full of nodding pimps and drunken, screaming women. Ray had quit the job that afternoon. I had a couple more days to go. He was to take the bus to a remote northern outpost where his wife and kids would meet him and drive him to the lake. He was happy to be going back.

After a while, Ray went to a room upstairs with a stumblebum prostitute, a hideous addict with needle marks between her fingers. When he came down his face was a mask of sweat, and he was grinning. He threw the room key on the table for me to go up and join the girl. No thanks. We grinned at each other like fools. I was so glad that he was out of that halfway house I felt I'd just gotten out too. When the girl came down from the room she lolled against the table, right out of it, as if somebody had just kicked her in the back and broken her spine. Wicked Wanda we christened her. A cop in uniform wandered in off the street to check the place out. He saw the girl and came over to say something to her. As he reached the table Ray, drunk now, pushed a bill at him, right into his hand. "Here's a dollar, now fuck off," he said. Uh-uh!

I said he was with me, I'd take care of him, to forget it, he was drunk. I knew if the uniform so much as checked Ray out he'd be right back in the can. No more halfway houses. The cop finally left, and after a while I left too. I couldn't drink any more, and I had to go to work in the morning. Ray drew me a map of his reserve, and I said I'd visit sometime.

"Al? I'm all right, Al."

The slow voice came over the telephone in the office trailer the next morning. They'd called me in from the plant to answer it.

"You mean you're not all right, Ray, is that what you mean?" I said.

"Yeah, well . . ." The voice was thick, hungover.

7

He'd been robbed of everything: money, clothes, bus ticket, identification. He didn't have the fare to get home, and he'd already missed the bus he was supposed to take. I pictured his wife and kids sitting in some old car outside a bus depot in some godforsaken wilderness.

He said he was in his room upstairs over the tavern, naked. He'd taken the addict back up after I'd left, and two men had come in behind her and taken everything out of the room but the bed. They'd also beaten Ray.

"I'll come down, bring some clothes, and put you on the bus. At noon. Wait there till noon," I told him. But when I got there the desk clerk said he'd checked out. I went up to the room anyway, but he wasn't there. There was nothing there but the bed.

"What was he wearing?" I asked the desk clerk.

"What d'you mean?" he said.

Few people have left behind scantier evidence of their culture, they say, than the Plains Indians. In his *Letters from America*, Rupert Brooke wrote: "They left no arts, no tradition, no buildings or roads or laws – only a story or two and a few names, strange and beautiful."

Ray, then, was true to form. He disappeared and left no trace. I hope he got home.

That was my first job, in that stinking, poisoned sweatbox of a plant. But it was just the first of many, some harder, some easier, but almost all falling roughly into the category known in casual labour hiring halls everywhere as "bull work". My plan had been to take to the road, a transient with no particular skills and no money, and get an existence in whatever way I could. It was late summer. Now I moved on westward, like hundreds of other transients, to the coast, to escape the snow.

# 2

*I don't like money, actually,*
*but it quiets my nerves.*
—Joe Louis, 1914

A panhandler was working the street outside an old residential hotel, and as I got out of the car I heard a woman say bitterly: "Why don't you go to welfare? They'll give you money." I checked into the hotel with what was left of my prairie money and then took the woman's advice myself. I called welfare. A worker came and sat in the one chair. I sat on the bed.

"You will be eligible for full benefits," she told me. She was plump with braces on her teeth. "Don't worry. Lots of people who have had good jobs come to us for help to get over a tough spot. The only thing is you will have to look for a new place to stay. This will be much too expensive."

"Can you suggest anywhere?"

"There is a place just behind here. But it is full of psychiatric patients. They bang their heads on the walls . . ." Her voice trailed off sympathetically. "You don't want that. There are better places just as cheap." But she didn't know of any. The vacancy rate in that area of Vancouver was 0.01 per cent. I went out to look.

I did find a filthy basement sleeping room no bigger than a closet for forty dollars a week. There were half a dozen rooms partitioned off in a house-sized basement, with a rusty communal shower stall. The pest-control truck was parked outside. I passed that up.

Around the corner was a fairly comfortable board and lodging spot mainly occupied by pensioners. The caretaker took me around, even introduced me to the cook in the communal dining area. But the rent was $350 a month, more money than I'd be getting.

These were the only two places I could find for rent in an eight-square-block area. I began to wish I had taken the sleeping room, if only for a week, because I couldn't pick up my cheque until I could give an address. In the end I stayed at the hotel but gave the case worker the address of the sleeping room, gambling that she wouldn't check. I got the money, but the rent for a week at the hotel was virtually the lodging lodging for the remaining three weeks. Even a room at the "Y" was was up, if I ate sparingly, I'd have four dollars a day for food and lodging for the remaining three weeks. Even a room at the " Y " was thirteen dollars a night. And the worker had told me: "When the money's gone, it's gone. We can't give you any more."

I had a couple of beers, pondering ways in which I could put a roof over my head and food in my mouth for four dollars a day, and then, short on other options, I went to the racetrack. As a concession to the source of the funds I bet to place or show, but it didn't help. *Tant mieux*. I moved my suitcases back into the car. I had stuff all over the back seat, so I had to sleep in the front. I parked in an alley behind a Chinese grocery and, soaked by the coastal rain, crept into my car after dark. I rose at dawn so as not to be detected by decent people on their way to work, or patrol cars checking the alley. I wasn't sure whether I was committing a crime, but it sure felt like it.

I tried the Employment Centre but there were no labouring jobs, and there wasn't much else I could do. I felt the ignominy of coming so quickly to a dead end.

That evening there was an obscurely worded ad in the newspaper, inviting applicants to a certain room in a large hotel the next morning. It was not clear what the job was, exactly. And it was no clearer the next morning after I and sundry other applicants had spent half an hour listening to a red-faced shyster. "Unlimited money for a good person . . . public relations for a major company . . . good dress important . . . meet the public . . . major marketing project . . ."

At least there was free coffee.

It turned out to be peddling books of special-offer dry-cleaning coupons door to door.

The crew chief would pick us up in a battered, stinking, station wagon, crowded with derelicts and simpletons, and take us to an area of the city, usually an arboraceous suburb, where we were required to knock on doors and offer the dry-cleaning books, containing coupons ostensibly worth $27, for $9.95. For each book sold we peddlers pocketed three bucks.

The first day I walked the streets for about ten hours and made $24.

The money was paid at the end of the day by the man who had the contract to sell the books. He wore gold bracelets and chunky rings, and he ran a stereo shop where he bragged the markup was 300 per cent. It was at the stereo shop that we got paid. He asked me if I'd ever sold before.

"Never," I said.

"Well, you're a born salesman," he said seriously.

Twenty-four dollars in ten hours!

I did make more, however, in the days that followed – almost a hundred dollars, in fact, one day. Enough, anyway, to get a room at the "Y" and to permit me to move on to something else. This was a meat-packing outfit selling bulk food orders. Again I got the job from the newspaper. Again it was all commission. The ad boasted that salesmen made upwards of four thousand dollars a month.

"I'm the Meathead," the sales manager introduced himself. "Everybody calls me the Meathead. That's the highest praise you can get in this business."

He took me to lunch at McDonald's, which seemed a little lowbrow for a meat sales executive in charge of men making more than $40,000 a year. "My wife works there, and I get it free," he offered by way of explanation. And, over hamburger and fries, which his wife, a thin dark girl, did not ring up, the Meathead explained why we were there and not at the Hyatt.

"I went down the tubes. I'm working for this other outfit, same deal, selling meat. We're making a fortune, setting our own prices, the sucker trade's biting like fish. We're pocketing hundred-dollar bills. Vegas on weekends, big house, three cars, the whole shot. Then I hear a commotion outside my office one day, and there's a hundred fucking television cameras in the hallway. It's an exposé. I'm a racketeer, they tell me. I'm on television right now. They tell everybody I'm a racketeer. Right on the tube. I lost everything. One day I have every-thing a man could want, the next day I have a station wagon, a wife, two kids, and a Hibachi grill. Not enough money for a campsite. I drive out of town, set up the grill and a tent, buy some tube steaks for the kids, and when the guy comes around for the money I tell him I don't have any till the banks open on Monday. This is on Friday night. I give him some ID to hold, and I go out with a bunch of sales leads the boss of another outfit – meat again – has given me, and I sell fifteen deals that weekend. Fifteen. More than two thousand in commission. I'm back on track. But I don't ever want to go through that again." He shook his head. "You know what it's like when you try to talk to your father-in-law and he turns his head away because he's ashamed of you?"

I suppose it would have been provident to walk away from it right then, but I admired the guy's frankness. One other factor was that, after three days of training as a meat salesman, I was once again broke. And in any case, even before the Meathead's confession, the sales manual for his company had prepared me for a certain dearth of altruism.

"It is a positive fact," the badly typed tract trumpeted, "YOU CAN'T BE ALL THAT NICE AND POLITE AND STILL BE A GOOD SALESMAN."

It went on: "The top salesmen that I have known personally are more inclined to be very direct, and in the eyes of many people they are considered to be RUTHLESS.

"The prospect says, 'I can't afford it,' and the sweet, nice, courteous, gentlemanly salesman says, 'I understand,' and leaves again with no sale.

"The way to handle that is to look them right in the eye with all the persuasive conviction in the world and say, 'Why not?' It will bring them out of their shell and make them think . . ."

The author of this misspelled, twenty-six-page manual was the president of the company, a man called Lachine, an Irishman despite the name, whose background had been in the aluminum-siding business during an era when the aluminum-siding business was as queer as a three-dollar bill.

Lachine was the epitome of every snail-backed bunco artist who ever left town in a hurry. He was a small, light-boned man who had suffered many operations for heart problems. He was constantly unbuttoning his shirt to show visitors his operation scars. "I'm like Frankenstein," he boasted, puffing on a big cigar and holding his shirt open with hairy little hands, revealing a plundered mine of a chest. Railway tracks, tailings, rivers of scar tissue, spurs, burrowings, the glitter of abandoned bones, the darkling of old spilled blood, and the myriad gougings and bypasses of a lost mine were all there on his chest.

There was no hair at all on his torso – none could grow – but the hair on his head was parted low and trowelled around his ears. He regaled anybody who would listen – and many were spellbound – with tales of his successes in the siding business, which was still his first and oldest love even though he had now moved on to meat.

He would sell the siding, he explained to me, by offering to use his prospect's house as a "show home".

His pitch went something like this:

"Normally this siding costs $6,000. You can have it for $3,500 if you permit us to use pictures of your house in promotional brochures. Every deal we make using your house as the pitch you get a hundred-dollar bill. But whatever you do, don't tell your neighbours about the special deal you got because we're going to be selling in this neighbourhood, and if they hear about the price you got they're all going to want it."

Of course, everybody was being given the same pitch and the same price, but they all thought they were getting a good deal so they all kept their mouths shut.

Lachine and his cronies would let some days go by after the siding was installed and the photographs taken before returning to hand over a solitary hundred-dollar bill to the pigeon. Sales are slow, Lachine would complain. Your house doesn't look quite as good in the brochure as we thought it would. It would look much better with shutters on the windows. "If you had shutters, we could take new pictures, and sales would skyrocket. It will only cost you another $1,500 for the shutters, and you would get all that money back on the hundred-dollar bills you would make."

Once the customer's name was on the contract for shutters as well as siding he would, of course, never see another hundred-dollar bill.

What happened if somebody got awkward and refused to pay after realizing what a pit they had fallen into?

Lachine beamed. "A wrassler would be sent to remind them of their contractual obligations," he said sublimely, through a cloud of smoke.

A wrestler?

"A wrassler," confirmed Lachine. "In full wrasslin' costume, with a mask with eyeholes and carrying a gun."

Lachine leaned back in his black leather chair, swivelling. "Ah, the good old days in Montreal," he sighed, his mouser's eyes glistening.

With my sales manual and leads I headed out just like any old drummer, assured by both the Meathead and Lachine that times had changed and that my errand was a legitimate one.

Actually, I was becoming less concerned about whether it was legitimate. Poverty was a gathering wave that threatened to smash me on the rocks. I was facing the skull's head of hunger and would do nearly anything to avoid it. Before I left, however, I did venture one question: "What happened to your other salesmen?"

The Meathead responded easily, casually. "Well, Jacob, he's made so much money he sits all day drinking martinis and talking to his cronies in the Timber Lounge. Manny's in Hawaii for a couple of months; he takes six months on and six off, nowadays. I don't want that. I'm cutting them all off. I want a new crew I can train myself."

The training I had received had consisted of a couple of warnings, the first of which was: "Don't waste time on tire kickers."

A tire kicker, from what I could gather out of the Meathead's virulent screed, was anyone who asked an intelligent question like: "How much will this meat cost me altogether?" or, "How much meat will I actually get for two thousand dollars?" In direct sales, I had concluded, you're looking for some imbecile who has to have a pot or a pan or a bathtub or a freezer full of meat right now, and who has a pen handy to sign the necessary contracts. To my surprise I was to discover that the world is full of such people and that there is, as the Meathead suggested, no need to waste time on tire kickers.

I went through little places. Mining towns in the southeast. Fernie, Sparwood. There was still plenty of money around, though General Motors had already reported the highest corporate loss in history, and something bad had begun. Still, if you had tried to tell them in the Black Nugget Motor Inn that by the time 1983 was a week old two thousand Sparwood miners would be laid off – in a town of five thousand people – they would have laughed at you.

I brushed off tire kickers as instructed and kept away from two other specific categories I had been warned to avoid, native people and the clergy. Neither had any credit, the Meathead had said flatly.

And I seemed to do pretty well.

The first setback came when I ignored the Meathead's other serious warning: "Never sell to the woman alone, but always to the husband." Even though the wife might be gainfully employed; even though she might be the sole wage earner. If you sell to her, the Meathead said, the husband will cancel the deal as soon as he hears about it, every time.

Well, I turned a deaf ear to that piece of chauvinistic advice – to my cost. I sold to a couple of teachers, man and wife. Both were working, and they lived in a beautiful house on a hill in fruit-growing country. The husband wanted time to think it over. The wife said, "No, dear, we have all the information we need." The husband left the room. Remembering for a moment the Meathead's caution I said: "I don't want to do a deal with you without your husband. Are you absolutely confident he'll agree?"

"Anything I do is all right with him," the woman replied. She was a strong, vivacious, intelligent woman. Surely, I thought, these people have the type of arrangement that would permit the woman to make her own decisions in a matter of this kind. She signed the deal and gave me a cheque for the full amount, drawn on a joint account. No financing, no fuss. It was a cash deal, a big deal. But before the order ever reached the office, before the Meathead ever got the cheque, he got the cancellation. A telegram from the husband. He'd stopped the cheque; he didn't want any meat; and he didn't want anybody to contact him or his wife.

Never sell to the woman.

One thing about the Meathead and Lachine. They knew what they were doing. They knew people, and they knew sales. They also hated each other. Their relationship in the office was rather like that between the rats of India and their deadly enemy, the yellow-tinted snake called the dhaman; both are sacred, but they bite each other. (The Meathead was the rat; Lachine the snake.)

There were two highlights to the office day. The first occurred early when the Meathead telephoned the finance company to find out which contracts, if any, had been approved. He spoke to one girl, always, and his greeting never varied. "Hi, Josie," he would say. "This is your morning smile."

The second highlight came in mid-morning when the mail was delivered, bringing in deals and cheques from the salesmen on the road. There were in fact a couple of other salesmen, but the staff complement was almost permanently at a low ebb, for reasons that will become clear.

Even though he was the boss, Lachine spent most of the day folding the direct-mail coupons that were the source of all the sales leads. The tactic was to saturate a small, preferably remote (away from supermarkets) area with leaflets advertising the bulk freezer-meat deal. The areas that yielded good returns – two responses for every hundred advertising flyers – were well known. So Lachine laboriously folded the flyers as they came from the printer, all the while watching the Meat-head out of the corner of his eye, eavesdropping on the call to the finance company, sniffing around the mail. When there was little of interest in the mail he would threaten to fire the Meathead. A volley of insults would follow, culminating usually in the Meathead's current favourite, "I wouldn't piss on you if you were on fire." After this, Lachine would oil back to the wooden counter, where he would fold hundreds upon hundreds of flyers while continuing his surveillance.

So it was a blessed relief to get out of the office. I left with a clipboard full of leads – the tear-off, direct-mail coupons returned by potential customers – and a bundle of conditional sales contracts for those who might wish to finance their purchase, which turned out to be almost everybody.

The food was sold in freezer lots worth around $2,000, $3,000, or $4,000. That way the price of any particular cut of meat, or the price per pound of the whole deal, was hidden. Despite the formidable sales manual, the basic pitch was simple. "I will take fifty per cent of your present food budget," the salesman would promise, repeating the line for effect, "fifty per cent of your present food budget, and provide seventy-five per cent of your food needs."

It was a brilliant pitch, presumably Lachine's, as effective as the aluminum-siding dodge and much easier. The assurance was so simple and straightforward, so cut and dried, and the truth was so hard to get at, because nobody knew the price per pound of the meat – certainly I didn't – that it was almost irresistible to many.

"How much do you spend a month now on food?" I would ask the wife.

"Three hundred dollars."

"Okay." And I would pull out a plan that would cost around $1,800 – half the woman's yearly outlay on food. There were many such plans, one for every eventuality.

*Voilà*! Half the present budget, and it would provide the family with 75 per cent of their food needs. Or would it? The missing ingredient, of course, was how long the food would last. Quality was looked after because the purchaser had the right to have any inferior produce (vegetables were also sold on the plan) replaced. But would there be enough of it to sustain a family for a year? People unused to buying in bulk found it hard to assess – and sometimes got fleeced.

Meanwhile, I appeared to be making quite a lot of money. Making money wasn't what I had in mind when I set out to take any job I could get, but I would take it. I sold to one out of every two or three families I saw and wondered at the bounty I had stumbled on. My commissions were growing each day. Of course, the expenses were high – hotels, meals, booze, gas. Whenever I wanted it, the Meathead would wire me a hundred or so as an advance. Still, I thought I was doing well.

When I got back at the end of a three-week trip the Meathead said: "You did well. Don't worry, you don't owe us much."

And so the bubble burst. I learned how much times had changed. Salesmen were now fairly legitimate. It was the customers who were crooked.

"Nobody has any credit," the Meathead explained gently. "It's not just me – it's everybody."

He shuffled my contracts on the desk. The finance company had already sat in judgment on them. "This guy's just a bad risk. This character is going to jail as soon as they catch up with him. This old man died on you, and his wife cancelled. This fellow's an undischarged bankrupt." And on and on.

Eight or nine of my deals had gone through out of twenty-five signed conditional sales contracts. The rest had either cancelled out or failed to get financing. Commissions totalled about eleven hundred bucks. My advances had been more than a thousand. I had twenty bucks coming.

The Meathead shrugged. "We made money on you. You're a born salesman," he said hopefully. But I left, through the revolving door that had swallowed so many commission salesmen before me.

# 3

*The city of Victoria is a community*
*of dignified matrons.*
—Ted Czolowski and Balynn Richards,
*Victoria Calling*

I fell asleep to the rhythmic sound of drip-
ping snow off the car roof. It was November of 1980. I was parked on a
quiet street in Victoria between a cathedral and a graveyard. It was
a good spot, a block from the YMCA where I could shower for a
buck-fifty.

A tapping on the steamed window woke me. The dashboard clock
said 3:15 A.M.

I lowered the window, and a flashlight shone in. "Your hazard lights
are on," the policeman said. The sound I had mistaken in my sleepy
state for the drip of melting snow was the click of the hazard lights, on
and off, flashing all night long in that dark space between the cathedral
and the graveyard. A restless foot or sleep-drugged hand must have
triggered the switch as I lay in my sleeping bag on the seat.

"I saw your car here. I ran a check," the policeman said. He
shrugged.

I struggled upright, still half asleep. "I can't afford a place. I'm looking for work," I said. There was a terror in being confronted like that,
in the middle of the night.

"That's okay," the policeman said soothingly. "Just those Ontario
plates is all. No law against it. Wanted to make sure you were okay.
What's your name?"

I gave it, and the policeman nodded, as if he recalled it from the
license-plate check.

"Just give me a couple of days and I'll be out of here," I said.

"Sure." He walked away, but the fear remained. Up to now it had
been a bit like a silly game. But, like Gulliver, I had discovered, in the
middle of the night, abruptly, "the great power of habit and prejudice".

18

This was not my world – welfare, sleazy selling jobs, sleeping in the car. Now, suddenly, I was afraid of it. I had covered newspaper and magazine assignments in many parts of the world, including Russia and China, but I had never felt so alien as I did at that moment in my own country. What the hell are you doing? I asked myself savagely. I felt the need to move quickly, before the officer returned. I turned the starter and got only a grinding, heaving sound. Battery. Sweat started to run down my face, cold as it was. I tried again and again to start the car until all I got was a solenoid click. Then I realized how stupid it was. I had no gas anyway. No money. Nowhere to go. I walked down to the bus depot and brushed my teeth in the washroom. Then from a pay phone I tried to call a friend in the east who was holding some of my money in case I needed it in a hurry. I was going to quit. There was no answer. I had deliberately left behind all credit cards and other easy ways of getting money so that I would be, as nearly as possible, in a similar position to other transients. My car had been the one indulgence, a bit of cowardice. Now that was gone. Reality was crowding me. But wasn't that just what I had sought? Hadn't I realized I was going to be homeless and broke? It settled me to think of it once again in that way, as an assignment. I had never quit an assignment in my life, any more than the coal miner would shy away from the blackness of the pit.

That afternoon I waited on the steps of the hostel in Victoria. The street outside with its cracks and smears and its swaybacked neglected look was like a dry riverbed in the heart of the city. When the doors opened at four I told the young lady I was busted, could not even pay for a bed.

"Will you help with the dishes?" she asked.

Almost nobody in the chow line has washed, cleaned their teeth, or done anything but stumble from their bunks. They lurch into place like rubber dolls kicked from behind. The few disgusting grunts are bad manners or the remnants of dreams.

At the food hatch a row flares. The Television Man is, in a flash, overwhelmingly angry. He is a tubby, myopic moron who spends his evenings glued to the communal television set in this very room, determining the choice of programs with jealous persistence, one trashy show after another. Now he cannot get his breath. His face colours furiously. His big gut heaves, and his hands claw a warning inches from the face of a man in a battered Stetson who is behind him in line. The Television Man has some sort of speech defect, and his words when he is agitated come out in great grampus breaths that sound as if he is yawning and trying to speak at the same time. "Ooh, I rip your face off. A punk like you calling me an idiot, a faggot like you . . ."

His antagonist is white-faced. "One thing, buddy," he says. "Don't call me a queer."

Then a third voice, this time a woman. "You want an egg?" A magic phrase, a flophouse hymn. There is no fight. The line moves. One egg, hardboiled, one bowl of porridge, one spoonful of brown sugar, one apple, one mug of tea.

One by one we file past this young woman who feeds us from the kitchen through a hole cut in the wall. She rarely smiles – doesn't want to encourage the men. She wants to keep the line moving, go home. She is young and brusquely shy with dark hair, and some dark hairs growing on her cheeks, gently.

I follow the gypsy-like Québécois, Jean, to a table. The tables are long wooden ones. Jean slams down his porridge bowl. "She's lucky there's a warrant out on me, that bitch, or I'd beat her," he says. "One fucking hegg." He comes from Quebec City.

"I'm thirty-four. They can't kick me out in the street. If you're over thirty they have to help you. I'm going to give them shit. I'm not sleeping in the streets."

The director of the hostel has told Jean he must leave soon. He has been there too long, sleeping and eating for nothing. There is a sign right by the registration desk. "Three-day maximum stay. NO EXTENSIONS." There are always extensions, but now it is more difficult with so many men needing beds.

Jean grins sideways at me. We are seated at the end of one of the tables, near the window and the silver Christmas tree. "They want to kick me out in the street," he says. "But I'm old man." He shovels porridge into his mouth, the spoon gripped in a clenched fist. I am getting used to his restless energy. He behaves like an immigrant at a train station, sitting on his bags, playing his squeezebox, a man from a race of singers, gallant, swaggering, tragic. His every move shows the impulse to dance.

"Everybody knew me in St. Michel Street," he told me the evening before. "Have you ever seen a man in a white suit walking the streets at this time of year?" He faked a shiver. "That was me. Stupid."

He had a white suit, two apartments, two women, big money. He made $92,000 back in 1977, he said. He had a good job on the docks, but he also was in on some racket.

Then he found his sister's body after she took two hundred pills. "She was blue . . . three days dead. I knew she would do it. It was my father's fault. I phoned my father. I said: 'She's dead.' He said: 'Oh, go on.' I said: 'I'm drunk, but I'm serious. She's dead. What you gonna do about it?' "

All this Jean told me the night before. His one ambition, he says, is to go to his father's funeral. He hates his father. He wants to see him dead and buried. But he loves his other two sisters who are still alive.

"I bury him," he says with real anticipation. "I go back to funeral. I stand at back. I be drunk, but my sisters they see me. I love them. They love me. They see me. They say 'Jean . . . Jean.' I be drinking from a bottle . . ."

After we finish breakfast I follow the Frenchman back from the lunch room to the dorm. The old man on the bunk next to Jean's is still sleeping. He has a brace on his neck, an ugly plaster monstrosity out of which he peers, waking or sleeping, like a turtle. He has just been released from hospital. Jean shakes the man awake. "Wha . . . what?" begins the pitiful figure, his eyes half slumbrous, half frightened, making as if to rise but then keeling over on his side.

"God damn it, no snoring tonight or I knock you out of that bed," Jean says, thrusting the old man down again.

A few shirtless, bootless men raise themselves to listen, then sink back. The Frenchman sits on the edge of his bunk, takes off his own boots and, with a pocket knife, begins to cut the hard skin and sappy blisters off his ruined heels. Jean has work boots and western boots. The western boots cripple him, make his whole body ache, but he will not wear the more comfortable work boots at night, even on the back streets where he spends most of his time. Instead he suffers, and every morning he carves off the raw blistered skin and the callouses, lifting his foot like a pony as the knife does its work, and cursing with the pain. His western boots have big, heavy, clickety-clack horseshoe taps on the bottom, and he is proud of them. At night you can hear him coming a block away.

The evening before I had approached the hostel leerily. The building

21

looked as if it had once been a church, but the simple geometric elements had dissipated. It had obviously been a place of straight angles, but cracks had dragged the building to one side, distorted timbers, and pulled windows out of shape. At least, that's the way I remember it. The doors were closed when I got there, but there was one youngster outside waiting. He was very young, his features so well-defined and moist they could have been painted on. He told me he had wanted to join the armed forces to get off the street, but because he had recently been on probation he would have to wait six months even for an evaluation. So that day he had been getting ready to wait out the winter. He had bought a good sleeping bag for sixty bucks, work boots for forty-five, and some other things. The last thing on his list was a towel, and he had run out of money before he got to it. "You know how much a towel is? Nine dollars," he said disgustedly. "They don't have none at the thrift shop. No coats, shoes, nothing. Lots of guys getting ready for winter, I guess."

Or for the long winter of a recession.

"You don't get on with your folks?" I asked him.

"Ah, they used to get on my case a lot," he said vaguely. "Throwing this whole trip at me, you know."

When the doors opened we were given bunks and a blanket, and then we went for supper. We formed a line and got a plate of chili and salad. "Just salad," I heard somebody tell the girl. From behind him came a natterjack complaint: "Most guys would get it [the chili] and give it to the next guy. I'm right behind him. I ain't eaten for three days. I always take it an' give it to the next guy . . ." He droned on about the chili, and I awakened to real poverty. These things mattered when a guy hadn't eaten for three days. I was myself to be hungry enough in the coming months to accept gratefully leavings shovelled onto my plate. But that complaining voice in the chow line was my real introduction to the transient life.

I spent my first night in the hostel in an upper bunk, lying awake mostly, listening to people talk in their sleep. There was a rhythm to it, a kind of trance poetry.

I am forced back to the present by a commotion outside the dorm. Leaving Jean I walk down to the door between rows of two-tier, steel-framed bunks, about a hundred of them in all in the big room. The walls of the place are yellow-orange, the bedsheets orange, the floor bare concrete, the roof high. Several of the men are still sleeping, even though they have now missed breakfast. The voice of some dreamy baby talker – "Oh me, oh me, da da me, oh me " – like the cry of an animal trapped in the rafters, cuts through all other sounds. From an empty, unmade bunk, a dirty white corset trails down obscenely from the grey mattress, a man's supporter left behind, presumably by someone with a back or spine injury. Men cough, early morning coughs with the cadence and phlegmy clatter of a bank of Vegas slots. The only light in the room comes from two red exit signs over the doors at each end of the dorm, and in the gloom I almost trip over a figure crouched in the space between two bunks. The figure is holding some sort of unmoving posture of meditation or prayer, supporting himself on his hands, with his legs thrust out behind him and his head thrown back at a seemingly impossible angle so that he is gazing up toward the roof. Massive amounts of ragged clothing hang loosely on the stiffened body.

I step around and out into the lobby that adjoins the lunch room. The director, the man in charge of the hostel, is trying to prevent a man from entering. The intruder has evidently been out all night. Vomit clings to the grizzled beginnings of a blond beard. His eyes water. He wears a brown coat of fairly good quality that, years earlier, might have been fashionable. He is slightly overweight, between twenty and thirty years old.

"Come back when you're sober, Derek," the director hollers, still trying to hold him back. The director is a vigorous man in his thirties with curly black hair.

"I want my suitcase," Derek protests, voice breaking, head bobbing, feet shuffling.

The director sends somebody to get the suitcase from Derek's bunk, but when it arrives the drunk still refuses to leave. He wheels like a weathercock and throws himself in melodramatic fashion on the cracked stone steps in front of the building in the rain. It is just getting light outside. With his dishevelled, bunched clothing, he looks as if he is acting the part of a hunchback throwing himself before the gallows in a movie.

"I'll call the police, and they'll give you a nice warm cell, is that what you want, Derek?" the director insists, stretching out his vowels as if he is talking to a child.

The crowd spills around, silently, curiously, watching this confrontation.

Derek, still sprawled on the steps, rummages with one hand in the suitcase, which has fallen open. "I just want a bed," he drools. He throws himself forward, pushing the director aside, and launches himself into the lobby, screaming that he has been robbed. A blanket is missing from his suitcase, some clothing . . .

He tosses everything out of the suitcase onto the floor, and the police are called. When they try to usher him outside he kicks out the glass from the door, and they take him away in a police car.

"You're so shit-faced you don't know which end is up," the director yells after him angrily. It will cost $85 to replace the glass in the door, he moans.

Later that evening people ask about Derek. He has been at the hostel some time. Usually he is quiet, mooching cigarettes but doing no harm and seldom getting drunk.

"He phoned from the jail for his toothbrush," the director says. "I just laughed at him."

I stuck with the Frenchman. Jean's routine was painstakingly constructed around his voracious appetite. He ate at least four times a day, never spending a nickel, with his head down to meet his paw, like a bear grubbing ants.

Residents were not permitted to remain in the hostel during the daytime. They were kicked out at nine and could not return until later afternoon. This was to encourage them to look for work, but there was very little work now, and most people spent the days foraging for food, aid, and cheap pleasures, on a perpetual round of soup kitchens, street churches, pool halls, pinball arcades, flophouses, welfare offices, community health clinics, street corners, and park benches. It was a strange thing, but very few of them went near the ocean, which was only a short walk from downtown. The ocean seemed anathema to these men, as distant from their lifestyle as good from evil.

There was a strange, unexpected impatience, too, to the younger ones especially, that kept them downtown, in the centre of things: a hardly repressed urgency to their vagrancy. There was not an ounce of real boredom in most of them, not even enough to let them sleep; in the early hours, they could be found sitting like refugees, half-dressed, on the single long bench that ran the length of one wall in the yellow showers at the hostel, smoking cigarette after cigarette. In the daytime they hit the streets with the blind vigour of a snowstorm.

Jean was like a cock sparrow with his constant pecking at this meagre life. But he was talented. Once, when he'd been drinking, he dragged me into a Radio Shack store and played chess against a computer. The Frenchman lost the first game and then racked up win after win. Each time the machine flashed the message, "I AM CHECKMATED, I AM CHECKMATED," until the store manager kicked Jean out. And he played a magic game of pool, making incredible bank shots and jump shots, playing with one hand or the wrong end of the cue (once with the tip of an umbrella) gently patronizing his opponents: "I think you didn't call that shot, eh?"

He had no desire to go back and join the massive numbers already unemployed in Quebec. He would spend the winter where it was warmer, scrounging whatever he could, working if possible. Once, later, I actually saw him beg from a minister during a church service. "I don't have a nickel for coffee," he said, not whining, just telling it, keeping his eye on the minister. "If you're that hard up, here," the minister said, leaning down with a quarter. "God bless you."

Washing up – pearl-diving – was shunned by most hostel residents. Those who couldn't afford the three bucks a night bed fee were supposed to do chores, but they usually made themselves scarce after a meal. Jean, on the other hand, would volunteer. Once in the kitchen he would ransack the fridge and cupboards for fruit, eggs, leftovers, anything he could eat on the spot or smuggle out.

He was philosophical about life's setbacks. Whenever anything went wrong for him, or anybody else complained to him about their lot, whatever calamity had occurred, Jean would shrug and issue his invariable Gallic response: "We are men, we have experiences, *oui*?"

He said he really wanted to go to California and then to Mexico, but his passport had expired and he couldn't get another one because there was a warrant out for his arrest. He had hitchhiked from coast to coast nine times, and the names of foreign towns he claimed to have spent time in rolled off his bastard tongue easily. Yet there was always a suspicion he could have learned them in the same dogged way he improved his English. I'd say: "I'm going to lie down," and the Frenchman would cock his head and become suddenly serious. "Lie . . .

lay . . ." he would ponder in his cyclonic patois. "Lay is past?"

Each morning we followed a well-worn route from the hostel to downtown, a route of leery shopkeepers, such veterans, in fact, that one knowing doctor had a terse sign in his window. It said: "Acupuncture. No drugs. Do your breaking and entering elsewhere."

Each night we would return to a kedgeree of rice, macaroni, tuna fish. Some faces would be missing, and new ones would arrive.

A cowboy with a face filigreed with dark cracks like coal-dust tracings was kicked out the Saturday before Christmas. I thought about him as I lay in my upper bunk and listened to the rain drumming incessantly on the roof all night long. The next morning he dragged himself in for breakfast. "I got real wet last night," he said. He put his sopping sleeping bag up against a heating duct. He sat down on the floor and prepared to wait patiently, with the slouch hat he always wore half over his eyes. There was a laundry across the street, but he didn't have fifty cents for a dryer, and I knew he wouldn't ask for money. In the time I'd known him I'd never seen him handle so much as a nickel. He got his meals at the hostel, and where he spent his days I don't know, though I saw him at the library a couple of times. He didn't seem to drink, didn't work, didn't care to work; and money did not seem to matter to him at all. I'd offered him money before – by this time I was working occasionally out of the temporary labour pool – and he'd just declined it. I gave him fifty cents for the dryer, and this time he took it. "Thank you kindly," he said in his straightforward way. "One thing I can't afford to lose is my sleeping bag." He was about forty, and he'd been all over – Africa, New Zealand, South America, just hiking around. He called the bedroll he carried his Old Turkey, an expression from the thirties.

The cowboy was self-sufficient despite his lack of money, but there were tragic cases at the hostel, far too many people who needed help badly. One of them was an old girl in a cheap, imitation fur coat, who, coincidentally, I had seen in a greasy-spoon restaurant my first day in town. From my booth I watched her come in the door carrying a suitcase. She put the case down inside the glass door and stood alongside it, just stood there, literally wringing her hands. When the waitress reached the till, which was close to the door, the woman went over and said something to her, maybe asking if there were any jobs. The waitress gave her the rush, and after a few minutes the woman left again with the suitcase she could barely lift. On that occasion she had been distraught; but the next time I saw her, at the hostel, her condition was more acute. She swayed and talked to herself, but shrank in terror if anyone went near her. She was totally emaciated, her white, thin face riven by stress and nerves, framed by rat-tails of reddish hair. She hung back, refusing to join the food line – even though many were sympathetic and would gladly have let her go ahead of them – so that she often got no food at all. Her skin was translucent, her veins prominent but dry in appearance. She was all bone, and the bones seemed to shake, one with the other. Her hands were talons that hung at her sides, dumbly, like umbrella ribs or chopsticks. She would not talk. A slash of tires from the street outside made her cringe. She stiffened, as if with the ague, at every rip and clatter. She couldn't have been less than forty, yet her eyes were good, in a birdy way, and in other circumstances she could be imagined as the lively, artistic, slightly cuckoo wife of a businessman.

It was in this quality, this air of potential, that the horror existed in the women who found their way to the hostel. It was as if some germ had invaded them and laid waste the part of them that might have wanted a better life. To a greater or lesser degree this element of ultimate hopelessness was in all the women I saw there. The women had their own dormitory. While I was there the night-time segregation was maintained, and there was no trouble; but I heard later that a woman was sleeping with a man in the men's dorm when a jealous male rival poured gasoline over the bedsheets, tried to set them on fire, and then stabbed the couple through the blankets.

For the rest, there were epileptics who couldn't sleep, and narcoleptics who couldn't wake up, paralysed by sleep seizures. There were sexual deviants, slatterns, manipulators, bedwetters, pushers, and plain old-fashioned lunatics. There were people who wallowed in their own degradation, philosophers who embraced failure as the only virtue, people with dropsy and canker, swamp fever and scurvy, and folks who were just plain fiddle-footed. There were also those – a growing number – who had been laid off their jobs, had no benefits coming, and had nowhere else to go.

I was not prepared for the amount of mental sickness I found, either then or later in my odyssey. We assume that these people are being taken care of. We don't see them in our daily lives. But so many are on

Skid Row in the meanest rooms, nursing their jalopy visions, getting no help at all. Luckily, the community of strays at the bottom of society's heap accepts them with minimal discrimination – an amazing tolerance, which, if we could muster it as a society, would alleviate much heartbreak.

In their sleep it came out. One man would scream, over and over, night after night: "Die, bastard, die." Others moaned and sobbed. Sometimes the place resembled an asylum more than a hostel. There was one jaunty fellow, the best-dressed man in the place – he talked like a parrot – who took off his astrakhan hat one day with his back to me and there was a button dead centre in his skull. The operation was so recent the hair around the area had not grown back in.

Welfare day was the quietest. Even though they weren't supposed to be collecting while staying at the hostel, some kids managed to cash in fairly consistently. They would share their wealth with others, so that most of the residents would end up at the bar, one way or the other. One or two were collecting cheques both on the island and in Vancouver, so they took the ferry – they called it the Love Boat – and were gone for days.

In the laundry, the day I loaned the cowboy the money for the dryer, I watched a kid produce a crumpled piece of paper, which he spread on a table. "Sign this," he said to his friend. Printed on the paper, which was directly in front of me, I read: "To the welfare. I hope ——— will be able to pay forty dollars rent due ———." Underneath was a name and address and, in brackets alongside, the word "Landlord". It was simply a forged rent demand. Half an hour later the kid came back with a cheque.

This type of petty rip-off can largely be blamed on Catch-22 welfare regulations, which stipulate that to get relief you must have a place to stay, a room. A person without an address cannot get any real assistance. But without money it's hard to rent a room. So the rip-offs are often simply survival tools.

But others earned their money – the hard way.

# 4

*For myself I found*
*the occupation of a day laborer*
*was the most independent of any,*
*especially as it required*
*only thirty or forty days a year*
*to support one. The laborer's day ends*
*with the going down of the sun,*
*and he is then free*
*to devote himself to his chosen pursuit,*
*independent of his labor;*
*but his employer, who speculates*
*from month to month,*
*has no respite from one end*
*of the year to another*
—Thoreau, *Walden*

I held my hands out toward the sun so that I could see the glitter of silver particles embedded in the pores. I had worked the previous couple of days helping fibreglass a sailboat, a thirty footer. We'd put on five coats of robe and mat, and then I'd mistakenly run my hands under hot water, which had closed the pores on the fibreglass particles. Now I was tortured by the itch, especially around the wrists. When the December sun caught my hands the right way, they flashed like two fish.

"I hope the old man stays away this afternoon," my partner said.

We grinned at the thought of the old man, the boss. He wore carpet slippers in the mud and hopped around on his bad feet complaining about the way the work was being done. At least that's what he'd done all morning. "When you've shovelled as much drain rock as I have, you'll shovel it this way," he'd whine, making massive vague scooping motions with his arms. "Always shovel straight and never shovel the same rock twice." He could keep the same complaint in the air for hours.

"Don't matter," Rollo said. "He pays cash and he pays every day."

Rollo wore a red hard-hat with his name stencilled on the front. He had an economical build and short-boned, slightly rattish features. A teardrop was tattooed on his right cheekbone.

The old man was gone to some other job, and we sat on a pile of lumber, looking down across the fields to the freeway, smoking marijuana. A mud-clogged shovel stood by Rollo.

"Might be a couple of days' work in it for us," he reflected. We'd been hired out of the labour pool that morning.

"That's what the man said."

"Well," said Rollo, "it beats chasin' turkeys."

He was sick of chasing turkeys. He wouldn't do it any more, he'd told me earlier. But for a while it had been the only job he could get out of the pool. He'd never liked it, but then he started having nightmares. You go into a barn full of turkeys and toss them into a chain-driven steel barrel that whirls the birds around and is supposed to knock them unconscious but often doesn't. They go around, feathers flying, and when you pull them out they're mad, especially the big Toms. They scratch and bite. You grab them and stick their thin necks on steel prongs set in the wall, and they hang with the spike through their necks until they die. The pay is all right, and Rollo was good at it, but then he started having the nightmares, and he wouldn't do it any more.

He passed the stick of pot. "Beats bein' at home, too," he said. "The wife's a religious fanatic. She used to be a drug addict. She says she's had enough. 'I can't live with you,' she says."

He squinted down, narrow-eyed, into the glare from the sun, which gave the steep fields a quality of illusion, an ethereal laid-out look, as if they were a figment of the imagination or a map of some imaginary place like Atlantis. Occasionally, a scarf of smoke would blow from the fire in which we were burning waste wood, pieces of smashed drain tile, and scraps of tarpaper. It was a thick, black smoke, but it came from behind, and most of it dissipated overhead. A breeze stirred all the appendages of my skin: nails, hair, follicles, sweat glands, ducts. Or maybe it wasn't a breeze. Maybe it was anticipation. I could listen to Rollo all day.

He settled into his story. The Story. Himself and the wife. I'd had a taste of it in the morning. He took his hard-hat off and scratched his scalp.

"She has her ex-boyfriend over the other night. She says: 'I want to go to a meeting with him, then bring him home.' I say: 'Right on, that's cool, bringing your ex-boyfriend home, but if you're out till two o'clock in the mornin' don't come back and tell me you've been to a church meeting.' She knows the score.

"She came at me with a knife. Three times she's done that. This time I pick up a cushion and a lamp and I say: 'Okay, lady, you might get me once but I'll bust your fuckin' melon with this lamp and you'll be in hospital for a long time. I'll go down to Wilkinson Road for three, six months, but you'll still be in fuckin' hospital when I come out.' "

The brutishness of Rollo's words, emphasized by the gunshot crackling of the fire, was belied by their delivery. He spoke in a serious, half-bemused way, as if genuinely perplexed by the domestic scrapes he constantly found himself in, as if he wanted advice. Self-defence was his basic theme. A man can't let people walk on him, even his own wife, especially his own wife. But there was a question mark after it all. One suspected he had hoisted this harsh, jury-mast philosophy because his original, gentler one had in some way been damaged, blown over by a tempest that came out of the blue to scar him.

He was in his thirties, runty looking, with the shadow of confused dignity in his features. His thin, dark-brown hair was cut short and bore the marks from his hard-hat.

He took a bite out of a sandwich, shifted his weight – rattling the lumber pile and went on:

"Used to be this guy, twenty-six, moved into our house with this couple we knew. They had no bread, right, so we let them stay, and they brung this guy with them. So this twenty-six-year-old guy is home with the wife all day. I'm not stupid. I know what's going on. I go downtown one night after work, have a few beers, smoke some dope, then I decide to go back home. I'm out in the yard and they come out and I say to this guy: 'I don't want no twenty-six-year-old guy home all day with my old lady.'

"He says: 'I screw my own broads. I don't need nobody's old lady.'

"I go inside and he follows me. I say: 'Right, well then, beat it out of here.'

"He says: 'You say I'm screwin' your old lady, come outside.'

"I say: 'If I come outside I'll pound your melon on the concrete, an' I won't stop poundin,' buddy.'

"He says: 'I'm a black belt.'

"I say: 'I'm a pink belt.'

"Anyway they both jump me, him and my old lady. Can you believe it, right in my own yard? Cops come. I do three days. I say, why me? They say to cool off. They invent some warrant somewhere. There's no warrant. They know me. They know when I get out I'm going to kill the sonofabitch. So they send a cop with me to my house. I say to the cop: 'Why don't you take him? It's my house.'

"The cop says to this guy: 'Yes, you seem to be in the wrong. Have you nowhere to go?'

"This guy says: 'No, I don't. I've got no record, you've got nuthin' on me,' he says.

"Anyway, then he takes one look at me and he says to the cop: 'I think I'll go back east.' He knew the score."

Rollo sat there for a minute after he finished, a poor cuckolded sap trying to understand it all. He gave up travelling around because his wife wanted to settle down. He gave up drinking because his wife did not agree with it. He passed the roach. Drugs, he said, were now his only pleasure.

"Last night," he said, "we're puttin' tinsel on the tree. She's puttin' it on piece by piece, an' I'm slingin' bunches on. She says: 'You always have to mess things up,' an' whacks me on the head. I punch her on the arm. The wife says: 'You mean cocksucker, you're not supposed to hit a lady.' I say: 'Right on, I'm mean enough to trade punch for punch with you, lady.' "

To hear him tell it there was never a cloistral moment in his marriage. He had a three-month-old baby, and a twelve-year-old boy from his wife's first marriage. The boy had also started to give him trouble.

We saw the old man's truck on the road and went back to work, laying drain tile around the raw cement frame of a house under construction. When he got to the site the old man jumped up and down. "What's this?" he ranted, pointing to a spot of ground. "This is supposed to be sand. What you put fill in there for? Sand. It has to be sand. I said sand. The goddam inspector's coming tomorrow. Cover it with sand so the inspector can't see it. Jesus Christ, there's going to be a sidewalk there." He tore his hat off his head and flopped in his carpet slippers back to the truck, despair eating at his very genes. "Jesus Christ," I heard him say.

We went for the wheelbarrows. "Mine's a Ford, yours is a Dodge," Rollo said without enthusiasm.

"What the hell, maybe you'll get something good for Christmas," I said, to cheer him up.

"I want to get my guitar out of pawn, also the old lady's gold cross," Rollo said. We started to shovel.

"What does your wife do?" I asked. "She work?"

"Yeah, she's studyin'," Rollo said gloomily. "Studyin' daytime TV."

That night the old man paid us for the day as we sat in the cab of his truck. Forty-one dollars and fifty cents each. Then he drove us downtown. He was a different person when the work was finished, a thoughtful old man, a small independent builder.

"You must have had some losers out of the labour pool," I said, curious to know what he thought of the men he hired.

He shifted gears. "I never had a bad worker out of that place," he said flatly. "Not once."

When we got out, Rollo said to me: "Where you living?"

"The hostel," I said.

"That hostel . . ." Rollo began.

"I didn't know such a place existed," I said. I was still self-conscious about living there.

"Ah, I bin down there," Rollo said. "People say, what you doin' down there, them's tramps. I say, what the hell, I get on with 'em. I'd go there tonight." He looked at me. He didn't want to go home.

"We don't want to go there," I said. "Nothing to do but watch TV. Let's get a beer."

# 5

*What comes next you never know,*
*Lady Luck runs the show.*
—Petronius

The Labour Pool. Some sit like stunned lizards. There are wolfmen, with fire-blackened faces and bundled offerings, peering out of whiskers like fabulous beasts.

The card players always sit around a centre table, the only object around which people can circulate freely. There are other tables, long, mess-like, wooden ones, but they are shoved up against the back wall. People are sprawled on them, some asleep.

One of the card players is crudely taunting the government man in charge, Lenny, a slight man, neatly dressed in brown slacks and a white shirt with a tie.

"What you want for Christmas, Lenny, a new job?"

The government man, standing behind the check-in desk adjacent to the door, replies with a half-feigned weariness: "I want you to get a full-time job is what I want."

"Get me one." The card player is cutting the deck energetically, with his back turned to Lenny. His hair stands up in tufts around his cap. A cigarette is bobbling from side to side in his mouth.

"I got you one at the zoo," Lenny jokes.

"Yeah, suckin' water out of dead fish."

The laughter is little more than a rumbling of cleared throats, as inane as the quip that prompted it.

A minute later a huge man swings through the doorway to confront Lenny. They talk together briefly and Lenny shouts: "Four men, four dollars an hour, to dig a ditch, one day's work."

The cards go on riffling and slapping and rasping like a cage full of birds. The big contractor leans his back on Lenny's desk and surveys the room awkwardly. Between the rolled bottoms of his work pants and the tops of his hiked socks a segment of white longjohns shows. Between there and his cap blooms a mountain draped in castoffs. There is a pinched look about his eyes as if he has been working too hard. He moves further into the room and leans his arms on a partition, coarse-grained and warped so freely it swings and buckles under his weight. The partition protects Lenny's private area – a desk, a file cabinet, a coat rack, a telephone.

The contractor waits. He has presumably been told these men are desperate and will work cheaply. He looks at them. Their clothes are worn and stained. Some have on work boots, but others just wear running shoes. Some are clearly drunk, though it is only a little past seven in the morning. There are smeared drunks with bleeding eyes, red rough faces with heavy bones pushing out like dislocations, faces rimed with not enough sleep, great mops of dirty, tangled hair, and chipped teeth. Those lying on the long tables at the back continue to sleep. There are a couple of women in the room. There is even a dog. There is no sign anybody even knows the contractor is there. He clears his throat.

"You need heavy boots," he says finally, to hear himself speak. He frowns at Lenny.

"You," the government man calls, singling out a thickset, middle-aged man. "You have good boots. You want to work, four dollars an hour?"

"Nope."

"You?"

"No way."

"Nobody want to work?"

"We want to work, Lenny," whines a thin man, a chronic complainer, a useless worker. "We want to work, but four dollars an hour is a disgrace. Disgraceful."

Lenny says nothing. Don't give me that, he might be thinking. I know most of you men. You're yard boys who'll take fishhooks or elephant tails in payment if it suits you. What suits you mainly is money for liquor and the time to drink it. He might be thinking that if he's feeling down. He'd be mostly right. It is in the manner of Aristotle and Herodotus that these men regard money. The temptations of inflation and debasement, rates of credit or investment – all the grave dangers –

35

they have escaped. Their monetary rectitude is unsullied. They work one day to provide money for two days of leisure. By this archaic value relationship, seven hours' work at four dollars an hour is insufficient. It has little to do with the hourly rate, though the big contractor's offer is a meagre one even by labour pool standards. Ten hours at four dollars an hour might be acceptable. Eight hours at five dollars an hour would certainly play. These are the most practical of men, closer to the civilization that erected the pyramids or sculpted the sphinxes.

Still, this is a highly unusual development. Invariably there is someone desperate enough for anything, someone who has just got into town broke. But this day they just sprawl there, all of them, as if they are anchored in rim rock by eye bolts.

And then there's Lance.

In the silence Lance steps forward, ready to go to work. He is only slightly retarded, but the simplest instructions confuse him. Boxes he stacks will fall down, a ditch he digs will cave in. Few employers retain him for more than a day, and because sensitive employers find it difficult and embarrassing to fire Lance alone they often also get rid of the other temporary men who have been hired along with him. For that reason few men in the labour pool want to work alongside Lance, and he is known as the Widowmaker. My first job out of the labour pool was with Lance, unloading and stacking bales of insulation in a warehouse.

"The other guy's no good. You come back tomorrow but not him," I was told at the end of the day.

But Lance has good rubber boots. "I'll take it," he says, his whole being a stupor of innocence, projecting such willingness that certain of the men, hardened as they are, never fail to be touched.

The big contractor takes in the dangly arm from which hangs a ridiculous orange lunch bucket, the hunched shoulders, the flop of near-orange hair, the unnaturally clean chin, and the look of baffled wonderment. Lance looks as if he was born yesterday, or, more accurately, as if a large foetus has been unfurled and dressed for work.

"I don't want him," the employer says. He is angry now.

"Later," Lenny says quietly. "Later there will be men who need work. Give me the address of the job site and I'll send men out there. We'll get four men for you." He steers the contractor to the door.

A very short time later, as the recession spawns more and more itinerant job-seekers, this contempt for certain work will all but vanish, of course. These labour pools will become the trenches in which men wait to hurl themselves on any kind of job, thousands of men all over North America, milling for a job like blind kittens for a teat. The dawn line-ups will be shown on television and in the newspapers, and people will say: "Just like the thirties."

By now, early 1981, that recession is a gathering cloud.

It was a sluttish place with greasy green walls, relieved only by the massive, twin-panel windows that dominated the street side. At this hour the windows made little difference to the gloomy character of the place. Even in mid-morning, any sun that shone in seemed to contribute a timorous aspect that, instead of bringing freshness and lustre, managed to make everything look still more dispirited.

The room was on the main floor of a large, old, federal government building, next door to the post office. It was the only room off the tiled lobby, which, from eight-thirty in the morning onward, was crowded with office workers taking the elevator upstairs. Most of these people, out of embarrassment, contrived to ignore the growing cluster of jobless around the labour-pool doorway.

A crazy wall, directly opposite the door where people entered the pool, had been built to partition it from the post office. It was a jerry-built thing constructed from pieces of castoff plywood of various shapes and sizes and was undoubtedly the only wall of a federal government department in town cobbled that way from waste pieces. The very wall seemed to mock the people inside. At its base was a ragged line of plain chairs, from which newcomers were scrutinized as they entered through the door.

Many a day I sat there. They really were an awful lot. When I saw a couple of guys go out to a private house to do some work, gardening or painting maybe, in a posh part of town, I imagined some old dear eyeing them through the window and frantically locking up the family jewels and hiding the booze.

The room had a high ceiling and the tall windows on the street side opened only at the top, so that to release the cigarette smoke Lenny, a fastidious man and a non-smoker, had to take a long pole with a hooked end – like an elongated boat hook – from its resting place in a corner behind the partition. Throughout the morning he could be seen, his tight profile lifted high, fussily opening and closing the windows to release the dense build-up of smoke. The men worshipped the cigarette the way primitive tribes worshipped larger totems, and everybody seemed to smoke. This was true everywhere I travelled, among working men and transients.

The windows were tinted so that people passing on the busy sidewalk could not see inside, though the men could look out onto the street. From the outside the tinting created a mirror effect, and pedestrians would often stop to comb their hair and put on lipstick, posing momentarily, to the delighted contempt of the ragged audience invisible behind the quicksilver. (Later the pool was moved to another, much smaller place a few blocks away.)

It is worth taking time to consider the labour pool, for it is the last refuge of the day labourer and a lifeline to the transient and it was to become a public symbol of the recession, a measure of misery that could be photographed, like the soup lines.

The labour pool works like this:

Each morning you sign, giving your name and social insurance number. The first day you will get a very low-priority number: let's say thirty. The chances of a job that first day are theoretically small. Each day, however, so long as you continue to sign in each morning your priority will increase as men ahead of you on the list bid on and are assigned jobs.

I say theoretically number thirty is unlikely to land a job because, in fact, it might well do so. On my first day I was number twenty-four on the list and got out almost immediately, simply because nobody ahead of me bid on the job. There are many reasons why they wouldn't. A man with a high priority, for example, will not want to give up that priority for a one- or two-day job. He will want to wait for a job to come along of longer duration, or at top money. Some of the men might be on welfare or unemployment insurance and might thus want to be even more choosy, requiring a job where the money is paid "under the table" so as not to interfere with their benefits. Some want to wait for a half-day job, for beer money, because they know they are allowed to do that – work a certain minimal number of hours – without endangering their priority.

Played by men who know the ropes, it can be a fascinating game. A man can sit at number one on the list for weeks, taking small, part-time jobs (often in addition to welfare or unemployment insurance pay-ments, or even a full-time night job) and still remain in an unassailable position if a really good job should come along.

But most of the labour pool jobs are not good jobs.

Digging a ditch, for example – the job for which there were no takers. Digging a ditch means digging to the other side of the world. It means having a package of smokes because the only acceptable excuse for a work stoppage is to foul your lungs, to swap one suicide for another. Roll your own, it takes longer. Roll your own and lean on your shovel and wish you'd never heard of the labour pool or some cheapjack gyppo who wants a ditch dug. Because when a guy comes to the labour pool for ditch diggers you can bet it's the deepest ditch in the world. Deepest and cheapest. Digging a ditch is . . . well . . . a euphemism. Shovelling sand is another one. Shovelling sand, in its most saintly manifestation, means shovelling drain rock, pebbles that wouldn't fit in your mouth, transporting the rock by wheelbarrow across a swamp or over a mountain and dumping it gently . . . ever so gently, slower with that barrow now, gently does it . . . on top of a plastic pipe. If the barrow should tip in the swamp or topple off the mountain, the rock must be reclaimed, for drain rock is expensive, much more expensive, anyhow, than the time of a labour pool bull. And then there is clean-up. Sounds easy enough. Clean-up. It means pulling salvageable lumber from a quagmire of mud, rooting like a pig, until you're carrying so much mud and you're so wet and your back is so bent that your knuckles scrape the ground. "Bull work" they call it. Shovelling sand. Clean-up. Digging a ditch. The labour pool.

A motel is being renovated, upgraded to get the tour-bus traffic. A bunch of mattresses were being stored around the pool, but some children went and pushed them all into the water. Now they're soaked. The pool is full of them. The water has turned into a brown scum, and the mattresses are coated in slime.

"We'll have to pump out the water, then haul out the mattresses."

"And who the hell is going to do that, eh? Them suckers'll weigh a thousand pounds. They's filthy too. How we gonna get 'em outa the water, eh?"

"Phone the labour pool."

"You mean you want a union man to get in that crawl space and cut that concrete with a masonry saw, right?"

"Right?"

"That's a good joke, man. I don't care how scarce work is, that's a joke. They's no air in there, they's no light in there, he's not going to be able to breathe. He like to kill hisself. An' you say you don't have no goggles, no mask. Shit!"

"Forget it. I know where I can get a man, cheap and no bullshit."

"I gotta get the pipe laid by the time the inspector comes or I lose that eleven per cent mortgage. I got a special deal. Who ever heard of an eleven per cent mortgage these days? I lose that I have to pay twenty-two per cent. I can't afford no twenty-two per cent. I gotta have the pipe laid, the water working, and the septic tank in."

"Well, then, you gotta dig a ditch to drain off the water first. Then you got to dig another sonofabitch for the pipe. And you want it done by hand? That's bull work. The guys are going to be up to their neck in shit. That's nothing but mud out there."

"Well, tell me, who's going to do it?"

"Phone the labour pool's all you can do."

Barbed wire to unload, chickens to be caught, fruit to be picked, hand-bills to be delivered, stumps to be dug. Don't want to pay medical insurance, unemployment insurance, workmen's compensation, union rates, danger money . . . ?

"C'mon boys, let's go, this is a highball outfit. What's that? No, we don't pay no highball wages, ha, ha."

"Lunch, you wanna take a lunch, eh? You don't wanna work through, eh?"

You pull until your arm is strung out like one long vein.

"What the hell you doin'?"

"Ripping out the weeds."

"Those are strawberry plants, for Christ's sake. You're fired."

"Anybody asks, you're union, okay?"

"Can't give you cash today, boys. Them cheques are good this time, though. Sorry about last time."

"Hide around the back. The boss don't like me hirin' guys with beards. I don't know why, just hide around the back when he comes around, okay?"

"The inspector's comin' tomorrow."

"Ever use a compactor? Yeah. Well, I gotta tell you this machine is the shits. Got an almighty kick on her. Knock your arms off. And you gonna be on her all day, you lucky sonofabitch."

"The inspector's comin'."

"Slap a line. Pour that slab."

Recalling now all the labour pools I worked out of I have an impression of darkness, a nigrescent ominousness. Yet those rooms were surely always full of colour: T-shirts, slickers, eyepatches, lunch buckets, tattoos, headbands, bandanas.

All this, though, left only a dark impression, as if the essence of all that manhood was in fine particles beneath the skin, where the blackness of negroes was once thought to reside. Perhaps it was simply a darkness within myself, a reaction to the surroundings, a sort of dyslexia.

An Indian in a brand-new beige raincoat one or two sizes too large stares dully as his friend speaks. He has the belt of the coat draped around his neck with the ends dangling as if it is the latest fashion. On his feet he wears blue sneakers. His friend is saying: "I got ripped off for a hundred. You saw that hundred-dollar bill, right? Ten hits, man, this chick rips me off. I find her, I get hold of her hair an' I drag her down to the water an' push her face in till she pays. I don't care she is a lady."

"Tha's no lady, she rips you off, man," the Indian replies uninterestedly. "Tha's like my ex-old lady."

An old fat man with grey hair flung right back from his forehead and a grey fleshy face stands over Lenny's desk. His hands are curled on the desktop. He wears mittens with the fingers cut out. He has lost the shopping bag he always carries, he complains. It contains all his possessions. Has anyone seen it? He lost it yesterday. The old man spends his mornings in the labour pool, sleeping. He doesn't sign in, but he brings his bag in every morning and sits in a chair and sleeps.

"Anyone seen this man's bag?" Lenny asks.

"You din' have no bag yest'day," somebody shouts accusingly.

"Yep." The old man nods vehemently.

"Not yest'day. Yest'day you just brung yourself."

There is laughter at the image of the old man just brunging himself down to the labour pool. The old man also laughs at this, to himself, and then dodders past the card table toward one of the vacant chairs backed up against the crazy plywood wall. "Back to the drawing board," he mutters, with unexpected, maybe unconscious humour, and within minutes he is asleep, his head thrown back to the wall, his mouth open, snoring.

There are kids who have obviously been out all night who are also seeking not work but sleep. One youngster, sprawled out on one of the long tables, puts his head down on a bundle of clothing. A thin girl, her black hair plastered to her head, tells him: "Get your greasy head off my coat." But she says it kindly, as if she is his girl, and she doesn't try to move the coat.

A young Oriental carrying a bulging green garbage bag slung over his shoulder ferrets with his free hand through the ashtrays, and then on the floor, for cigarette butts. He puts the bag down on the floor, splits the snipes, empties the tobacco into a paper and rolls a smoke. He wears a torn black coat, an old gentleman's coat with braided holes for buttons that no longer exist. It hangs on him, open at the front like filthy drapes. Crotch-wrinkled black pants, the cuffs hanging off in strips, are worn on top of brown pants, which show through. Everything the Oriental has on is rotten, and possesses in its shape not only the body of the present owner but the folds and foibles of previous wearers. They are the clothes of somebody who has dragged himself for miles before dying in them. He is bareheaded and has hair so smooth and black it shines like the finish on a new car. He is oblivious to the other men unless they offer him a cigarette. Then he sidles up to the offering or swings on it dramatically, as if he fears it is about to be withdrawn. He brings to this action an amazing intensity and concentration. His eyes burn, and the light in them never seems to change, as if he is confident he possesses some influence that is stronger than any other. He never speaks. It is rumoured that he has very rich parents in Calgary who keep pleading with him to go home and share in the family wealth. One of those rumours. Meanwhile he lives at the hostel. It is this man I almost tripped over while he was meditating on the floor a few days earlier.

Buchanan, a lanky regular at the pool, suddenly rages at him. "Are you stupid? You'll get a disease. If you want a cigarette ask for one."

The Oriental takes a cigarette from Buchanan, then a young man, a Christer, beckons him, but instead of a cigarette he proffers a religious tract with a bright yellow picture of a grossly suffering Jesus on the cover. The Oriental throws it down on the floor with the sort of agitated motion an angry child might use, then dives under one of the tables onto the floor, dragging his bulging garbage bag with him. The tables, backed up against the wall, form a sort of cave where the more wasted elements find gloomy refuge, dark shapes strewn like socks under a bed who are to be imagined – outside this room – only in some awful place where slime glosses the walls and planks sag underfoot into shallow pools of sewage.

Two middle-aged men are listening to a small plastic radio that dangles from a nail in the wall. One of them pounces on a reference to leisure time and grumbles savagely, "Leisure time. Should come down here, wait for a job three, four hours, that's leisure time."

His partner says: "It's not leisure time if you don't have no money," and there are nods of agreement. The room is packed with people waiting for work or killing time.

A man occupies one corner of the card table, away from the players, a pencil in his hand, notes and diagrams in front of him. He has been coming for a week. He is working out the date of the end of the world. One of the card players keeps looking over at him, shaking his head, and saying glumly: "Bug ward . . . bug ward."

Outside, the streets are becoming busy. A policeman is writing a ticket for a kid who rode his bike on the sidewalk. A young guy, watching from inside the pool, from the window, wheels and runs out the door to confront the policeman, who waves him away impatiently. The young guy returns to the room, flushed, excited. "I said to him, 'Cracked the mafia, eh?' Just like that. 'Cracked the mafia, eh?' " He cackles loudly. Nobody pays any attention. Most of the men have already been there two hours. They are tired.

In winter the West Coast has always attracted the true planetary citizens, loners, men not hobbled by the parasitic drag of government, free traders in the profession of getting by. Transients. It is the reason I came.

They do not come for the beauty. Indeed, they seem at first blush to have an aversion to beauty in any aspect of their lives, as if they are fighting against renewal, against life itself. Yet they live like weeds, in chinks in the sidewalk, and rely on nature, especially the climate. The weather brings them. They do not want to freeze to death further east. It is a natural, time-honoured migration. So the labour pools and the hostels are always full in winter. Only this year it is much worse.

The supervisors of these government labour pools seem to have long since lost the power to kick out the idlers and strays. Instead the current of their lives – the lives of the transients – often seems to have gripped the supervisor, so that he, like them, no longer recognizes any compulsion at all.

Some supervisors are better than others. In many pools the barbaric practice of having men stand outside most of the night to have a shot at a job persists. The men freeze and curse and camp all night on a piece of cardboard for a lousy day's work – if they are lucky. It was these scenes the newspaper and television cameras captured during the recession.

In other pools this was not the practice. The priority system did away with the first-come, first-served method, and even the first-timers had their priority chosen by lot so that it made no difference who arrived first and nobody needed to wait outside half the night.

It was striking that at the height of the recession so many labour pools still forced the men to line up in the early hours, bringing cardboard to sit on, lighting fires in the street to keep warm, brawling for position, suffering the drunks and the deadbeats, only to find that there were twelve jobs for two hundred men. Even more striking, perhaps, was the fact that though newspapers from coast to coast featured the thirties-style dramatic dawn pictures of the stamping men and their steaming breath, not one editorial that I saw questioned the need for such a reprehensible lockout. Few people actually saw the lines of jobless in person, of course, for the labour pools are normally opened around seven in the morning, long before the rush hour. If people had seen those lines they might have wondered what country and what brave epoch they were in. They might have been angry enough to demand changes in the system used by the government pools. But they saw only the way the sidewalks outside certain buildings were littered and streaked, and many of them probably pulled a face and wondered what they paid their taxes for. Often they were spared even the soiled sidewalk, for many of the pools are situated so that the men line up in alleyways, off the beaten path. This is true also of the soup lines, which are generally on Skid Row and thus hidden from the general population.

Once inside, the men wait for the jobs to come in by telephone. Occasionally, an employer will visit in person, but not often. Some days the phone doesn't ring more than a couple of times. When it does, however, two questions are likely to be asked before the men bid on a job: "Does he pay cash?" and "Does he pay every day?" (in the event the job is to last more than the one day).

The men want cash because many of them don't have bank accounts, or identification that a bank will accept. And they want to be paid every day so that if they get drunk or don't return to the job for any other reason they are paid up.

One additional question invariably put by the regulars is: "Does he pay under the table?" This is to ascertain that no tax or other deductions will be made, that if they are hired at five dollars an hour they will get the full five dollars.

These three things, the payment of cash, payment every day, and no deductions are the unwritten rules of the labour pool, appreciated and accepted by most employers who use the places.

There are several ironies in these arrangements, not least that the federal government, which runs the pools, appears to be aiding and abetting the evasion of certain formalities by both employer and employee. The jobs the government pools often have the hardest time filling are government jobs, where the pay might be high but the workers know they will have to wait at least two weeks for a cheque that will be studded with deductions. Much better to take the five-dollar-an-hour job with the cash paid at the end of every day "under the table."

There is no way for the government to keep track of these underground payments. Even if they keep a record every time a man goes out on a job they have no way of knowing how long the job lasts. For even those who are working will often go each morning before work to the labour pool and sign in, and so get back on the priority list so that when their current job is ended they will have the priority to get another one, if and when they want it.

The supervisors have no illusions, of course, either about their "clients", or about the men who hire them, the high-pocket slavers who use the pool as a source of cheap, exploitable, non-union labour. Neither, if they are at all imaginative, are the supervisors confused about their own role. It is partly to keep the men off the streets, to give the unemployed a place to go and some hope for a day's work, and so help minimize social problems that, if unchecked – especially during a recession – could lead to angry mobs, looting, and rioting in the streets, as they did in the thirties. These dismal rooms with their *Playboys* and their *National Enquirers* are much more than a place for down-and-outers to get the odd job. That was why Lenny might, just might, have felt a peculiar tremor when as one man the labour pool stood mute that morning in the face of the big contractor's job offer. Lenny did have imagination. Instead of becoming slovenly, as one might have expected, he dressed consistently well. He emptied the ashtrays himself and kept the room free of flies and smoke. He never kept the men waiting in the morning. At Christmas time it was his habit to hand around a large box of candy, and this small kindness alone had the effect of quieting the men in a way that suggested for a moment their many heartaches and heartbreaks. He kept the lid on as best he could. Such an imaginative man must have seen dangers in the solidarity that day, must have thought that, with decent jobs getting scarcer every day, with more and more men pouring into the pool, it might only take a spark to set the place afire.

He must have been horrified when the spark was struck so quickly . . .

"There's been a bunch of animals using it. Blame your buddies. They don't know how to use a bathroom."

The abrasive voice of the building superintendent, a stout Britisher in coveralls, explained to the men of the labour pool why they would no longer be allowed to use the bathroom in the federal building.

The labourer who had made the awful discovery that the washroom was locked to him retorted angrily: "You nearly had a filthy mess on the floor in the corridor, old man. You want me to shit my pants?"

"Blame your buddies," the superintendent repeated defiantly, enjoying his punitive, capricious authority, backscuttling gleefully toward the door. "There's some animals around in this room."

The yells followed him, threatening excrement on the floors, in the elevators, on the roofs, in the basement. It was a ridiculous development. They had to have access to the bathroom. Some were very upset. The air was full of bitterness. For a time it looked as if there might be real trouble; then, gradually, the mood passed. Most of the men, used to defeat, expecting nothing else perhaps, deserted their anger for humour.

Rollo, my erstwhile buddy on construction, broke the back of the anger with his rank humour, recalling laconically: "Once I ripped off two doors in a restaurant because the washroom didn't work. I was pissing in the hallways. I got thirty days. I said to the judge: 'Where should I piss? In Granville Street? That's ninety days.' "

The room filled with low laughter. At the back an urban cowboy with shaking hands spilled his coffee on one of the long tables. He looked at it, stubbed out his cigarette in the mess, and walked away. Lance, the boy rejected by the contractor, back from the cafeteria upstairs, immediately sat in the mess of hot coffee and swimming tobacco. He remained there, showing no distress. The card player who had joked with Lenny earlier was saying: "I'm gonna be evicted 'cos my hair's too long." His hair sprang out like wire from under his hunting cap. "I wash it every day, an' I'm usin' too much hot water, she says, that bitch of a landlady."

All the time he was telling this preposterous story his eyes were flicking over Lance.

"You sat in a pile of coffee," he said finally, stolidly, as if the other man had just dealt a stupid card.

"I don't feel anything wet," Lance lied in a challenging tone bordering on the beginnings of hysteria. He blushed. He was tremendously sensitive about his lapses. He sat there in the coffee, blinking fiercely under the attention of the men, staring back at them. There was nothing blank about his stare. It was piercing, gripping, as if he were trying to grasp something equally damaging about others in the room.

"Dummer'n red bricks," the card player muttered, disgusted. "I'm tellin' you this for your own good, Lance. You better shape up."

Lenny, probably feeling he should step in to help Lance, warned the card player: "No gambling today."

"Fuck off, Lenny. Get out of here," the card player told him.

So I moved furniture, ran a jackhammer, installed insulation and office furniture, loaded and unloaded trucks, dug stumps, poured concrete, humped drywall, and did a whole lot more. Jobs to dream by. I dreamed of the place I could be, should be, and how on good mornings the sky would be orange and turquoise at this time of year, a staggering, gentle colour. The water would have a mist on it, rising past the forest on the other side of the lake. A light frost would cover the sand, probably, near the water's edge, as well as the cabin roof, picnic table, and dock. There would be almost no smell to the land now, especially in the morning. Brown fallen leaves everywhere, but if you fell to your knees and scooped the leaves to your face they would smell of nothing. Even the pine would fail to scent the air with a hint of tar and turpentine – and pine grew everywhere, around the cabin, over the hills, and in the wheel ruts on every abandoned road. When the wind got up the whole place would whistle and rattle, from screen doors to garbage cans. The rusted silver fishing lure above the door would swing and jangle, too, a peaceful, faintly Oriental sound in the cold air, like the tinkle of prayer sticks. The fretted tops of the trees would slowly fill with darkness. And then . . . only the dark rounded eminences of a mountain and the feel of the log-jammed earth.

In my dream the first snow dripped from the roof down past the windows onto the perspiring ground. A great windstorm drubbed volleys of melted snow up against the windows. The fishing lure swung like a metronome. Steam almost obscured the lake, giving it an evanescent quality. Then a slippery glaze of black ice formed where the water met the shoreline. Small ducks flew squeaking over the water, some black and white, but most black and grey. The lake froze early in this daydreaming of mine, and with snow on top it lay white and unmarked all the way to the treeline on the opposite shore. A sepia image of winter. There was nothing as pure as that lake just after it iced over. It would be like the promise of some great confession. When the wind blew, huge clumps of snow would fall from the trees, hitting the ground with a fat dead skunk thump, making pockmarks. Wreathing spindrifts of snow would hook in the air like a solar wind, meeting and

48

merging with the spume of ground snow. The trees would look like ghastly, dripping hands, or maybe they'd just be dumb-looking, like soft, white toys kids might roll around on a weighted base.

I thought I knew what some of the other men I'd met, my friends now, were thinking about, too. Take Ricketts, for example. . . .

# 6

*What people are ashamed of
usually makes a good story.*
— F. Scott Fitzgerald, *The Great Gatsby*

His name was Ricketts, first name Benjamin. I met him when he took a bed in the Victoria hostel, and we became friends. If he had stayed in the navy a year or two longer he would have been eligible for two-thirds pension. But he got out, drank his money away, and drifted. He became a first-aid attendant in a forestry camp and, in a year and a half, saved twelve thousand dollars, which he then went through in less than two months. Before long he was in Alaska harvesting kelp eggs for the Japanese. Then he worked on a salvage vessel that was never successful in salvaging anything much during his time on board. The crew used to kill seals out of boredom, shoot them from the deck, and leave them dead on the ice or in the water. After that he drifted down to the Queen Charlottes, flat broke, and lived by digging razorback clams on the beaches and selling them door-to-door. He slept in his old car with a dog he'd picked up somewhere and drove the car right down along the beaches hunting for clams, with deer no bigger than his dog trailing along behind, picking for food in the tire tracks, snuffling for cigarette snipes he dropped. They loved tobacco.

The Indians tried to drive him off. They didn't want a white man horning in on the clams, even though they no longer dug them commercially. Once a bunch of them chased him out of a bar. But in the end the Indians were his best customers, and one of them, a well-known carver, would always buy any and all he had left at the end of the day. Ricketts did that for a year. Then he found the Lord. It happened through a paperback book he picked up in a dusty island store. It had a bleeding dagger on the cover, and he thought it was a thriller, a murder mystery. It turned out to be the testimony of a Russian convert, a man who had found the light by reading the literature he seized from Christians he was supposed to persecute. Ricketts read the book many times and then began to go to the library to read the Bible. And then he joined the Shantymen, a group of missionaries, and was enrolled in their Bible college. He had no money, but his tuition was paid by an anonymous American supporter of the group. "God laid a burden on his heart," Ricketts always explained to people later, with the piety that marked his conversion.

After two years of Bible study and training, he was sent out to preach in far-flung places: logging camps, Indian villages, isolated ranches.

He showed inspirational films and gave away Bibles from the trunk of his old car, the same old car he had driven on the beach for clams. And he ended each meeting by asking: "Would you like to accept the Lord into your heart at this moment?" Everything in those early days was calculated in terms of his own mortality and that of others — in terms of damnation and salvation. He had no doubts about his faith. And then, unaccountably, he began to backslide, and in shame he quit the Shantymen. "I was not walking with the Lord," he said.

Again drinking heavily, he drifted back to the port on Vancouver Island from which he had first put to sea. He had no car now, nothing but an old seabag in a locker at the bus depot, and he used to walk for hours on the shore. It was said that nowhere in the world were there rock pools of such beauty and variety, of such incredible luxury. The confusion of land and sea was such that it was hardly possible to walk in any direction without coming to the ocean within a short space of time. Ricketts, whose vocabulary was largely composed of portentous homilies, described it exactly as one would expect. "It is," he would say, "God's country."

Amid the anguish of this external beauty and his inner remorse reality intruded, and he began to go to the labour pool. His first job was as a driver for a drunk who wanted to go from party to party, from bar to bar. He made $29. At the labour pool he learned about the hostel and moved in because he could not afford a room. The hostel disgusted him. He was a navy man with neatness drilled into him, and the hostel was a mess. He kept his seabag in the locker at the bus station so his things would not be stolen. Every couple of days he went to the locker to get a change of clothing and then took a bus back to the hostel. He was so ashamed of his situation he got off, rain or shine, at a stop

51

almost a mile away from the hostel. He didn't want the driver to know where he was staying. He worried incessantly about being tagged as a bum, a welfare recipient. Every imagined slight bothered him, and he was convinced that the hostel staff had him pegged for a bum. It got to him so much he went to the director. "Look here," he said, "I'm not taking welfare and I don't intend to. I'm trying to find work, and meanwhile I'm supporting myself." He held out his hand. The director, who knew Ricketts's worrying nature and was irritated by it, didn't shake the hand. Instead he made a sort of slapping motion toward it and then turned his back. Ricketts brooded even more savagely after this. There is a widespread persecution complex among men who are down and out, and especially among those who are meeting obstacles in a genuine battle to retrieve their lives, and Ricketts was prey to this feeling.

There was one staff member at the hostel, a part-time helper, a prissy young acolyte of the director with a sheepish look about him like a rich fellow going off to war as a private. He had spoken to Ricketts at first, but then had become stiff, or so Ricketts thought. He became furious with him after a couple of minor skirmishes. Once Ricketts, employing his first-aid knowledge, advised the young man to check a drunk, who had vomited in his bunk every hour during the night, to make sure he didn't choke. The advice was ignored. Another time he tried to get help for a young drug addict. The young staff member said, in a superior manner, "Before you help them you have to stop and ask yourself: 'Am I being conned?'"

All this built up so that Ricketts finally collared the young man.

"Look, you are going to be around this town for a while are you?" he said.

"Yes."

"Well, so am I, we'll see each other again, remember that."

He let this sink in and walked away. When he realized what he had done – practically threatened the man, reverted to the heathenism of his seagoing days – he became more anguished than ever. He prayed furiously in his bunk at night. The wino on the next bunk heard him. He sat on the edge of the upper berth, his feet drooping forward uselessly, toes pointing downwards. "I can see you're a big drinker," he said approvingly, when Ricketts stopped praying. "I can tell by your nose." Ricketts had a disfiguring red pimple on his nose at the time. He hadn't taken a drink for weeks. He began to feel he couldn't win. He felt himself better than these tosspots and maimed soldiers, but immediately he thought that, he cursed himself for false pride.

Every way he turned he stumbled. He imagined everybody was against him, was snubbing him, even the waitress who served him eggs with whites that were too soft. He had such a lack of presence that he rarely got any satisfaction even when he complained. When he sent back the runny eggs, the cook popped his head out of the greasy kitchen, took one look at Ricketts, and told the waitress nothing doing. "Take it or leave it," he shouted across the crowded diner. Ricketts indignantly left the breakfast, but when the cheque came he paid it like a martyr. It was just another humiliation, another testing. He steeled himself to disregard these worldly trials, willing himself to focus instead on the death, despair, flood, fire, and chaos that would descend before the coming of the Great Peace. He concentrated on keeping himself clean, keeping his pride, diligently looking for work. But there was no work now.

As time went on he was forced to take refuge in old memories. He thought of a Japanese whore he had, in his days at sea, been very fond of. The whore would get on top of him. She would always be chewing gum. The clock was on the wall behind her. "How much time?" she would ask after a very few minutes, and Ricketts would look at the clock and tell her. He had never met another woman who was like that. Around the clock, filling the walls, were pictures of naked black men, dozens of them in various poses. She loved black men.

So Ricketts thought of the whores and the he-she's, as they used to call them in Singapore. . . .

Ricketts understood, to his damnation, the prodigious fantasies of celibacy: the wasting sickness, the desire without rest, the inflamed belly. And drink, too, he understood, for the lure of drink had tortured him always. And he had never been more tempted or had to battle himself more fiercely than during his time of desolation at the hostel and the labour pool, among men who had no brakes. It only served to make him realize, though, how much he wanted to walk again with the Lord.

He looked into new trades and skills. He applied for jobs as a dog groomer, a baker, a bus driver, the only jobs there were, but he had no luck. For one thing he was an unprepossessing man, as I have suggested. He was short and full-bellied, with thick tattooed arms. He walked with the roll and wallow of a seaman. The articulation of ribs and vertebrae was so pronounced, in fact, that he appeared to be breaking some law of mechanics. Sometimes it seemed as if he would shake himself to pieces. He had a neat beard, though, his thinning brown hair was always clipped military-style, and his plain clothes were always clean and neatly arranged.

However much his troubles multiplied, he would not go for help to welfare. I'd say that for every welfare cheat there are ten or twenty people who really need help but refuse to ask for it. Ricketts was one of these. "If you get involved with government like that, once they get you pegged, well . . . it's bad," he used to say vaguely.

Time and again he was forced back on temporary stuff out of the labour pool, but that too had almost dried up. One morning, however, through a lucky circumstance, he was hired by an Italian as a bricklayer's helper, and it turned into a permanent job. The Italian, however, worked him so hard, shovelling and carrying fifty pounds of bricks under each arm up a ladder, that his back just above the kidneys began to hurt continuously. He could no longer stand to shovel, but needed the job so badly, to start him back on the right road, that he dropped to his knees and continued to shovel from that position. It was if the fallen preacher were praying and doing penance at the same time. And in the end he was delivered, I suppose you could say, by a tendon pull in his arm that made further work impossible. He was at the end of the line. The Italian refused to pay him. Then the director told him he must leave the hostel. Within days he would be broke and homeless. One would think he could not sink lower – but he did.

He ruled out going back to the labour pool. He was disgusted by the place. In any case he could no longer do heavy work. And he had been uplifted and strengthened in this determination by a scene he had witnessed the day the Italian had hired him – a scene that, in fact, led to him landing the job.

The place had been bedlam. Guys were rolling on the floor fighting. Tables and chairs were being scattered. Lenny was helpless to stop it. Then a young guy near the door, a guy who had worked his way up the priority list, announced suddenly to Ricketts who was next to him, standing with his back to the wall: "You can have my priority. I'm leaving."

"What number are you?" Ricketts asked.

"Number one."

That caused a bigger commotion than the fight. It was unheard of for anyone to give up number-one priority. There were no other jobs to go to. It was throwing away the investment of many pre-dawn attendances, tossing out the chance of a good job.

The fighting had stopped.

"Where are you going?" someone asked suspiciously.

"I don't know, but I'm not coming back here. It's a goddam cesspool." And he turned and left.

So Ricketts got the job with the Italian. At the time it had seemed like a godsend, a helping hand from heaven. (Like most Christians, Ricketts saw the work of the Lord in everything. When he had attempted, at the Bible college, to give up cigarettes and had succeeded — with no withdrawal symptoms — he had been elated and had boasted of his will power to others. But his resolve had quickly crumpled and he had begun to smoke again. He reasoned that God was punishing him for his false pride. He tried again, this time giving thanks and credit only to the Lord, and his success was more enduring. These small miracles buttressed his faith.)

Of course the job with the Italian had ended badly, with the injury, but the boy's proud sacrifice had endured in his mind. The boy had been right. The labour pool was no good. But where then to turn for a job? He had heard of one job opening in the north in a bar, a job he felt he could do with his still-tender arm; but it was impossible . . . immoral . . . it would be hypocritical and sinful even to think of doing such work. Yet he had to have something.

He telephoned the tavern. They had already hired a waiter. I will work for nothing, Ricketts told them desperately, just a room and some food. And so the very thing that had caused his downfall and that of so many others became his lifeline. Hooch, suds, sauce, juice, booze. He would have to serve people who had already had too much to drink, he knew that. And he called himself a Christian. But he had to have a job.

He lasted three weeks. It was even worse than he thought it would be. The tavern was always full of drunken Indians, the very type of people he had ministered to and tried to wean from the bottle. Now, as long as their money was on the table, he was supposed to serve them. He couldn't sleep for the guilt. Once, after being served all night by

Ricketts, a native man put a piece of timber through the windshield of a white man's truck outside the tavern. He believed the white man had cheated him out of something or other. The white man caught him and beat him half to death, kicking his face with steel-capped boots. Everybody stood around. Nobody tried to stop it. And then a young native boy who had drunk too much, wandering drunkenly, fell face down and drowned in two inches of rainwater in a puddle in the street.

Ricketts prayed for hours, but he could not concentrate because, of course, he already knew what was right and what was wrong. He kept thinking of his mother who lived on the prairies and who still believed he was preaching. Ricketts and his father had been reconciled just before the old man's death. The father was a cantankerous bigot who beat his wife consistently, but had finally, almost on his deathbed, accepted God into his life at his son's urging.

Ricketts told me: "I hated my father. After I started to walk with the Lord I said to my advisor: 'I don't know if I can forgive him.' He said: 'Oh, that's the last thing you have to worry about. The only thing you have to worry about is whether he will forgive you.' "

Mrs. Ricketts had been overjoyed and proud of her son when she saw what a change his work could bring to all their lives. To know he was now working in a tavern as a waiter would break her heart. Though he did not exactly lie to her, he allowed her to go on believing he was still preaching the gospel with the Shantymen. At one point, while he was in the hostel, he allowed her to think that a friend's address was in fact his own, and picked up his mail from her there. These deceptions bothered him constantly, until the thought of his mother was like a Judas finger forever indicting him. He was ashamed.

So he quit the tavern, and it was the right thing to do in more ways than one, because on his return to the city he found a cheque waiting for him, compensation for his earlier work injury, for which he had fought bitterly, but which he now saw only as God's work. For, through all his tribulations, this backslid itinerant preacher, this piece of religious flotsam, had retained his faith.

# 7

*This is what you shall do:*
*Love the earth and sun*
*and animals, despise riches,*
*give alms to everyone that asks,*
*stand up for the stupid and crazy...*
— Walt Whitman

The sidewalks were very crowded, but she kicked a stone as if there was nobody around, and the dog chased it madly. The stone bounced off ankles and shoes and confused oncoming pedestrians. The girl laughed like a gypsy and kicked the stone each time she came to it, until she turned down a street leading to the waterfront. Already she could see the crowd congregated outside a scratched red door. The voices came to meet her.

"You have a smoke?"

"You kiddin', I've bin pickin' butts up all the way down the street."

The girl, Luba, sat on the sidewalk a little way from the crowd. The dog raced back up the street and then came bounding back with its mouth open. It was a mangy black dog with a humped back. Luba watched the line-up outside the red door.

There was some pushing and shoving between an old derelict and a gangling longhair wearing a khaki army greatcoat with a U.S. Army insignia on the sleeve, and underneath it a U.S. flag. The greatcoat went down past the longhair's knees. The old man, an indignant veteran, tried to tear off the insignia, but the younger man kept jerking his long arm away and holding his shoulder up in a lopsided fashion so the old man couldn't reach it. The old man was beside himself. "Knuckles up," he screeched, dancing and banging on the arm of the younger man with his fist. "Knuckles up, boy." The longhair kept his shoulder up and his arm straight down by his side, stiff as a fence picket. He was smirking.

A bald hag with plastic bags over her feet kicked out at a boy in a jean jacket. The bag flew off her foot, along with an old carpet slipper and a piece of foam. Her feet were swollen purple by disease, and the foam, tied on underneath the slipper, was to make walking easier. She sat down on her coat in a doorway and gropingly put everything back on, sniggering to herself in an eager way. Then she jumped up like a young girl, kicking and screeching and scratching at the boy and pulling at his jacket so that his cigarettes fell out of a breast pocket onto the sidewalk. "Cigarettes, cigarettes," she screamed.

A derelict smelling of some poison he'd been drinking lashed out with his foot at Luba's dog, and she tied it up in an alley and went to stand next to the Frenchman, whose features she had finally picked out of the crowd. She had seen the line-ups get longer and longer for something to eat, and today, of course, Christmas 1981, there were more than ever. By the time the red door opened there would be hundreds. Hundreds who were out of work, as well as the regulars. One night last week Luba had spent the night in a parked car in an alley. One window would not close properly – it was just an old junk car – and she had no sleeping bag, only the pink blanket she had stolen when she was kicked out of the hostel. In the morning she had gone to warm up in the labour pool. And the telephone had not rung once all morning. Not once.

She stood quietly by Jean and myself as the tall character in the army greatcoat, strutting like a grandee, now tried to bum a cigarette. He was wired.

"And one for him." He indicated Chino, the Oriental from the hostel, from the labour pool, who seemed to be everywhere, his shoulders slouched, his coat flapping open, never saying a word. When singled out he turned sideways, not dissociating himself exactly, willing, but not presumptuous, like a trained seal taught to jump for fish, but not too soon. He looked like a seal, with his black hair and black coat.

Jean snorted. "I give you one," he said to Greatcoat. "But if he wants one he comes ask me. He has not courage to ask himself?" He acted indignant.

Greatcoat clicked his heels and shouted to Chino: "Hey, front and centre." To Jean he said, in an aside: "He's my spiritual master. He's a professional cigarette bum. I'm his servant."

"Crazy," Jean said.

The Oriental showed no sign of having heard anything. He simply moved forward and Jean handed him a cigarette.

I had made up my mind to leave soon. The night before, Jean had got into a stupid argument with an old drunk. The Frenchman kept demanding to know whether he had served in the war. Finally, the old man said he had.

"Did you kill anybody?" Jean insisted.

"No," the old man replied.

Then Jean said: "My father was in war. He was captain. He kill." He said it proudly, as if he had never had a moment's disagreement with his father. It was a reminder that however long I spent among these people I might never know them.

I'd watched Luba come down the street kicking the stone. I'd talked to her briefly in the labour pool a few days before. Now she was humming softly and leaning toward Jean who stood there proudly, as he always did, as if he was the centre of attraction.

A tour bus went by – forced into the area by a detour for roadwork – and people in the line-up cheered. The bus passengers waved. I was mad at both groups. I felt, it must be said, superior. I felt like a king journeying through the guts of a beggar. This life was getting to me.

Luba cheered me up. She was a big dark girl with red cheeks and a red sweatband. Her story was a fascinating one, if it was true.

As rumour had it, she had been a performer whose job was to ride the back of a whale during an aquatic show somewhere on the coast. Three times a day in the summer she performed for tourists, until the accident.

Whales are extraordinarily tidy creatures. Luba's whale, Birdie, would pick up floating wrappers and cigarette cartons tossed or blown into the pool, and would take them deep underwater to a certain corner, to an outlet pipe around which they would lie, sodden, until the circulation of water eventually carried them out the pipe to the sea.

Luba rode the whale with her long black hair halfway down her back for effect. She was very attached to Birdie. One day she slid off the whale, and her hair hung on the water like a web. The whale, seeing only the floating hair, seized it in his mouth and dived. He dragged Luba deep, holding her hair in his mouth, until she was close to drowning. Another performer, a man, dived in and attempted to pull Luba free, but when Birdie finally released her, Luba was unconscious. She was revived but never again rode the whale. In fact, she simply wandered around after that, this way and then the other, as if still pulled by her hair by the whale. Perhaps she had seen something in her state of near death and been changed by it, but if she had she never spoke about it. She simply drifted in a blue pool within her head, alive, apparently, only to things that had happened to her before the accident. Of the things she remembered she spoke in an almost hypnotized way, and once she began to speak it was hard to shut her up.

As we stood there waiting for the door to open, chauffeur-driven cars and taxis occasionally pulled up at the curb with food donated by those who had money, and the drivers carried hampers and boxes up the alley, past Luba's tethered dog, to deliver them at the rear door. It was to be a Christmas meal, provided by a coalition of churches who regularly provided sandwiches and coffee behind the red door to those who needed it.

Some of the people waiting began to chant for the door to be opened. The street was now full of people in a haphazard line, and when the door opened they poured onto the stairs as if they were storming a truck that would take them away from a death camp. A sort of roar came from the stampeding crowd, the voice of real hunger. It filled the narrow stairway, causing those at the top of the steps to move back involuntarily. They were the representatives of churches who were helping cook and serve the meal, good-hearted people who, looking down on the forging, kicking mob, must have felt fear mixed with their faith.

Upstairs, the large room was set with rows of pristine tables, every place arranged similarly with cutlery and side plates for a sit-down turkey lunch.

In those days before Christmas, Jean had introduced me to many places where food could be obtained for nothing. The Frenchman was completely mercenary about his exploitation of charity soup kitchens.

Some churches served food only to those who first attended a service. During one such obligatory attendance, Jean, consumed not by religion but by the thought of food, pointed to the word *manger* in the Bible, as in babe in the manger, and, in a fat whisper, told me: "You know what that means in French. It means eat. That's what we do after we finish this shit. Eat."

The Salvation Army provided a sit-down meal on Sundays, and had a back room full of donated bread, buns, and cakes, which people carted away by the boxload. Some needed the food, others, affluent enough but stingy, drove up in pickup trucks to load up with free food. The back room was always full of children fighting on the floor amid a riot of bread and buns, people going through cardboard boxes full of baked goods looking for something fresh, and others just sitting around.

Anything could happen at the services. Once we had to sit through a presentation of washcloths to the brigadier's wife.

Others sometimes expected something more from the transients than mere attendance. At one such service the regular congregation of a certain street church erupted in a fervour of revivalism. They joined hands, wailed to the skies, clapped, swayed, and urged the visitors to join in, grabbing their hands in supplication. The children of charity, present only for the food that had been promised later, were bewildered. They found themselves holding hands with strangers, taking crude shuffling steps, their arms wrenched upwards as the hand-holding spread. It was funny to watch. Jean winked and joined in with a will, as if he was at a dance hall. The only person still seated was a blind man with a huge braille Bible on his lap and a black guide dog at his feet snuffling at a fallen page from the songbook (*Songs for Men*). Just then a bum came in the door, bent down, took the songbook leaf from the dog, and blew his nose on it. He looked around as if he saw such scenes every day of his life, and then went out again.

As for myself, I had begun to feel foolish and impotent wandering the same drab streets every day, being overwhelmed afresh with distasteful scenes and begging ways. One day I found myself flaring at Jean over a small, stupid thing. The Frenchman had stopped in the street to talk to a girl who was living at the hostel in the small women's dorm, which had about twenty beds. She was a heavy drug user, a zombie who moved heavily and silently in a world of her own, carrying as much misery as anyone could expect to see in another human being. I had only heard her speak once, when the exasperated director, obviously feeling she needed to break away from a certain harmful association, asked her: "Why do you hang around with that guy? You know he's a loser."

The girl shrugged her large shoulders and, with a chilling helplessness devoid of any self-pity or, indeed, any emotion at all, replied simply: "He buys me booze and dope."

In the street she spoke to Jean as I stood apart. Her long brown hair clung to her face in the wind. Her eyes were flat and silver, like the beaten heads of nails. She slouched down inside a baggy pair of farmer's jeans, the kind with straps.

Jean left her and approached me. "Give me a dollar," he said. "She needs it."

"You give her a dollar."

It was out before I could stop it, a reaction of pure niggardliness, but one I had no power to suppress. Indeed, I didn't regret it, but became more indignant and intransigent over the small request. The fact that this poor woman wanted a dollar and that Jean was demanding the dollar from me when I had never been introduced to her seemed in some indecipherable way a tremendous affront. There seemed some profound moral in the depths of the trivial exchange over which I had to make a stand. I was suddenly as angry as I could ever remember being, and Jean was outraged. We looked at each other. Up to that point, he knew, I had been completely free with my money.

"You really think I won't give it back to you?" The Frenchman was turning on his heels in indignation. "Man, you won't give a girl a dollar." His dark face, more Latin than Gallic, was indignant and confused. There was a revelation of genuine sensibility and tenderness in the way he spoke of the girl that only served to provoke me.

"You give it to her," I repeated.

"I don't have it."

In the end I handed over the dollar, but I did it with bad grace and couldn't rid myself for a long time of the irrational turmoil the simple request for a dollar had provoked. I still can't explain it except to say that perhaps it was some sort of turning point, that I was behaving in the way nine out of ten people do when confronted by a beggar. Perhaps I was still playing at being poor.

Though I didn't hear about it until later, for I had left the hostel by then, the girl I gave the dollar to slashed her wrists the day before New Year's, killing herself. For days afterward the hostel staff got calls from street people who had known her. "Did she really do it?" they all wanted to know. "Did she really do it?"

The truth was I had become afflicted with the very decay that caused dropping floors and rising damp at the hostel. It was an atmosphere in which nothing clean could thrive: slums, row upon row of sheetless flophouse bunks, rain, scenes of lewd enjoyment, macaroni meals, tired feet, crazy people . . . the mystery of it all enough, I sometimes thought, to spawn unfathomable, goitred creatures with enormous eyes.

That was the only time I had a difference with Jean, though. Working alongside him had been an eye-opener. A steel plate had to come off, who knew how to use a welding torch? Jean did. Who could run a backhoe? Jean could. And he did. He showed me his millwright's ticket and complained that his Quebec ticket was ignored in the west. He told how he had kept warm by running a welding torch inside the lunch shack on the Quebec docks. It didn't matter what he was doing, he gave it all he had. "We gotta hundig that pipe," he would say, making the earth fly. As he glued together sections of plastic water pipe his hands would literally shake with the desire to go faster. One time I got him on a job I'd been working at for about a week—a guy trying to build his own house cheaply. Very cheaply. He also wanted to get it up fast to qualify for a mortgage. On the day Jean joined us we had to move a six-ton septic tank into its berth in the backyard by hand. The guy was that cheap. The whole backyard was a steep, sloping swamp of mud. There were four of us altogether, and we eventually moved the tank about twenty-five feet into its spot by using timber levers, a heavy-duty jack, and lots of sweat. If it hadn't been for Jean it would have been much harder. He worked like a Trojan, and every time he thought we were slowing down he yelled: "Come on. We are men. I make you men," which stung us into extra effort.

In fact, nobody will ever be able to tell me that transients are lazy. It just isn't so. In truth they tend to be crazy about work once they get started. They work far harder than they need, and the longer I worked with them the more I understood the old contractor in the carpet slippers who had said: "I never had a bad worker out of that place."

I was seated across from Luba. She had her back to a wall and on her right was a Christmas tree with a white angel on top. Above it on the wall hung a sign that said: "God Is Able." As we ate, a drunk at another table said over and over: "I can't believe it, I can't believe it" his twisted, drunken face bathing in the food.

"Pass the sugar," somebody yelled.

"I'll stick it up your ass," the drunk drooled.

Luba's face was flushed from fighting her way upstairs, and she looked more gypsy-like than ever. She was febrile and fecund, like a sunflower with edible roots. Suddenly she began to speak across the table at me, one of her outbursts, a gush of stuff.

"I used to walk with a man and he used to say: 'Don't you see how they look at you? You're good-looking.' I used to say: 'Oh yeah? It's like Frank. When he wanted to go with me I stood him up a couple of times, then I gave him a bit of encouragement, said, 'How you doin' today?' Like that. He said to me: 'Why are you standing me up?' Same thing with this ticket taker. I kept company with him once. He used to say: 'Get away from me . . . get away from me,' using reverse psychology on me because I wouldn't have sex, see?"

That whole table was listening to her. People suggested this habit of launching into stories about her teens was a result of her accident with the whale – I always doubted that – but she was known for it. She could ramble on for a long time.

"This East Indian, know what I'm doing to that? I'm ignoring him. You know what it's doing to him? I went with him once to the movies, and he said because he's paid for me to the movies I should go with him to his apartment. I said: 'you don't appeal to me sexually.' People like him I don't need. He's like the ticket taker. I ignore him.

"That guy, that ticket taker. I saw him five months later after he got into trouble. Get that. Got into trouble. And he said he needed somewhere to stay. That blows me up when he wants me to take him to my place to stay, but while I know him he's never asked me outright to have sex with him.

"He's a virgin, that's what he says. Why is he using that psychology, tell me . . . ?

"He tells me about his problems. He can't have sex, he says. I know he's lying. What does he expect me to do, invite him up to my place to have him jump all over me? So he says: 'What is it with you, you don't want to get too close to guys, or what?' I don't see him now except when I meet him on the street then I take him for what I can get, maybe a meal, then boom . . . "

The whole room was quiet, even the drunk. The church people were listening. My food was getting cold.

"Ralph. Did he tell me three different stories? He had a swimming pool. I gave him my wrong telephone number, everything. Ralph is a

Cancer. Very generous with money. But he lied about everything. He had a Cadillac, a black Cadillac, lived in a big mansion. He wanted me to jump up and down. Except he never mentioned a profession. Get that."

She was still talking to me, with her head forward over the table. Bits of her hair had come free from the sweatband she wore and lay over it in a ragged fringe.

"He introduced me to his mother," she said, finally lowering her voice, conscious for the first time, I think, of all the people listening. "His mother is now dead. His mother said: 'He's a very bad penny, stay away from him. He's no good.' How'd you like that?"

After the meal we had to go out through a line of church people who were shaking hands and distributing small gifts. I was given a little parcel, which I took back to the hostel with me. The director was on his own back there. "I'd like to go out like everybody else and get snapped," he said, following me into the dorm, "but I can't get any volunteers to work."

He wanted to hear about the lunch, and when I mentioned the line of church people and the gifts he erupted with a jealousy that is strong among the charitable fraternity. "Those fuckers. Can you believe it? A receiving line. The pricks."

I untied the package. Inside were a pair of black socks and a package of cigarettes. I put on the new socks and left the cigarettes under the blanket on Jean's bunk.

# 8

*I slept till noon, when I looked*
*out the window I suddenly saw*
*an* SP *freight going by*
*with hundreds of hobos reclining*
*on the flatcars rolling along merrily*
*with packs for pillows and funny papers*
*before their noses, and some*
*munching on good California grapes picked*
*up by the siding. "Damn,"*
*I yelled. "Hooee! It is the promised land."*
— Jack Kerouac, *On the Road*

The heron stood out on the rocks, as it always did when the tide changed. Woody seaweed formed spreading canopies over the crusted rocks, and once in a while the heron would flap the loose plumage of one wing in a savage gesture.

"The Indians used to grind up the seeds to make flour," I said.

"Uh?"

"The seaweed. They ground up the seeds." I looked over at my companion who was almost asleep on the bench. A hundred yards down the coast, all muffled up, was a boy in a home-made boat with a dirty tablecloth for a sail. The little boat was wallowing in some tidal filth, waxed by a faint sun, near a natural breakwater. A chainsaw rattled distantly as someone cut up driftwood. And farther off a dog, as if in answer, ground away like someone cranking a cold car. Small stones fell unceasingly down the bank of sandy clay. We were seated at the top on a green bench. Seals could often be seen from here, sometimes whales, and always a few filching sandbirds, no bigger than leaves.

Great twisted masses of tubular weed at the foot of the cliff gave off a slightly fruity odour. A few saplings grew out of the bank, scarred and ripped where people had scoured a route down to the pebbly beach.

Behind us golfers beat along in the wind like sails.

Cliff was an old ex-convict with the tattoos between his fingers to prove it. He had that look, half mean, half bashful. Nobody did nothing to me, it said. I did it all myself. It was a face the colour of tree rust, a face full of busted plays. He had pale eyes, and he sat like an old woman with his hands in his lap.

Clouds rolled in, bringing a sudden depression. The heron suddenly took on the appearance of a hag.

We had met in the library. I had my usual seat on the second floor by the window so I could see across the street into the government office building. I could almost read the writing on the diplomas hung on the walls of the little cubicles. I watched guys pacing and turning in their offices, picking at their moustaches. They would move to the window from out of the gloom, gaping down at the street like hooked fish dragged to the surface. They were like battery hens gazing out at free-range hens. There was one particular fellow who would stand at his window for half an hour or more at a time, looking down at the sidewalk as if he wanted to jump. I liked to imagine everybody else, in the gloom behind him, turned savage, bent on raging bloody cannibalism, tearing the flesh off each other the way pigs do imprisoned in factory farms.

A bunch of pensioners were cruising the stacks this night.

"Are you looking for romance, mystery, or murder?" a woman asked her husband, covering all the bases. Maybe he was blind and couldn't pick the books for himself.

"Naw," he said.

"*The Saint Turns Pirate?*"

"Naw, I read one of them."

"Mazo de la Roche?"

"Who?"

"Mazo de la Roche. All them Whiteoaks."

"Naw." I could see the husband now. He was stooped, bent over as if somebody had just whacked him.

"This sounds good," the wife said in her whistling old voice. "*The Night They Killed Joss Barron*. We can swap. This other's a romance, so we can swap."

"Hokay." The old man gave a laugh.

Then another woman's voice piped up. "He won't like romance," she said.

"Now don't tell me he's too old for it," the wife giggled.

The husband laughed.

I looked across at the office building. You never knew what you might see. People didn't expect you to be looking into their offices. Once I'd seen a beautiful thing. A man and a girl had curved their necks and put their foreheads together, like swans.

I was thinking about that when I met Cliff. He was a far less beautiful thing. He came into the library drunk and sat down on one of the chairs in the open space reserved for reading. He said, very loudly, "Oh God," and began to roll up his trouser legs. He rolled them right up to his knees. His legs were chicken white and veined like Gorgonzola.

A library girl went past collecting books to be restored to their places on the shelves. She picked up one big volume.

"Is that what they call a heavy book, miss?" the drunk shouted. "Heavy reading." He gave a loud, raucous, ignorant laugh that ended in a crippling smoker's cough. He waved his arm over his head. "Have a happy," he gasped. "Have a happy." Then he went to sleep sitting up like that with his pants rolled up and his lower lip rolled down.

When the library closed I helped the girl wake him up and get him out the door, and then I propped him up until we got to the place where he was staying. In return, the next day, he got me a temporary job at the golf links. It was a lifesaver, for I had not been able to get anything for quite a while.

By now we had been working together for almost a week, in hard-hats to protect us from flying balls, carrying simple implements, trooping lethargically like serfs on some great estate.

It was a treat. Mostly what I'd had out of the labour pool had been pretty rough construction jobs, up to my ass in mud; or cutting windows in crawl spaces with a masonry saw, choking in the airless dark, my body hunched in a three-foot space lit only by the spitting sparks as the saw reduced concrete to dust, going for air every few minutes through the black damp dust to a single hole through which light and air fell; or dragging a bunch of sopping, slime-covered mattresses out of a motel swimming pool where they had been dumped by vandals.

However bad the job, though, always afterwards I felt that a hammer blow could not buckle my knees, felt as if I had just walked out of an earthquake – the euphoria, no doubt, of a man rediscovering muscle and open-air work.

I'd seen a couple of bad accidents, though – a sobering experience. In one a piece of heavy equipment just about to be loaded on a truck toppled sideways. The operator clutched at the cage as it fell, and his hand was severed. He was in shock, his eyes rolling.

"If he'd just set there he'd a bin' all right," a man with a toothpick in his mouth said. "But because we were just leaving he didn't have the belts on. He had to hold onto something."

On another job the contractor was inspecting a skylight on the roof of a completed home when he fell off. It was early morning and the side of the roof away from the sun was still coated in frost. He slid almost from the apex of the cedar shake roof. There was nothing to hold on to. Nobody could help him. In slow motion, he slid quietly off the edge of the roof and fell twenty-five feet onto a concrete patio. He broke both ankles and both wrists and telescoped his spine. His wife claimed afterward that the judo lessons he had been taking had saved his life. "He knew how to fall," she said.

The most touching story came from a youngster, a teenager with whom I worked construction. His body was covered in burnlike scars, and his delicate face was striped with the same embossed redness. He told me he had once hit an underground high-power line with a jackhammer. The power line had not been on the plans furnished to the contractor by the municipality for whom the work was being done. The boy was in hospital for many weeks. Then when he was finally in a position to sue for damages, there was some hassle over the time that had elapsed. He was supposed to file suit before such and such a date. He had to settle in the end for some minor amount, a few thousand dollars. He told me one lunch hour that when he was excited or making love to his girl a blush would suffuse his face and body and make him helpless and impotent. This affliction had only begun after the accident. He wondered if it would ever go away.

It was a hard thing for me, as a rookie, to discipline myself to be careful all the time, to watch for everything from heavy equipment and excavations to protruding nails underfoot.

The only danger on the golf course, on the other hand, was from flying golf balls, especially to Cliff who was half blind and couldn't see them coming.

"They can't hurt you, them little balls," he'd say, not even aware that one had whistled within an inch of his head. I kept watch and tried to drag him away, but Cliff couldn't move too swiftly anyway. He had a crooked leg, picked up when he was with the army of occupation in Germany after the war. Attempting to demonstrate to gape-mouthed Germans how paratroopers had won the war for the Allies he took a drunken leap from the third-storey window of a beerhall and crippled himself for life.

The work was edging, trimming, raking sandtraps, laying turf. For the first time I could wear sneakers instead of huge, steel-shank skidoo boots. We spent our breaks looking out to sea from the bench on the fourteenth tee. The tee had to be constantly rebuilt, as the sea claimed many feet of land each year. It was a beautiful links course, split by the coast road.

There was always something for the crew, mostly temporary men, to watch and comment on. There was so much merriment the foreman finally said to cut it out, keep our voices down, didn't we know the members paid $3,000 a year? "You're the worst," he said, turning on Cliff. "Yap, yap, yap. Get that edger going and fix these sandtraps and then walk down to the twelfth and take up the sod where it's marked. After that I've got some tools want fixing."

Cliff squinted at him. "What's my left foot doin' while all this is goin' on," he asked indignantly. "Crackin' walnuts?"

He paced himself like a slug. He stopped to roll and smoke a hundred cigarettes a day, littering the fairways with his butts. Nothing would get him to move any faster, to the chagrin of the permanent work crew, a bunch of miserable East Europeans. They sat out their breaks morosely in a little shed, surrounded by scum and clinker, speaking only when they lost their tempers or were excited, when they became just like a bunch of strutting Nazis. One Teutonic moron, a sort of assistant foreman, a little guy with a burgomaster manner, stormed in one day, incensed. "This woman says you should cut it here and it'll grow higher next year," he yelled indignantly, flapping his hands to indicate what he was talking about. "I said: 'Stick it up your ass, lady, mind your own business.'" The others grinned at him. They slapped him on the back and repeated the story, even though they knew it couldn't be true – the man hadn't the guts to talk like that to anybody.

The golfers would put up with anything. They lolled in their golf carts like a bunch of sandbagged Caesars, abstracted, half asleep most of the time, or maybe thinking about the office. It was interesting how difficult it seemed to provoke these captains of industry and civic leaders. "The acquirers vast," Whitman called them. They seemed paralysed by the sight of work clothes and filthy hands. Not afraid exactly, more ashamed. At first I thought I was imagining it, but it wasn't so. The golfers went out of their way to curry favour with the labourers on the course. There was almost a wistfulness in their tentative approaches, as if they would rather be edging and raking than golfing. Had their creations reneged on them? Was it possible that these men felt the same pull toward a freer, wilder life that I had when I began my wandering a year earlier? Or were they just conscious of the recession and bestowing a kind of big-brotherly interest on people who had jobs, however menial?

Each night the temporary men walked across the links to the club-house where we each signed a chit and were paid, in cash, thirty-two dollars and fifty cents.

Cliff and I would often take the same bus. He was the sloppiest man you ever saw. All his pockets were invariably turned inside out, and there was ash all over from the hundreds of cigarettes he smoked a day. Even his hair didn't seem to be on straight. Once we got a block from the golf course and he discovered he'd lost his pay. We walked back, and the bills were just lying on the sidewalk – luckily there was no wind – where he'd dropped them from his pocket. He lived in a district of industrial enterprises, marginal shops, full of the scum of molten metal, brass dust, the usual inner-city squalor. He was waiting to go back into the bush. He'd been a logger most of his life. But now everything was shut down. At his age he might never get back. He'd been out for a long time anyway, which was why he didn't qualify for unemployment insurance.

He had a fund of stories:

"I got drunk with a guy was a gardener one night. He said come back with me, I've got a house to myself. But we had to get a ferry, he said. I was so drunk, I didn't care.

"We got on a ferry and went out to this island. There was this big house with a garden going right down to the water, a big place, empty. We drank everything in the bar, everything in the house, and ate all the food. After about a week, the boss, the owner, came back. He was a geologist. I was in his bed upstairs. The gardener had taken off. Knew what was coming, I guess. The boss took one look at me – I didn't know where I was – and he said: 'Right, well, you stayed. You drank all my liquor and you stayed. You robbed me. Now (he pointed out the window) stand by that gate outside this house and don't ever let anybody else do what you did. Either that or you go to jail.' I stayed five years. There were two ducks there, tame. I couldn't shoot 'em and I couldn't leave 'em. If it hadn't been for them ducks I'd have left long ago."

That was the type of stories he told. You couldn't make them up if you tried. He said: "The feller who had this house, he used to have a racehorse. Kept it on the mainland. It was the only time I got off the island. I used to give the horse a bottle of rum before a race. It did his heart good. He ran better. I'd just stand there and pour it down. He used to come back puffin' an blowin' like Demerara."

He could give beautiful, funny, capsule portraits of people he'd met, never more than a paragraph.

"I knew him years ago in the bush. He got married and he used to bring an alarm clock to work in his lunch bucket. His wife would set it every morning for quitting time, and then if he was on his own somewhere he'd know when to quit. He was clever and a good worker, but he couldn't tell time or money. His wife is dead now."

# 9

*And down there, in the squalid*
*and as a matter of fact*
*horribly boring sub-world of the tramp*
*I had a feeling of release,*
*of adventure, which seems absurd*
*when I look back, but*
*which was sufficiently vivid*
*at the time.*
—George Orwell,
*The Road to Wigan Pier*

My ride waved his hand out the truck window. "They've done nothing but drink for forty years," he said. "If you rated Indian reservations from one to ten that one would be off the bottom of the scale."

He took a drink.

"You like it here?" I asked him. We were in ranching country.

"Hell, yes. I don't want to live nowhere a man can't step outside and piss in the bush."

"They built this country, the old-timers." I was tired from walking; I said it without thinking.

"They didn't build it, they raped it. Who built up this country were the Mennonites, the Hutterites, the religious, you might say, the what-you-call 'em . . . the Doukhobors. Only the Doukhobors were not such good farmers. The Mennonites were good farmers."

He sucked on his beer like a starved wolverine. His eyes were sharp as fishbones.

Up the road a way, after I left the redneck, an old man called me into his yard, gave me a drink of orange juice.

The Indians? The Indians, the old-timer said, were the hardest workers a man could wish to see in the old days. They were also smart. He told me how some big politician came to look over the lake one time. How he stood on the dock with the other officials in their

73

suits, lashed by rain, pretending they knew what they were looking for (something to do with a logging project) and spotted an Indian paddling out of the storm toward the dock. They all laughed at the Indian, and when he got close the big politician said: "What kind of weather you call this, son . . . ? What kind of weather you call this, eh?"

The Indian got out on the dock and pulled off his boot. He poured the water out of it onto the dock and then he said: "I tink this is white man's summer. Indian summer a mite better'n this."

The old man rocked with laughter at his story.

I was heading north, thumbing half-heartedly, awkwardly, feeling my age, not yet used to begging for rides from the roadside. It's not an easy thing to do, to put your thumb up for the first time. I was outside of Prince George, my back to the traffic, hiking along, and an alcoholic stopped. They all tell me something. This guy said he was an alcoholic. Sleeping in alleys, going through garbage to find food, as low as you can get. Finally, after he'd had umpteen visits to a treatment centre, a priest said to him: "You have been back here so many times, Red. What can we do . . . ?" It was so pathetic, this helpless priest who had done his best over so many years and was admitting he didn't know what else he could do . . . so sad.

"Father, I've had my last drink," Red blurted out.

And since then, Red said, he had indeed been sober. He'd built up a business, starting with $1,500 he had borrowed from a woman with whom he was now living. And he'd been kept on the straight and narrow, he said, by a man he unashamedly called "an angel of mercy" – an old man who had suffered eighteen heart attacks but who believed God had allowed him to go on living to serve a particular purpose – to help alcoholics.

This man had helped hundreds, Red said, by making them face the truth about themselves. For example, Red had blamed his drinking for many years on the fact that he had been denied custody of his daughter. The old man had said to him: "Do you really think you would have been a better parent for your daughter? You were a drunk. It would have been hopeless." And with that impetus from the old man, and from Alcoholics Anonymous, Red said, he began to explode all the other lies he had told himself. He had not had a drink now for three years. He should have been dead, he said, with the liquor he'd consumed and the terrible falls and beatings he had suffered and sleeping outside in all sorts of weather. Now he helped others as much as he could, through A.A. He pointed to a dent in the dash in front of me. Made by an A.A. member who had fallen off the wagon and, desperately drunk, had brought his head down in anguish. He always picked up hitchhikers or helped out people in whatever way he could. Many hitchhikers tried to con him out of money or a meal, which amused him because he'd been on the wrong side of the street so long he knew all the tricks.

He stopped at a café. "Have anything you want on the menu," he said. "Have a sirloin steak, have some milk, have some pie."

He took me two hundred miles all told and dropped me off at a truck stop after giving me his business card on which he also wrote his home address and telephone number. He used to employ thirteen men, he said, but now, with the recession, he only had three full-timers.

I walked about a mile from there and got my next ride in a tiny jeep jammed to the roof with camping equipment. I had a big, old-fashioned backpack myself, and I took a look and said I didn't think we could get it in.

"Sure we can," my ride said, and that was that. He was an administrator on big construction jobs, but he was out of work and heading toward Prince Rupert, to the coal port, to see what he could find.

He was a small fussy man called Jacob, originally from the Channel Islands. He had quit his last job "to protect my integrity," he said. He confided that he had been known on the job site as the Road Runner and was regarded by the men as a fink, forever darting around self-righteously querying overtime claims and mysterious inventory shortages, trying to keep the men honest and costs down.

"I was caught between management, which was trying to appease the unions, and the men, who didn't like me," he said frankly.

"A guy would put in for twelve hours and this would be noon, and I'd say: 'How can you have worked twelve hours when you clocked in at six?'" To Jacob it was straightforward. Either a thing was right or it wasn't. But that's not the way life is, and he had to leave.

Now he was sleeping in a tent, driving his little yellow jeep from place to place in the middle of a recession, looking for work. He was an unlikely wanderer, with his precise little moustache, hat, and raincoat – all very English – and his tent, which he said he had owned for twenty years. It was a brown canvas tepee with a single pole in the centre.

I camped with him near a lake he knew about past Houston, and he made a fire in the wet with no trouble, using jack-pine branches and moss. He was a handy guy. But he was terribly afraid of mosquitoes for some reason. It was early for mosquitoes (June 1982) and there were none I could see, but he took a great many precautions against their possible appearance.

As we drank his tea I edged around to the subject of alcohol. I had become fascinated by the number of alcoholics I had met, and I wondered if this prissy little man was yet another running from the spectre of the bottle. I told him about Red.

His own father had been an alcoholic, he told me, but he himself never took more than three drinks. He never took a fourth. "I'm a stronger man inside than my father," he said.

Jacob built a fire outside my tent as well as his own. (He was right down by the lake, almost in it, "because of the mosquitoes," and I was way back.) Then he made more tea in a huge kettle. When he opened the back door of his jeep all sorts of things fell out: teapots and packages of crumpets, hot water bottles, crab traps, fold-up chairs, axes, chainsaws, tam-o'-shanters, barbecues. You name it, Jacob had it.

It rained all night, but then cleared in the morning, showing patches of blue sky.

I left Jacob sleeping and hiked about five miles before I got a ride, with a trucker carrying groceries for Safeway in Terrace. He was an older man, but he still had a dream. His dream was to find two or three nice hookers, take them up to Tumbler Ridge, the big coal project outside Rupert, and set them up in a camper, pimping them to the workers. He let me off in the Safeway lot, still speculating on the money he'd make.

It was raining again, and I took a bus to Rupert. The fare was seven bucks. Soon I'd be broke again. I defy anybody with money to do a real job of researching poverty. Jack London did it in London, England, by acting the part, dressing in rags, but he cheated a bit, since he had a place to retreat to when he could no longer stand the squalor. George Orwell *was* broke in Paris and London, and his book has more poignancy and humour for me than London's book, for that reason. There was one point on which I differed from both of them, though. London in *People of the Abyss* and Orwell in *Down and Out in Paris and*

*London* both said that changing their clothes changed everything, that they were immediately accepted, despite their accents, their obviously superior educational backgrounds, and the like. This was not my experience. Many of the people I met were suspicious of me at first. Once, for example, when I went to the desk at a hostel to sign in, the telephone, which had accidentally been left off the hook, started bleeping. The girl behind the desk said to me, "You've left your bleeper on," and then realized it was the telephone and blushed. "You thought I was undercover," I joked. "Yep," she said. And later, when I'd been on the road long enough to know what I was about, a guy I got talking to in a bar said bluntly to me: "You're not what you seem. I don't know who you are, but you're not what you seem." Hard work was more often than not my open sesame. I'd work alongside a man and then be accepted. Or live in the neighbourhood a while.

In Prince Rupert, I hooked up with a bearded, balding hiker from Oregon, a former Peace Corps volunteer in Costa Rica. He was going to the Queen Charlotte Islands, and I thought I'd tag along. The fare was $10.50. The guy from Oregon had exactly $1.80. With my money we could just make it, but we wouldn't have anything over at all. He said he thought he could get some money from a girl he'd met in the city hall licensing department. He'd left his backpack with her the day before.

I went to check out the longshoremen's hall. If I could get a day's work, I could get us a decent stake. The hall was a yellow house in the middle of a vacant lot with wooden steps up to the door. There were a dozen guys sitting around waiting. On the back wall was a blackboard full of the names of men who were already out to work and the ships they were on.

"Anyone left here with a number?" (any union members) asked the bearded guy who seemed to be in charge.

Nobody had a number.

"Anybody worked the boom before?"

Nobody had. The bearded guy pointed at a thin kid. "I'll take you, you're the skinniest."

I stayed a while longer but the phone wasn't ringing and the bearded guy was screaming, so I left, and went to a bar. When I got back to where we were camping, Jess, my partner, had borrowed the money for his fare from the girl in the license bureau.

77

It was a smooth crossing. There had been some rough weather earlier in the week, the crew said, and the year before it had been so bad the ferry had had to turn around and go back because it could not enter the harbour at Skidegate on the Charlottes. That one turned into an eighteen-hour trip. In the bar the bottles were all taped up to the shelves so they wouldn't fall and break in a storm. The tables and chairs were bolted and chained to the floor.

I bought us something to eat, and then I got talking to a waitress, an older woman who said I looked as if I had the numbers "666" somewhere in my life. She said it was the devil's number. "Revelation 13, look it up," she said. ("Let him that hath understanding count the number of the beast: for it is the number of a man; and his number is six hundred, three score and six.") She said her nephew had 666 in his social insurance number, and after trying every other method to get it changed he had finally driven all the way to Ottawa to personally petition the powers that be.

Jess and I got separated, and when I got off the boat I hiked into Queen Charlotte city and camped on the beach behind a huge log, which, at dusk, looked like a fallen totem with vague tribal meanings in the grain of the bleached wood. Clouds hung over the mountains, and the sky was light and dark in streaks. It rained that night, but not heavily.

In the morning I bought some supplies with money I had left and began to hike back past the ferry dock again and then on north toward Masset at the other end of Graham Island. I had to hike out of Queen Charlotte city on the road because the tide was up on the beach, and as I passed a row of waterfront houses I spotted Jess's pack stacked up on a porch. He was a man who seemed to land on his feet. Maybe it was somebody he met on the ferry or a "contact". Jess had many "contacts", most of whom had never heard of him. When we had first met we were talking about some island or other, and he said: "I have a contact there, a guy who works with whales, studies them. I can't remember his name, though."

"Paul Spong," I said.

"Yeah, that's him. Did you read *The Starship and the Canoe*? That's where I got his name from."

As soon as I could after passing the ferry dock I slipped down to the beach again and was soon within ten feet of a deer that appeared to be completely tame. It just ambled off after a while. Further on lay the legs and skull of a dead one. Only the black hooves seemed unaffected by decay. Still further, and a bunch of ravens were gorging on the red belly of one newly dead.

It was blowing a gale most of the time, the going was rough over the rocky sections, and I had a particular problem. My boots had given out around Prince George, and I'd bought another pair for three dollars in a thrift store, along with a pair of fifty-cent running shoes. The boots were Grebs and in good shape – a really good buy – but they were not broken in yet, were still walking with the previous owner, I guess, and I'd developed painful blisters on both heels. I cut the backs out of the runners and wore them to allow my feet to heal, but there wasn't enough support in them for the stony beach so I rejoined the road. Immediately, a guy driving a truck toward me stopped and offered me a beer out the window.

"I can't pay for it," I said.

"Hell, I don't want paying. I might get thirsty myself some day, going down the road."

It is fascinating how prevalent this is: the feeling, however subconscious, that by giving now you will get back later. It's a superstition, especially among those who have been down and know it might happen again. Ditch fantasy, they call it. There is nobody as generous as a man who has had a heaping of bad luck in his life. Later, thumbing over thousands of empty kilometres up north, I was to get to be something of an expert. Motorhome after motorhome would pass, and I could see the faces through the glass, and I knew, as every other hitchhiker knew, that there was no hope for a ride. Then a pickup would come along, and there'd be a scruffy old cowboy behind the wheel, or a one-eyed native woman with a bunch of kids, and my chances went up 500 per cent.

Toward the end of a rain-soaked spell of days, I got a ride to Masset in the back of a pickup. I went to a restaurant just off the main street, thinking to get a cup of coffee, took a look at the prices, and turned to walk away. Then I heard somebody hollering my name from inside the place. It was Jess. He'd spent one night in Queen Charlotte city with a forestry worker whose name somebody had given him, then got a ride out. He took me down to the dock and introduced me to a fisherman he'd met, the owner of a fifty-six-foot wooden boat that had somehow fallen over in dry dock. The planking was smashed, and he was patching it up with wood and some tarp. His hair was pulled back in a long pony tail; his face was tanned and lined. He had hip boots on and a bandana on his head. He looked like a pirate. Or Willie Nelson. His name was Paul. He'd let Jess stow his backpack on board, and I put mine in the cabin, too. The cabin was a small area with a table in an alcove and a sink. Down a wooden stepladder was a sleeping area with bunk beds. All this had been flooded when the boat fell over, but it had pretty well dried out now.

We went down and watched the fisherman work for a while, and a guy came over with some mushrooms in a bag. He was guided by a youngster, obviously a local. The man wanted to know if the mushrooms were magics. They weren't, Paul said, after no more than a cursory glance.

Then he said: "The way I do mushrooms is real religious. I fast for four days, no sex for three or four days, no conversation, or as little as possible. It's all about increasing your personal power, right? And pick a good time. People have a good time of the day, you know. Just before sunrise and just before sunset are good times. Full moon is a good time. Height above sea level is important, too. I have a special hill. Keep your mind empty, don't think about things, or you're going to mess up. An empty mind is real important.

"Once I saw a dog lying over two mountains, a dog with two heads. It was incredible. And every time I looked, it was still there. I'd look away at something else and, you know how you usually see these things and they vanish, well, it would still be there. For two hours, man. I walked away and looked back and it was just fading."

All the time he was talking he was working on his boat. He turned to look at the newcomer with the mushrooms that weren't magics, a middle-aged man, a pleasure boater. "Yeah, man," Paul said. "If you fast for four days I'll give you some stuff. With this stuff you'll see God."

The pleasure boater, who was fat and a little crazy-looking, said: "I saw God without any drugs." He went away soon, disappointed at the news about his mushrooms and still half convinced he had a bagful of hallucinations. He looked as if he was going to get a second opinion.

The fisherman said he'd pay us if we helped him out for an hour or two. He had to get as much work done as he could at low tide, and the tide was already starting to creep up around the hull.

While we worked he told us a story. It was a funny, cloak-and-dagger by way of Keystone Kops type story, but it was true – it had been in the newspapers and on television a couple of years earlier, and I vaguely recalled it. It was even funnier knowing that this piratical old hippie had been the protagonist.

Paul and his crew had found some sort of Russian sonar device while fishing off Vancouver Island. It was black, it looked like a bomb with tailfins, and it had Russian lettering on it. They towed it in to Masset, and it became a centre of attraction around the wharf, sitting there on the deck of the boat. Everybody called it the Bomb. A CBC crew filmed it, which excited other media interest, and finally the military dropped around. They wanted the Bomb. It could be of strategic importance. It could be dangerous. The fisherman said: "Not unless you pay for it." The military offered $600. Paul turned it down.

"They went frantic," he recalled as we worked on the boat. "Everybody called this thing the Bomb, and I wouldn't let the military near it. There was all this stuff about civil rights and property rights and civil defence flying around. I just wanted paying for it, just like a catch of fish. Finally, they said they were coming to get it. We sailed out around the point, took this thing ashore and hid it in some bushes. When I got back home the phone was ringing off the hook.

" 'Where is it?' they asked.

" 'What?'

" 'The Bomb.' Even they were calling it the Bomb.

"I'm going to burn the fucker."

It was then the military man called Paul a traitor, which made him more obdurate than ever.

"Eventually I got them up to five thousand dollars for this thing. I had a meeting with the crew. It would have been a thousand each, and they wanted to take it, but I figured if they'd pay five thousand they'd pay fifty thousand. Greedy, eh?"

But the military would not pay fifty thousand. Instead they threatened the fishermen with jail, and they meant it. They came and took the Bomb away and paid nothing. Some weeks later they returned the device to Paul. They did not tell him what or how important it was. The consensus was, though, that it had either dropped from a Russian plane by accident or been lost from a Soviet ship. Paul said he still had the Bomb.

I asked about camping spots – there didn't seem to be any in Masset –

and when we finished work the fisherman drove me out to a place he said he had used in the past. It was just off the road out of town down in a gully right on the inlet with a freshwater stream nearby. Jess was going to join me later. He thought he had a lead on a job and stayed in town. The fisherman had paid us ten dollars each for the work, so I was able to pick up some food.

The spot had obviously been used by generations of tramps. Anyone who didn't know it was there would never have found it. There were about half-a-dozen places to unroll a sleeping bag or pitch a tent, spots worn by use in the surrounding jungle of trees. They were like caves, in fact, so dense was the bush, and offered good protection from the wind. The fisherman's only caution had been that some of the local Indians claimed the spot as their own and had been known to wreck a camp and drive outsiders away. The place was empty when I got there, though. I got organized, started a fire, cooked something up, and waited for Jess. I went up onto the road in case he missed the spot, and when it started to get dark I walked back toward town. I got as far as the tavern across from the bridge into town and settled down with a beer. I would be able to see Jess if he crossed the bridge. I remembered the backpack on the porch in Queen Charlotte, and I wasn't too worried.

How he found people who could be useful to him, one after another, was a mystery to all. St. Christopher, the patron saint of wandering scholars, vagabonds, and travellers in general certainly seemed to be watching over Jess – I have no doubt that right now his backpack is up on somebody's porch.

Jess, though, had a special problem. He was American and could not, without difficulty, get a regular job, or welfare, or anything else. So he had to hustle. What he really wanted to do was find somebody who was going away, maybe for the winter, who would loan him a social insurance card. Jess would get a job, if he could find one, using the card, and would work for the winter. Then his patron, when he returned in the spring, would be able to collect unemployment insurance. It was a mutually beneficial arrangement – one of a hundred minor-league swindles.

I had got it in my head that I wanted to hike right around the tip of the island and then south on the beach back to the Tlell River. I set off down a road that would eventually lead me to the beach. It was a dusty road with very little traffic. A huge dog loped toward me. I had never seen a more menacing-looking dog. I could see it snarling at me and sort of cantering sideways, as if to cut off my path, from way off. The back of its neck was up, the fur spiked. I'm not normally fearful of dogs, but this thing was different. There were no houses on this stretch. I had a knife, and I put my hand on it. Then a car came out of the dust from the direction of the beach. The dog was right in front of me by this time, snarling. There was just me and the dog and and old Indian leaning out of the window of an older car.

"Are you frightened of that dog?" he asked me. He talked as if he knew the dog.

"Yep," I said. "Is he dangerous?"

"I don't know anything about him," the Indian said. He gave me a look of real hatred. I've known a lot of Indians, but not one had ever looked at me quite like that before. Then he drove off, real slow, so as not to scare the dog.

Haida. Children of the Spirit of the Raven. Something stuck hard in his craw. Well, I guess they've got nothing much to thank the white man for on these islands.

Which left me and the dog. But somehow he'd calmed down. He tracked me for a while down the road, and then I lost him.

A car with the worst wheel wobble I'd ever seen passed me after a while and pulled over ahead. It was Paul. He had his wife and child in the car. The little boy had a bunch of chicken feathers stuck in his hair, I don't know why.

After I got in, the car wobbled away again, and Paul's wife said: "I thought you'd fixed it."

The steering wheel was shaking like an earthquake in the fisherman's hands. "I did," he said. "The spare wheel didn't fit right, so I banged it on and now I can't get it off."

"Why don't you just put the spare tire on the old wheel? That one fits perfectly."

Because he can't get the wheel off, I thought, but the fisherman didn't say anything, just gripped the steering wheel a little tighter. It was kind of neat and unexpected that he had a wife like that who sometimes didn't listen too good, and an old car, and a kid with chicken feathers in his hair. It wasn't what you'd expect of a guy who looked like the last buccaneer.

They ran me out to the beach where they rented a big wooden house right on the saltchuck. When we hit the driveway, the first thing I saw, big as the house, was a huge sandhill; and on top, like a missile on a launch pad, pointing directly out to sea, big black and Russian . . . the Bomb.

Stunted shore pine were twisted like conch shells by an everlasting wind. One tree would lean forward out of a clump on a headland, giving, from a distance, a tropical-island effect. The bleached roots of bigger fallen trees held walls of matted earth. A haphazard belt of kelp fronted the driftwood, which was scoured and splintered. Where the rivers ran into the sea the ocean was stained brown in a great arc because of the iron in the fresh water. This brown gives a peculiar, grotto-like atmosphere to the recesses of the rivers, and pebbles and sand and shells can clearly be seen through the dark tint. Deer came down steep sand cliffs to the beach. Others I could see lying up on grassy ridges. They watched me, remaining completely motionless. When the rain came down on the tent at night, which it frequently did, it was like being in the middle of a crackling fire.

I thought of it as a bonus, this trip. I'd seen few enough perks to this life so far. Scratching to stay even was about all I'd seen. But there were no jobs in the cities now, or anywhere else. Might as well be one place as another. I didn't know how I was going to get off this island, but meanwhile, as long as the food held out, it was nice, part of what I'd had in mind when I thought about the transient life before I'd set off. But the rain did come down.

It took me just a week to get back to the Tlell River. My boots were broken in now. I walked a couple of miles back toward Queen Charlotte and the ferry, on the side of the road, and then a girl stopped to give me a ride. Every ride I'd had on the Queen Charlottes – apart from the one from Paul, the fisherman – had been given by a woman. A woman took me into Masset in her pickup, a woman picked me up as I walked back to my camp from the bar in Masset that night, and now here was another one.

I talked about the rides I'd got on the island. "Sometimes," she said, "we just drive up and down the island for something to do. It's such a small place. We'll go in the wrong direction to give a guy a ride. It's something to do."

But there were more than thirteen hundred men out of work on that tiny island, she said. There were no jobs.

84

She took me into Queen Charlotte. I was flat broke. I went to welfare.

There was a gum-chewing fat girl slouched in a chair talking to a man and a woman behind the desk. After she finished I told them my problem. They said the best they could do was a ticket off the island.

"This is a designated area," the man said. "We can only help you further if you have a job or a promise of a job. What do you do?"

"Construction," I said.

"You'd be classified as unemployable in the present situation. All I can do is give you a ticket to the mainland."

Then the fat girl chimed in. "You wanna babysit?" she asked me.

"Not really," I said.

She turned to the guy behind the desk. She hadn't been listening. "Well, there you are," she said. "This guy looks after my kids and I go to Vancouver and get a job and become a respectable woman."

We all laughed, and then the fat girl said: "Have you tried Wagner Funk at City Centre Grocery? He's sort of into the underdog thing, you know."

I thanked her. Underdog or not, she was a damn sight more helpful than the pair on the other side of the desk. I went looking for Funk, who owned a grocery store and had a small logging operation besides. I found him in a sort of basement office with some other men.

I told him I was looking for work. He shook his head and kept on shaking it. "No, this is a disaster situation up here," he said. He was sympathetic, but there was nothing he could do. Probably the other men in the office were looking for work, too.

I went back to the welfare office. The girl was behind the desk, and the man was in his office at the back with the door closed. "I need a ticket off," I said.

She didn't look up. "The ferry doesn't go until ten," she snapped.

"I know what time the ferry goes," I said sharply.

She became quite apologetic and started to make out some forms. A minute later a man came into the office in shorts. He looked hot and harried. He was a young man, the girl's husband or boyfriend, and he said, "Can you give me ten bucks." He wasn't asking, he was telling.

"What's going on?" she asked.

"I'm trying to get that car fixed, that's what's going on," he said. Now he was snapping at her. The snapper had become the snappee.

She gave him the money, and he took it and left. The girl didn't look at me. We've all got our problems. Her problem didn't happen to be catching a ferry. Mine didn't happen to be a car or a spouse. I felt better toward her. I felt she might not snap again for a while.

She handed me a form to sign. It said that I was destitute and had no job. It was in triplicate, if not quadruplicate.

"Where does this go? In the files?" I said.

"Yes."

"Do you get many people in for these?"

"Not many this year. It's surprising." It wasn't surprising to me. I knew most transients were staying close to the cities, to a welfare source or a place they could get food.

Then the girl produced not a ticket but three pieces of B.C. Ferry Corporation scrip. They were cardboard things – two blue and one pink – the size of an invitation to a Royal Garden Party or a Governor General's Ball, perhaps. The blue were worth five bucks each, the pink a dollar.

Why not a ticket? The answer was right there on the scrip. "Refundable only to original purchaser on application to B.C. Ferry Corporation head office." They didn't want people cashing them in. They wanted the riffraff off the island.

The girl indicated the closed office door at the back. "He asked me to tell you the hostel is open in Rupert," she said.

As I hiked back to the ferry dock a guy gave me the finger out of the passenger window of a red truck. At the ferry I offered my scrip to the girl on duty. "Is this funny money any good?"

"Don't you know?" she said sweetly. "Where did you get it?"

I didn't have to tell her where I'd got it. She knew. You can't steal off the Charlottes incognito. Not if you're down on your luck. She took the eleven dollars in scrip for a ten-fifty fare. I didn't ask for change, and I didn't get any.

"About the worst stretch of water I've seen, and I've seen a few," the barman was saying, about the very waters in which we were sailing. "Shallow, you know. Boils up. Once it took fourteen hours to go one way. A truck fell over below decks." But again it was an uneventful passage, nothing more than a few bumps.

In downtown Prince Rupert a bunch of kids were fishing with a string in a big puddle of rain water outside the Overwaitea Store. I headed for the Tourist Bureau to find the address of the hostel. On the way I passed the Ford Mercury dealership on McBride, a landmark business for many years. There was a big bright sign in the window: Home of the Little Cheeper. But inside there was not a cheep to be heard. The showroom floor was bare except for fallen promotional banners, which were strewn all over. And on the door was a more recent sign: "This Dealership is in the hands of the Receiver."

It was July 1982. There were distress warrants all over town. One was pasted up on the door of Eric's Steakhouse on the mall, right alongside the fancy, expensive menu. "Owed: $13,800."

At the Tourist Bureau a young boy in a very white shirt and pressed grey slacks and wearing a nametag marked the hostel on a map for me.

"Is it a halfway decent place?" I asked him.

He shrugged. "I have no idea," he said. Not used to dealing with that class of tourist. As it turned out he didn't know where the place was, either. It certainly wasn't where he'd marked it on the map. I asked a couple of native men on the street, and the younger one said: "It's behind Kentucky Fried Chicken." He pointed to the familiar symbol. "Brown building."

I set off, and the Indian caught up to me. "I'll go watch some TV in that place," he said. He had the usual jean jacket, jeans, and missing teeth, and he spat in the street, but at least he knew his way around.

Down on the wharf where the fishing boats are anchored in rows under the hot sun, an old lady from Monterey, California, was waiting for her husband. He used to play poker with John Steinbeck and now he was walking around somewhere, looking, smelling, thinking. He was a retired fisheries researcher, his wife told me. He worked out of Monterey in the days when the purse seiners came in slopping over with sardines, or, more properly, pilchards. As she put it: "In those days you could smell the scenery." Now the canneries of Monterey were nothing but a tourist attraction, the sardines long gone, fished out as her husband and his scientific colleagues had predicted they would be.

Her husband, she said, watched in anguish as the industry died – killed by greed, or natural human behaviour, whichever you prefer. It was a familiar story: no co-operation between states with a common interest, a powerful fishermen's lobby . . .

The woman and her husband had come to Prince Rupert in Canada for only one reason – to watch the hundreds of fishing boats come in or go out or lie in the oil-slicked dock reflecting the sun. Again they smelled the scenery. "It almost makes me cry," the woman said to me.

Salmon fishing was closed until the following day, and the boats lay there: *Courtney Main, Bon Accord, Miss Cory, Adriatic Sea, Windward Cloud, Beaver Isle, Reubina.*

Later I told a young fisherman what the woman had said about Monterey. "We did that to the herring," he said. "But the salmon are pretty strong."

He hadn't done so well in the preceding days, he told me, but some boats had big catches. They were after sockeye, because it took eight pinks to make the value of one sockeye. The buyers were paying forty-five cents for pinks last year, he said. This year their best offer was thirty cents, and the fishermen were going to take a strike vote over the issue in the coming week. They were scheduled to take some sort of preliminary vote, in fact, the following day. "They [the buyers] are trying to set us up for next year, when there will be a huge run of pinks," the fisherman said. He had short, fair hair, a white sweater, and gold-rimmed glasses. He looked like an accountant, but he and a partner had their own boat.

It was a beautiful, sunny day, the first one, he said, since he left Vancouver on July 1, three weeks earlier. Way out in the channel there was a Lilliputian dimension to the sight of two tiny tugs turning a huge grain ship, one pushing at the stern, the other, on the opposite side, at the bow. To my right a crewman was urinating over the side of the *Lana* into a perfect sunset. Across the channel were green hills topped with snow.

The next day I talked to an older fisherman about the vote. This was before it was taken.

"They're going to say, 'Any questions?' and forty idiots are going to stand up, half drunk. Then the Indians are going to make speeches, and then the Slavs are going to get up . . ."

After the meeting I met the same guy again, a short, sharp-featured, sharp-eyed fisherman. He was sitting in a fish-and-chip shop around the corner from a bar the fishermen use. I asked him how it went.

"I just said nuthin', moved we take a vote. Get the ballots in. The chairman gave me hell. 'We gotta have ideas from everybody,' he said. I just got up and walked out. They've been in here pumpin' everybody up like a bunch of communists. [He was talking about the union.] I just walked out, did something constructive, bought myself a shirt." He fingered the shirt he was wearing.

"My crew didn't like it, and I got some other buddies in there didn't like it, but I bin hearin' the same stuff now for thirty years."

Then he grinned and said: "Now I gotta go to the beer parlour and take my lickin'."

She was a runaway who hoped to get work in the canneries or as a hairdresser. She had taken no formal hairdressing training, but she said her uncle was an undertaker in the small town she had run away from, and she had practised cutting hair on corpses as they lay in the coffins. "It wasn't too bad," she said. "I only had to do the front and sides."

The uncle extracted everything he could from the bodies, she said. Gold teeth, fillings, metal hips or pins, false limbs. He melted them down and sold them. He then made an extra dollar or two by donating the remainder of the body to a local university for tests. The bodies were suspended in a lab and hit by a machine at speeds of up to twenty-five miles an hour to simulate injuries received in traffic accidents. When they came back (they were required for only an hour or two by the university, by which time every bone and organ was smashed) they were patched up some, and laid out, and then this girl, the niece, got to practise cutting hair. The hair she cut off was sold to a company that made dolls.

That's what she said.

The hostel. Two boiled eggs. Two pieces of toast. Here we go again. There's a sign in the lunchroom: "We can't all be heroes. Somebody has to sit on the curb and clap as they go by."

That's us. There's always a sign like that. That's how they cheer you up in these places.

"*We be clappin', massuh.*"

"*Harder.*"

"*We be clappin' harder, massuh.*"

There's a logging bum in the next bed to me, a faller. He's in five, I'm in six. He's run out of timber to cut. He's got a solid-silver belt buckle, gleaming brown leather boots. He's about six-five. He just got back from New Guinea. "Bad jungle," he said. "Ninety per cent humidity.

Lost sixty pounds, caught malaria. I was there four months. Made six thousand dollars and was cheated out of fourteen thousand more. Sent it all back to the wife and kid. Came out with nothing."

He'd been offered a job at Mount St. Helen where they were trying to get the wood out after the eruption, the big one, but it was a rotten job, all that ash, and he'd passed it up in favour of an ill-fated trip north.

"An old cuttin' buddy of mine called me. Get up to Rupert, he said. Two hundred a day. I take a fifteen-hundred-mile Greyhound trip. My buddy's not home. His wife says he's in hospital after a two-week drunk. There's no job. He made it up. I was pretty damn mad."

He lit a cigarette and put a gold cigarette lighter down on top of a pack of Pall Malls on the chair by his bed. He doesn't know about hostels, doesn't know you don't put anything down like that, especially not a gold cigarette lighter. He lay down, smoking and talking. He talked about snakes, scorpions, crocs, naked head-hunting natives, bugs, seven kinds of malaria, and shyster Aussie companies operating out of Hong Kong, cheating a man out of hard-earned cutting money.

Around him, perched on the edges of their beds, the other men listened. You didn't get this quality of conversation often in a hostel. Among the listeners was Rick, whose fire once got out of hand when he was trying to heat up a can of Spam. Unfortunately, he was in a fast-moving boxcar at the time. A railway bull on the side of the tracks spotted smoke and flame belching from the boxcar and had the train flagged down. Rick was fined ten bucks or a day in jail. He took the day, in a backwater jail, and the wife of the local cop cooked the Spam for him. There was T.J. the hippie, long haired, dressed all in flowing, white, East Indian-type clothing. In the Watson Lake lockup he had recently urinated in the pail provided for that purpose, then poured it under his cell door into the office, which happened to be next door. They made him take all his clothes off, he said, and mop it up, naked. Next morning they ordered him to wash all the police cars. "Fuck you," he told them. "I've done my nice time." His friend Lawrence, who was said to have five complete sets of ID for welfare and other purposes, had something else on his mind and only half listened to the logging bum's stories. He had found in the street the keys to a Harley-Davidson motorcycle. He had located the owner by phone and been told to go over to his apartment the following day. He expected his good deed to be worth at least a couple of reefers, Harley-Davidsons and reefers being linked inextricably in his mind. There was the usual Newfie – always one or two in these places – a professional story-teller, who listened with a more critical air; but even he would have had to admit that tropical jungles, headhunters, deadly insects and killer diseases ranked above the usual conversational subject matter, which might be, say, conditions in the Edmonton holding cells.

It was an entertaining night all right, but in the morning the newcomer was quieter, as if seeing the place with a fresh eye. He sat at breakfast with a piece of toast sitting flatly on top of his coffee cup, keeping warm, while he ate his cornflakes. He was a logging bum with nowhere to go. Nobody was cutting wood. He lived in Washington state, and now he was stranded in a hostel in Canada. He didn't even have his saws with him, because his buddy had told him he wouldn't need them. He would have gone up to Ketchikan where he had worked before, but he didn't have the fare. Things did not look rosy.

I had checked in the night before, just ahead of the faller. There were about twenty men staying there. The dormitory was a whitewashed room one storey above the street. A wooden shelf for baggage ran right around it above the beds, which were arranged side by side around the perimeter of the room. These were narrow, single beds, not two-high berths. There was a three-day maximum stay. After that, a man had to see a social worker from welfare. The place was cleared at 10:00 A.M. and nobody was allowed back in until 4:00 P.M. The lights went out at 11:30. The hostel was above the Indian Friendship Centre, which had a television set and a pool table.

The talk at breakfast was mainly about the chance of getting money out of welfare, and the threatened fishermen's strike, which could shut the town down completely for jobs. In fact, it had already done so. Neither processing plants nor fishing boat skippers were prepared to hire while the possibility of a strike loomed. In any case there would be twenty to a hundred applicants for every job. The employment picture was wryly summed up on a blackboard behind the B.C. Packer plant on the docks.

"I need a job," somebody had written in desperation, with a phone number.

Underneath had been added the cynical, no-hope response: "Shop Super Valu."

At the employment centre a handful of jobs were listed, for a desk clerk, maids, a couple of professional people. The place was full of people filing unemployment insurance claims. It was not quite as depressing, however, as Prince George had been a couple of weeks earlier. There the employment centre had been jammed. There must have been a hundred or more men and women in the place, some just sitting hopelessly, and the job boards were almost completely bare. It was frightening.

"You're not going to believe this," the receptionist at the welfare office said as she flipped through a huge diary, page by page, "but we have no free date until" – she paused – "August fifth."

It was now July 26. Ten days to wait, just to see someone.

"But this is an emergency," I said. "Tonight is my last night at the hostel. Surely there are emergency procedures? I don't really want to apply for welfare. I just need enough money to get out of town. There are no jobs here."

She was a nice woman, and she had me fill in an application. She said the best she could do was to ask me to come back in the morning and wait. An appointment might be cancelled, somebody might not show, and perhaps I could be fitted in. In the meantime I should see the social worker who was to visit the hostel that afternoon and ask to extend my stay there.

We chatted. She asked me where I was headed, and I said probably Whitehorse. She said she had lived in Watson Lake thirty years earlier. She had been practically the only white woman there. "We had it rough," she told me. "I loved it up there, but it was rough. And it's rough again now."

That day in the office and the following day I had the opportunity of watching this elderly receptionist deal with more than a dozen needy people. She was attentive, not in an insincere way, but genuinely alert and sympathetic. I saw her go from office to office to try to find a worker who could fit in a hardship case quickly. She did everything efficiently and always behaved as if she were there to help the supplicant. There were line-ups in that office, of course, but I never saw the type of restlessness or mouthiness I so often saw in other offices. Those waiting knew they would all receive the same type of hearing and effort on their behalf. The elderly woman's own dignity seemed to spread to others. I think I know why this woman treated the people who came to

92

the office in that way. It had much to do with her own past, with the hardships she had hinted at to me. She was part of a pattern that I saw repeated over and over as I drifted. The rides generally came from people who had needed a ride themselves, and so did help of other kinds. It might be axiomatic, an unsurprising thing, but it strikes one so forcibly that it is worth stressing.

That afternoon we sat on a line of chairs that had been placed in the hallway at the hostel outside the social worker's temporary office. She was a brisk, dark-haired girl. Her job was solely to determine whether we could remain in the hostel for a day or two longer, or whether we would have to leave. The door to the office was kept open, so that each man had to state his case, however embarrassing his circumstances, for those waiting outside to hear. One after another they told their stories.

T.J. the hippie said he'd had a chance of a permanent job but had been mysteriously turned down at the last minute. He thought it might have been because of his appearance.

"Why don't you get your hair cut, then?" the girl said to him. "You want the job." She was dressed in jeans.

"That's discrimination," T.J. said.

"This is a conservative town," she informed him. "You might lose a lot of jobs because you have long hair. It doesn't matter to me how long your hair is. You can cut off your ear if you want to."

"Van Gogh," T.J. muttered.

"What?"

"Nothing."

"But why do you stay in a town like this?" she persisted. "Go somewhere else."

"Well, I just want to get enough money to move on."

The girl waved her hand at him. "Well, I don't want to get into a philosophical argument," she said.

All this – in public, too – to determine whether a man could sleep one more night in a hostel (where there were certainly vacant beds) and get a macaroni meal.

While the girl was packing her pencils and forms I asked her how she enjoyed her work. She said she didn't care. She had only eight more days before leaving for Paris as an exchange nanny. A nanny!

"Don't run out and cut your ear off just yet," I muttered to T.J. He winked.

She allowed me an extra three days at the hostel and told me, as the older woman had, to go to welfare the following day.

The Newfie, meanwhile, had been busy. He had already managed to get welfare to fork over some getaway money. He came back to the dorm with a Coke bottle full of rum and Coke in a brown paper bag. He sat on my bed and filled my mug.

He nudged me. He'd already taken a few drinks. "Easterners are all right," he said.

"I never met a bad one," I said.

"I was a sailor for ten years. Sailors don't ask for five or ten dollars when they want money. They ask for fifty or a hundred. If you're gonna get drunk, get drunk properly."

He talked about how many easterners had left home to look for work elsewhere. There were sixty thousand in Toronto alone, he said. He told me he had gone back home three years earlier and there were very few men left. He went to a club, and there were girls all over the place. He said he took four of them home.

Even when easterners were away from home they looked after each other, he said. "I was in a doorway on Hastings Street in Vancouver once, looking at the rain, when a guy pulled up in a car.

" 'Newfie?' he shouts. He could tell just by looking at me.

" 'Yep.'

" 'What you doin' here?'

" 'Lookin' at the rain.'

" 'Are you tapped?'

" 'Yep.'

"He peeled off five twenties, gave 'em to me, and drove off."

After a while the Newfie went to use a pay phone. He was headed for Prince George by bus that night, and he wanted his girl to be waiting when he got in.

He had been pretty quiet in the preceding couple of days, for a Newfie, but now that he had some money, some booze, and a place to head for, he could hardly stand still. He wanted to get it on. Everybody had to drink from his bottle. He wanted to give me money, but I wouldn't take it. Welfare had given him $87. He told me to look him up when I was in Prince George. He said I should look only in the lowest, dirtiest bars; those were the places where he could be found. He gave me a list.

Almost everybody who had been at the hostel a couple of days or more was making plans to leave. An incident the night before had soured a few. The young woman who generally looked after things around the hostel had walked through on a cursory bed check, with no warning, embarrassing a couple of guys who were headed for the shower, and then had loudly and vindictively berated one man for leaving stuff untidily on his bed. Possessions were supposed to be stored on the shelf above, she lectured. She ranted on for a while in a frayed-nerves sort of way, a reaction completely out of proportion to the offence committed, and then dragged in the supervisor, a man, who felt obliged to give a stupid, condescending lecture, threatening a general clean-up during which all property not on the shelves would be thrown away.

Some, including T.J. and his friend Lawrence, were heading for the Okanagan to pick apples, despite farm labour pool bulletins warning that thousands of unemployed men and women had descended on the valley and were wandering around the fruit-growing areas looking for a day's work.

I was the only one thinking of heading north, and everybody warned me against it, especially those who had just come from there. If possible there was even less work up there, they said. Looking for work was hopeless. It was a long way to hitchhike, a lot of dust to swallow. And no possibility of welfare. They were much tougher up north, I was told, just kicked you out of town.

In the morning, I stopped in at the employment centre, and met the faller from Washington state, all the bounce gone out of him now, looking for work, any work. He had an appointment with the immigration people to see if he could wangle a work permit. Almost overnight, from being a man with a trade and supposedly a job to go to, he seemed to have become assimilated into the world of the nowhere man, the transient.

On the wall of the welfare office was a tearjerker-type picture of a woman hugging a child and, alongside, one of those nauseating homilies people insist on inflicting on those who have run into hard times. This one said:

Well I'm doin' my best gettin' started,
And I know I'm gonna be okay,
But it sure will be nice,
When we get together,
And the sun shines through all day.

95

A fascinating incident while I waited demonstrated the lack of flexibility or imagination in the system. A young native woman went to the counter and handed over a money order made out to Human Resources to pay back welfare payments she had received. She said she had been working for two of the weeks covered by her latest cheque and simply wanted to pay the money back.

The girl who dealt with her over the counter – in the absence of the graceful older woman – looked stunned. Thunderstruck. Her hand actually went up to her lips in the gesture you see in bad acting.

"You can't do that," she said. "You can't pay it back."

The young woman said: "Well, I've got the money order made out now."

Conferences followed in all corners of the office. People peered at the money order and at the young woman. They were helpless in the face of this sensible, honest gesture. In the end they simply sent her away, and she trudged out with the money order.

They managed to fit me in next. I happened to draw the same girl who had been at the hostel the previous day.

"I need help to get out of town," I said.

"How?"

"By bus."

"I can't give you bus fare to Vancouver. Just the ferry."

"There's a ferry?"

"To Port Hardy," she said.

"Then I have to get from Port Hardy on the Island to Vancouver on the mainland. Everybody knows there's no work in Hardy."

"Well, you can probably get some more money in Hardy, and you can get ferry money in Victoria."

I scratched my head. "Well, I don't know how this system works . . . I began.

"Neither do I," she interjected.

" . . . but it seems I'm being passed from one place to another. In the Charlottes they told me to come here. From here I'm supposed to go to Port Hardy, where there's no work but where I can get more welfare money to go to Victoria, where I get more ferry money to get me to Vancouver, where, presumably, I'll have to apply for help again."

She shrugged. I told her I'd rather go north. She gave me a cheque for $87. This seemed to be the standard amount of getaway money, for

Prince Rupert, anyway. It was the same amount the Newfie had received, and some of the others, regardless of destination. It was treated like a full welfare payment: once a man had drawn that amount he was no longer entitled to any more benefits for a full month afterward.

When I went to the bank to cash the cheque I showed my copy of the welfare declaration as additional supportive identification. "That's no good," the accountant told me. "They don't know who they're giving cheques to at welfare. They have no idea."

# 10

*The Northland is the Northland,*
*and men work out their souls*
*by strange rules, which other*
*men who have not journeyed*
*to far countries can not understand.*
— Jack London, *In a Far Country*

I was picked up outside of Rupert by a German couple in a rented camper van. I sat in the back at a small table. He spoke a little English, and she a little more, but it was hard to understand, and I had to lean forward and concentrate. She carried a bilingual dictionary on her lap. They lived in Cologne, I was told, a short distance from the polluted Rhine. The woman had grey hair pulled into a bun and kept intact by the sort of thin hairnet one rarely sees here any more. She asked me why so many of our trees were dead at the topmost branches, and I didn't know the answer, hadn't even noticed the problem. She said there were few undeveloped areas of forest now in Germany. There were areas where the trees were protected, but no wild forest.

We stopped for a while so the man could fish in the Skeena River. He caught three small fish in an hour. He was ecstatic. He said that in Germany all the lakes and rivers are on private property, and you have to get permission to fish them. Every time we got a new view of the Skeena from the winding road, he would point out good fishing spots. "Wunderbar," he kept saying.

They took me to Terrace, and I hiked through the town in a burning sun. I walked a long way before a retired forestry worker picked me up and drove me to a campsite on Kleanza Creek. He said he had passed me when he went into town to get a paper and said to himself he'd pick me up on the way back. He had been retired two years, he said, and he and his wife were worried that if things got much rougher the government might cut his pension. He showed me his home as we passed it.

"You don't have to take me any further," I said.

"I want to," he told me.

We talked about the shortage of work, and I said I was heading up to the Yukon. "I don't know whether it's any better up there," I said.

"I don't think so," he said.

The next day, in the morning, I made it to Kitwanga, the junction to the north, in the back of a pickup carrying three military types. I walked for quite a way uphill then, until a fellow in an old Volvo picked me up and took me almost to Stewart, to a place called Hanna Creek. There was just a bridge over the creek, no houses, nothing. There were lots of fish in the water, cruising, basking, turning back into the current.

It was windy, and the fine sand and pebbles on the little beach made it hard to anchor the tent, but I finally got organized, with a fire going. The creek was shallow on my side but deeper, dark and quiet, near the opposite bank where the fish were. I was hidden from the road by a bend in the creek. The fish were jumping, making big heavy splashes. I could see the moon through the fabric of the tent.

There's nothing much on those roads for hundreds of miles. When you're camped by the side of one it's eerie. There's virtually no traffic after dusk to remind you the road's even there, yet you know it is, and you can see that dust ribbon in your head, see it going on and on past nothing but nature, and you involuntarily send out antennae down the road . . .

Love of country is generally regarded as one of the soft passions, but up here it screams at you like a boss whistle from out of the silence. Bijou emotions are drowned in the Canadian north. Cabin fever only affects those whose love is somehow not big enough. For the rest there is an almost paradisal freedom.

I read once about Saltatha, an old Dogrib Indian from the barren lands, being taught the principles of Christianity by one of the first Catholic missionaries. "My father," he said, "you have told me of the beauties of heaven. Tell me one thing more. Is it more beautiful than the country of the musk-ox in summertime, when sometimes the mists blow over the lakes, and sometimes the waters are blue, and the loons cry very often? That is beautiful, and if heaven is still more beautiful my heart will be glad, and I shall be content to rest there until I am very old."

The next morning I was lucky. I got a ride from the second vehicle to come along, a camper van with a couple from Delta and their young daughter, and they took me to within about eighty miles of Dease Lake. They were stopping early, and I was trying to go on further, so they let me out. I hadn't got too far down the road, though, when they came up behind me and picked me up again. They were going to get groceries, and they had the wife of a provincial park ranger along. She was trying to catch up to her husband to pass on a radiophone message before his light plane took off from a nearby lake. A bridge had been knocked out up ahead, she said, and there wouldn't likely be much traffic until it was opened again, so my rides would be few and far between. She wasn't even sure I could get across the bridge on foot. We got to the lake and flagged down her husband's float plane just as it was about to take off, a melodrama that turned out to be unnecessary because he had already got the message his wife was to give him. But he did tell me there was a fire near Cassiar and that I might get firefighting work out of Dease Lake where the forestry office was. He turned to his wife. "Mighty Moe's place has gone up," he told her sadly. It was a resort on the highway. Mighty Moe was a local character.

I got a couple of short rides, then one from another German couple. I tried to repay the rides, as hitchhikers do, by helping in any way I could, primarily with information about Alaska and the Yukon, which I knew, and with recommendations about places they should see. My situation often seemed strange to me. I was older than most hitchhikers, and I was an imposter, I suppose. But it takes all sorts, and I often consoled myself with thoughts of a predecessor, a man who, indeed, might have been this country's first hitchhiker.

O'Byrne, first name not known, a gentleman of Ireland, found himself in Edmonton in a state of chronic destitution. The year was 1862. There he came across Viscount Milton and Dr. W.B. Cheadle, out from England, ostensibly to explore a route across the Rockies, but in truth looking for a sort of off-beat vacation. Mr. O'Byrne begged to be allowed to accompany them to British Columbia, where he felt sure he could retrieve his fortunes, and promised to make himself useful along the way.

Some months later, this odd party, guided by an Assiniboine Indian who had his wife and his young son along, had lost most of its supplies and ammunition and, living now on pemmican, was forced to plunge into pathless, virtually impenetrable forest, somewhere alongside the Thompson River. By this time all ideas of a vacation had been shelved.

"Under these trying circumstances," the doctor and the Viscount recorded in their memoirs later, "we had the advantage of Mr. O'B's advice, which he did not fail to offer at every opportunity.

" 'Now, my lord, now doctor,' he would say. 'I don't think we have gone on nearly so well today as we might have done. I don't think our route was well chosen. We may have done fifteen or twenty miles (we had probably accomplished three or four), but that's not at all satisfactory. "*Festina lente*" was wisely said by the great lyricist; but he was never lost in a forest, you see. Now, what I think ought to be done is this: the doctor and the Assiniboine are strong, vigorous fellows. Let them go five or six miles ahead and investigate the country, and then we shall travel much more easily tomorrow.' "

Later, when all the food was gone, they held a council of war. "Mr. O'B. laid down his one-eyed spectacles to suggest we should immediately kill Blackie, as he affectionately denominated the little black horse he usually took charge of on the way."

This was overruled in favour of attempts to gather food. "Early next day the Assiniboine set off to hunt, Cheadle and the boy went to a small lake ahead to try to get a shot at some geese which had flown over the day before; Milton (the Viscount) gathered bilberries, and Mr. O'B. studied."

Thoughts of the brazen O'B., the original hitchhiker, cheered me over many a rideless hour.

When we hit the bridge it was just being reopened. A long line of traffic was waiting to cross, had been waiting, no doubt, for hours, and the German imperiously drove straight to the head of the line and over the bridge, nodding to a dumbfounded policeman, without seemingly giving it a second thought.

I had them drop me at Dease Lake because I wanted to see about a firefighting job. At the forestry office, though, they said the fires they had were under control, and they didn't need any more men. However, they said, it was a day-to-day thing, and if I stayed around town I might get something. That night it rained, the first time in a week and a half. If my prospects of a job had been chancy before they would be even less certain after the downpour, so the next day I moved on, hoping to get hired further north. The fire hazard was high pretty much all over.

A Dutch couple from The Hague, who had given me a short ride once before, picked me up in their van the next morning. The Europeans, I was discovering, perhaps more used to what is over there a fairly respectable way of vacationing, invariably stopped if they had room. This couple had been given a special mission, they told me. They had been asked to deliver a license plate to a man who collected them. The Oregon plate had come off a car demolished in the accident that had wiped out the bridge. It was to be dropped off at Mighty Moe's place up the highway. (The Dutch couple had actually misheard and were looking for somebody called Mighty Mouse, but I recalled the park ranger's words to his wife – "Mighty Moe's place has gone up" – and was able to put them right.) The woman who had given them the license plate ran a roadside café where they had stopped to eat, somewhere near the bridge, and had said that Mighty Moe collected the plates and that it might help cheer him up a bit to get a new one because his place had just been wiped out in a fire. The plates were going from one disaster to another.

Mighty Moe's place was on our right, a campground and a bunch of cabins on a lake. It was a mess, but not quite as bad as we had heard. Somehow the cabins had been saved. The whole area right down to the lake was blackened, though, and a bunch of machines, a snowmobile visible among the pile, lay in a mangled and melted heap. There was no sign of Mighty Moe – the place was deserted – so we left the license plate with a note, after looking around for a while. One side of a central cabin was plastered with license plates from all over. There were also mooseheads, beer cans, hockey sticks, antique shotguns, toy pistols, a pair of crutches, a child's bike, and God knows what else on the same wall. Mighty Moe collected pretty near anything.

The Dutch couple had been travelling since February, they told me, when we got back on the road. They had flown from Holland to New York, and since then they had been all over Mexico, where they had lived with Indians, sharing their corn-based diet. They had also lived in the United States for a while and were now headed up to Alaska.

They had done a lot of work on the van, putting carpets inside on the floors, walls, and roof. There was a cupboard and a makeshift bed. "It is our home," they said.

They had driven hundreds, perhaps thousands of miles on gravel roads in this van, but, just as we hit a stretch of pavement up past

Cassiar, a stone spit a crack in their windshield. Welcome to the real north.

That night there was a drunken party in a campground by Teslin Lake. Beer, wine, moose meat, baked potatoes. Guitar music by a crazy Czech who said he'd gotten out just ahead of the Russians. Pickup trucks everywhere.

A girl asked me: "Are you from the Yukon?"

I was standing helplessly with a beer. I had nothing to open it with. I tried to reply, but my words were drowned out by the music. The girl threw me a plastic disposable cigarette lighter.

"I can't open it with that."

"You're not from the Yukon," she said shrewdly.

I was about 150 miles from Whitehorse now.

I got a third ride the next morning from my globetrotting Dutch friends. It was getting embarrassing. They'd stop early for the night, I'd get ahead of them, and then there I'd be the next morning, on the side of the road with my thumb up. As if I'd planned it. I kept apologizing. They kept laughing. We were running out of conversation. But it would be my last ride with them. They were going down to Skagway to take the ferry into Alaska. They let me out at a gas station at the turnoff, and I got another ride immediately. The driver this time was recreation director at a tungsten mine, five hundred miles away, east of Watson Lake. He made the ten-hour trip every two weeks to check on a house he owned in Whitehorse. He had come north four years earlier when things were booming. Now every mine but his and one other was shut down.

He was a sandy-haired, bucktoothed fellow. Divorced. His ex-wife and child were in Winnipeg. "She said things are so bad there, so terrible, she guessed more people were out of work than working," he said.

We talked about the economy a bit, and he said: "I think a lot, living in that bunkhouse. Why can't we have a two-tier interest rate, across the board?

"They say the problem is high interest rates, and that people won't buy Canadian. There must be a way to solve this. Why can't we set the interest rate on a loan to buy Canadian goods at, say, ten per cent, and to buy foreign it would cost, say, twenty-six per cent. It would apply to all sizes of deals, private or corporate."

He took me right into Whitehorse. It was just after noon on a Sunday. The only campground was way back out of town, and you had to pay, so I finally crossed the bridge and made camp right on the Yukon River, inside the Education Authority Nature Preserve. There was a big sign: "Visitors are welcome, BUT NO CAMPING."

The river was green. It's been green-grey every time I've seen it, the ice tinge always on it. Robert Service called it the big blue Yukon, but it's more often green.

On Monday I went into town to do some laundry. The laundromat wasn't open yet, so I walked down Fourth to the Klondike Inn. I was just crossing the road at the junction when I heard a fast, heartstopping thump from behind, and a white pickup, out of control and over on two wheels, flashed past me on the raised median, missed me by six inches at most, crossed the road, and slammed into a telephone pole. Embedded in the side of the truck, right in the metal like a spear, was a street sign it had picked up on the way. It happened so quickly I had no time to get out of the way, or even turn my head. A cab driver raced to the truck, which was on its side, smacked right up around the pole with the passenger door uppermost, and jerked open the door. The driver, very young and fair-haired, hoisted himself out as if through a submarine hatch. Incredibly, he was not hurt. And neither was I. But I was weak.

"You just missed me, boy," I said.

He looked at me as if I was a ghost. He was scared stiff. "I know," he said, with as much sincerity as a voice could get into two words. Another few inches and I would have been a smear.

You can read all sorts of things into an incident like that. There lies madness.

Just after I got started on my laundry a guy swung through the door, red-eyed, with a guitar wrapped in a garbage bag tied onto his backpack. He wore worn, floppy cords and a dirty-white peaked cap. He had a droopy eye, a stiff, protruding brown moustache, and a vaguely scarred face. His brows came together in a fairly narrow skull. He looked about half Gael, a quarter Russian, and the rest Micmac Indian. He was just down from Alaska. They'd seized his truck at the border because there was no insurance on it and he didn't have the ownership papers, and fined him $800 for impaired driving and another $400 for the paper offences, or twelve days in jail. Nine days later they let him out and deported him. His mistake was in trying to get across the border drunk, with six or seven drunked-up hitchhikers in his truck, beer bottles all over the place, and music blaring ... a rolling party.

"Guy's not supposed to be happy," he said disconsolately, dragging dirty clothes out of his pack.

He'd been mending fishing nets on the dock at Cordova in the last few months, he said. Before that he was trapping on Montague Island, shooting the odd bear, living off the meat, plus buttercups, asparagus, and any other plant life he could turn into protein.

In his backpack he had all sorts of gadgets: things for telling the weather – barometers, chronometers – who knows what they were. They spilled out onto the floor with his laundry. "You want 'em?" he said to the man who ran the place and who was watching.

"Sure," the man said.

I told the hiker where I was camping – over the bridge and down along the river bank – and I said if he couldn't find anywhere else there was room for another tent. Before I left I offered him the cool salute, palms up – I did it automatically now; everybody I met did it that way – and he turned it over into a real handshake, the old-fashioned kind. "When I shake hands with a man I do it this way," he said.

He was there when I got back from town that afternoon. I could hear the guitar from down the path. If we were trespassing we were obviously not going to do it quietly. It was a beautiful, classical sound, absolutely clean.

"I found what I wanted in Alaska," he said as we sat by the fire he had built. "But I also found I was a social person."

What he'd wanted, he said, had been to walk into a completely unspoiled, uninhabited valley, with a rifle and a few tools, and live there.

He found the valley and he trapped mink until he had two hundred pelts, but he could only get $28 a pelt so he had a girl make hats out of them. It took four pelts to make a hat, and he could get $380 a hat. He had a partner doing the business end, the selling, and they were to split the money they made. They could sell the hats right away, as soon as they were made.

Then Terry, who hadn't seen much money yet, decided to go check on the business.

"I came out of the bush like a wild man. You've heard stories up north about these wild men who stumble out of the bush, play great classical music in a bar, and are never seen again. It was like that. You freak out, you know, all these women serving you food . . . . To spend four hundred dollars a night is nothing."

Later he found out that his partner, a six-foot-six giant from Maine, had been cheating him badly on the mink hats.

He went to the boat the man lived on in Cordova and waited with two guns the man had loaned him as part of their deal. When he saw his partner coming, Terry said, he stood up and shouted: "C'mon you cocksucker, I'll knock your cheekbones into your eyes."

The guy wouldn't fight. "I don't want to shoot you," Terry warned, but he still wouldn't fight, and finally Terry threw the two guns over the side of the boat.

The guy from Maine said: "Terry, I'm just like you. I'm running just to survive. I'm an alcoholic, my wife left me, I've got thousands of dollars in debts . . ."

Terry spoke quietly, wearily almost, rolling cigarettes once in a while, splitting the tough rose hips from the bushes around us with a thumb to make tea.

From where we were we could clearly see the ss *Klondike* II, the tourist-attraction paddle-wheeler on the other side of the river, down near the bridge. Our site was a good one. We had a little dirt beach, and there was a small island about fifteen feet offshore, so that the river formed a fairly docile channel between the island and us, and our camp was pretty well hidden from view. Behind us there was only a thin screen of trees atop a bank between us and a path through the nature reserve, but few people used it.

It was a source of amusement to Terry that this boat, the ss *Klondike* was not in the water but up on piles. He'd look at this huge, sparkling-white, useless boat from time to time and say: "It's not even in the water." It seemed to be some sort of symbol to him of what the north as a last frontier had come to. He hinted that finding an unspoiled valley in Alaska where a man could live and trap and hunt without being harassed had not been as easy as falling off a log. "For a while I thought I was the only guy up there without ferry money to get out," he told me.

He said he was glad to be back over the border in Canada, which was his home. He seemed to have already chalked up to experience the loss of the truck, for which he'd paid two thousand dollars only a month earlier.

We sat there, stew in a pot over the fire, by the Yukon River, and he said: "My dad was an alcoholic hobo, and here I am." He grinned that lopsided, wrinkled way of grinning out of the corner of their eyes they have on the Atlantic seaboard. It was funny. We were squatting illegally on a riverbank in the middle of a recession cooking in a big pot we'd found in the bush and scoured out with sand, looking across at the lights on the road and from the big, dumb-looking, tourist boat. It was like a scene from a Chaplin movie.

After he and the guy from Maine talked things over, Terry lived for a while on the boat in Cordova and mended nets for fishermen, a skill he had learned in his youth in Cape Breton. At the start, he charged fifteen dollars an hour, but he found he was working as quickly as a woman he worked alongside who charged twenty dollars, so he upped his price. At the end he was charging twenty-five dollars, but the work was sporadic.

Before I crawled into my tent, Terry showed me the "Dear John" missive he had got from an old girlfriend in Alberta while he was still up in Alaska. No letter, just a colour photo showing a handsome blond girl about eight months pregnant.

I could hear him playing guitar and singing there on the riverbank until late. It was a clear soft night, with not a breath of wind.

In the morning I bathed in the river and walked across the bridge into town. The weather was rainy, cloudy, and sunny by turns, the town dismal. That day's issue of the *Whitehorse Star* said: "The once-thriving Yukon economy continues to be ambushed by massive layoffs and depressed metal prices."

A headline on another story said: "Repossessions up as economy crashes."

It was Tuesday, August 3, 1982, and I suddenly felt I'd been on the road too long. That hobo remark of Terry's, funny as it had been, had hit close to the mark. I was beginning to wonder about myself and my motives, and that made me uncomfortable. That, and the near miss with the runaway truck the previous morning. I was beginning to wonder if I wasn't courting disaster a mite too ardently.

I went to the employment centre, which, as usual, was a disaster area itself, then walked down to the library between the railway tracks and the river bank. The riverbank was littered with broken glass on that side, near the town, which is where the alkies go to drink. The glass has been trodden underfoot so many times it is like fake gold dust. But it is the glisten of a far more sordid piece of history, unfortunately.

The huge river moved past these decades of drained and smashed bottles as it had always moved, six or seven miles an hour, with a weight and power that tugged at the heart.

This end of town is full of drunks. The Indians used to live here among willows on the riverbank before they were moved out for an ugly park nobody ever uses. Now one was watching a group of canoeists prepare to head out on the river for Dawson. He offered advice, and the canoeists tried to shoo him away as if he were a dog. They were excited by their trip and preoccupied.

When I left the library I could see Terry at the other end of the bridge walking back to camp. I hollered to him and he came back. Terry was angry. He had got a twelve-dollar voucher for food from welfare and shopped for half an hour, carefully, as one does when one has only twelve dollars to last an indefinite period of time. Then, at the check-out, the manager had said he couldn't accept the voucher. Somebody at welfare had made a mistake and given Terry the wrong copy. He would have to go back and get it changed. But the welfare office had been closed for the day when he got there.

We walked down to the Salvation Army at the other end of town. Soup and coffee was the menu. There were about twenty people there, one guy with many fresh cuts on his face, thin rivers of dried blood like contours on a map. There was the usual assortment of beards, dirt, odour, and hacking coughs. Terry couldn't take the place, I could see that. He sipped some soup and left the rest. "I'm splitting," he said.

He was waiting for me outside. "I think I'm going to become a middle-class capitalist and make some money," he said, as if his eyes had just been opened. He was also still upset about the welfare gaffe. He walked on morosely beside me for a while and then turned his face up to the sky, stopped, and yelled in a pleading, joking voice: "Take me back to the joint." We sat down in a coffee shop and I spent what I had left, which wasn't much.

As we drank our coffee I told Terry to save the new welfare voucher he would get tomorrow. I still had some food left, we'd eat that first, look for work for a couple of days, and then, if we had no luck, I'd get a food voucher, too, and we'd hit the road. I was still hoping to find a forest fire, but there had been rain, and I was less hopeful. I told him we could probably get extra food from the churches the next day.

In the morning I went to St. Joseph's at Fifth and Cook. The church ran the only hostel in town. There was a little garden around the hostel building, and when I got to the gate a priest came to the open door and beckoned to me. "Come in and see me," he said, almost impatiently.

"Sit down," he said. I was in a small room with a kitchen table. The priest sat across from me as if he meant business. He had a grey brush cut and a brusque manner. A huge silver cross hung around his neck.

"I'm out of work and out of food and out of money," I told him. "I thought maybe you had some food."

"Where are you from?" he asked. I told him I had come up from Prince Rupert.

Without hesitation he said: "My advice is to go back there."

"I heard you served one meal a day," I said.

"We only serve meals to guys who stay here," he said. "But I'll give you something anyway." He went into the next room and came back with a brown bag. A small brown bag.

"Where you staying?" he asked. I told him I had a tent on the river.

"One night's all I'd give you here anyway," he said. "Then I'd kick you out. There's no jobs."

Outside in the street I checked the bag. Two cans of beans and half a loaf of bread.

But when I got back Terry had a whole bunch of stuff: moose meat, rice, potatoes, peas, green peppers, margarine, packaged food, bread, soup, some cans, orange crystals, six eggs . . . quite a spread. I put down my little bag. "Where did you get it?" I asked.

"St. Mary's."

"Where?"

He said he'd gone to St. Joseph's but the place was locked up and there was nobody around, so he went across the street, kitty-corner, to St. Mary's, which turned out to be the women's hostel, and the nuns there had given him as much stuff as he could carry.

"I guess I'm learning," he said.

We cooked everything up at once in the big pot, with the moose meat, and then we made tea from the reddening rose-hip buds. You couldn't ask for anything better. The lights from the ss *Klondike* were reflected in the river. We could see the odd glimmer of vehicle lights hitting the bridge, but nobody could see us. Terry's music. For that one night there wasn't a place either one of us would rather have been. It was a night we knew just how much tramp there was in us, and that it was considerable.

In the daytime Terry and I went our own ways. Usually one of us stayed with the gear while the other went into town. When Terry left he'd leave with me, for safekeeping, a bag of home-grown Alaskan dope he'd managed to pick up somewhere, probably in prison. At night we'd sit by the fire, and I got to know a bit about his background.

As a kid he was thin, nervous, and covered in acne – a real bad case. He was, as a result, extremely defensive, and fought like a wildcat at any slight, real or imagined. He learned most of the eastern-seaboard trades, ancient and modern – from running a dory to smuggling drugs. Once he was stopped in a roadblock outside of Halifax. In the trunk of his car was a suitcase containing forty pounds of marijuana. The cop went into the trunk and opened a guitar case. As he was checking it out, one hasp on the suitcase, which was lying alongside, clicked open. It was not fastened properly, and right there under the cop's nose it went click. The cop looked at the suitcase.

"Do you own a '74 Monte Carlo?" he asked. The Monte Carlo had become an obsession with them. They knew it was running drugs but they hadn't been able to catch it. They also suspected that Terry owned it.

"Yeah, did that cocksucker get into trouble?" Terry demanded. "I sold it to some guy for nine hundred bucks and I still haven't got the money," he lied. As he talked he fastened the guitar case and slammed the trunk lid. He said he would never have gotten away with it, but he had a very old man in the car, a passenger – "I'd turned him on to pot, and he was a friend for life" – and his presence made the cop indecisive.

At this time, Terry said, he was smoking forty marijuana cigarettes a day and chewing hashish.

Once, he said, he went to a hotel room to buy drugs. A girl was standing there with a syringe, which she had just stuck into the belly of a man lying on the bed. He was naked and a cripple. His legs were wasted and useless. She was shooting speed into him. He had a gun out and pointed when Terry walked through the door.

"I just want to buy some pot, man," Terry said. "I don't want none of that stuff."

The cripple lowered the gun, the girl sold Terry the drugs, and he left. Just as he hit the pavement he heard the gunshot. The next day the newspaper said that the cripple, described as a drug dealer, had been shot dead. Presumably the woman did it.

Busted on a fairly minor drug charge and in need of money, Terry started an escort service by advertising in the newspaper, using his aunt's telephone number. He got seven hundred calls in a week. He had to rope in all his male relatives, uncles, cousins, anybody he could get hold of, to make a dent in the trade.

One girl came to his apartment. When she took off her clothes she had more scars than anybody he had ever seen. She'd slashed her wrists, her arms, under her armpits, her neck, her crotch . . .

"Don't worry," she told him as he looked at her. "It's over now."

"It better be," Terry said. "I don't want no blood spilled in my apartment."

One woman client, married to a man who worked in an office, called because she said she had never seen a healthy male body. Her husband was fat and droop-bellied. She just wanted to look.

Another woman, a nurse yet, said she had never seen an erect penis. Terry charged $30 an hour and $150 a night.

The whole thing ended in disaster, needless to say. The relatives were feuding because the women naturally did not want their men involved; the aunt was pissed off because she had virtually been driven out of her house by the telephone calls; and the newspaper cut off the ad.

Throughout this period Terry had been gaining a reputation in the east as a fine musician. He had studied music extensively, though not formally, had appeared on television, and had played clubs and bars. But more and more he was turning toward a classical sound and studying the work and life of Segovia, as well as a broad range of philosophical literature. And he was living with a girl who taught him the craft of the silversmith.

Eventually, like so many from the east coast, he moved on. He started a trucking outfit in Toronto, but the tax man finally got the trucks. He drove a tour bus in Banff, and then got a job ferrying pipe casings from Alberta to Swift Current, Saskatchewan, a 1,200-mile round trip.

One day the boss said: "Terry, the boys down at the pipe factory say you're on something."

"What d'you mean, on something?"

"You're hauling much more pipe than anybody else."

"That's because I want to make money, man." He had been driving all night, sleeping when he could, and showering one night in six. But he'd been having a lot of trouble with the trucks, and he took the opportunity to say to the boss: "If I have to keep fixing this truck, I'm just going to dump the load."

Next time out, two bald tires went. The second time, Terry fixed the tire then dumped the pipe into a field, drove the truck back, and parked it outside the boss's house.

He wound up in British Columbia, in Kitimat, first playing guitar on the street with his black hair down his back almost to his waist and a gold ring in one ear, and then working at the mine. He was still playing guitar at nights for extra cash, though, and the foreman said: "Hey, Terry, I hear you're playing a couple of bars. We like our employees to have only one job."

"Do you?" Terry said. "Well, I had three, and now I only have two. Make up my pay." He collected $1,400 and left town.

He headed for Alaska to find his valley and pawned his guitar in Anchorage for fifteen dollars. He had been travelling with an American who was able to get $108 in food stamps from welfare. They couldn't cash the stamps, however, because to do so was a federal and state offence, and nobody would buy them. They needed gas for the American's truck, so they went from grocery store to grocery store, getting a few groceries in each, and getting change from the food stamps. They hit about thirty stores before they had enough to fill the tank, and they went to the gas station with the money in quarters, nickels, dimes, and pennies.

Terry raised the money for the rent on an apartment by laying carpet, but the American lost it playing pool.

And that was to be just the first of a series of trials and challenges that would end a couple of years later with the seizure of Terry's truck at the border.

With the rain coming down on the tent, I thought of how it must have been, settling in some desolate valley in a country not his own, building a cabin, trapping. He told me he had once been reduced to rubbing two sticks together to try to get fire, but he couldn't do it and, in the end, had to hike out to town. I imagined him walking out of the snow to a bar and playing music the way he'd described it. And mending fishnets on some pier. Now he wanted, he told me, a nice apartment, somewhere he could take a warm bath whenever he wanted, a woman, and time to work at his music. He wanted to be recognized for his music, but not to go through the grind again of playing to bad audiences in barrooms full of smoke to get that recognition.

He was thirty-eight years old, and every night he took pills for his ulcers.


Like Terry, I left the welfare office in Whitehorse with no money but with two pieces of paper instead. One said that the Department of Human Resources would accept responsibility for one night's stay at the per diem rate at St. Joseph's Hostel. The other authorized Food Fair to supply me with twelve dollars worth of groceries.

The name of the welfare counsellor was Elizabeth. She was plump and pleasant, but there was no way to get any cash out of her. If you hadn't lived in the Yukon for six months and worked for three of them, you were regarded as a transient. And the most she could do for a transient was a bed for the night and enough groceries to get out of town with a full stomach.

I picked up a bit of sausage, some rice, noodles, milk, bread, yoghurt, and tomatoes. I had to sign three pieces of paper to get out of the store.

Outside, across from Kentucky Fried Chicken, where the maddening, perpetually rotating chicken-box was a landmark in a featureless town, I met a native man who had been eating at the Salvation Army a couple of days before. He hadn't eaten much except soup for a couple of days. He had nowhere to sleep. Because of some bureaucratic dispute about his status, welfare would not deal with him, not even to the extent of twelve dollar's worth of groceries, and neither would Indian Affairs. He was in limbo. And he was starving. I gave him the voucher for a bed at the hostel, half a loaf of bread, some milk, and some other stuff, and he started to eat it right there on the sidewalk. "This is a tough town to survive in," he said.

I crossed the bridge with the rest of my loot. In a schoolyard some young forces cadets were being drilled. The instructor was simply trying to get two lines of uniformed twelve- and thirteen-year-old kids to face front and stop fidgeting. The kids were bursting to laugh.

"Don't laugh, don't touch your caps, don't look at me," the officer said vehemently.

The lines immediately collapsed in an unrestrained burst of giggles. The war goes on.

The sound of the river seemed to grow louder as the night wore on. We were staring into the fire like a couple of zombies. Terry looked at me. "I'll give you a pair of pants before we hit the road," he said. "And some socks. A couple of pair."

That forced my attention away from the fire and onto my condition. If Terry thought I needed sprucing up I must be in pretty grim shape. He was no *New Yorker* ad himself. The knees were almost out of my jeans, the Greb boots I'd bought for three dollars in Prince George were starting to look like three-dollar boots, my beard was pretty wild, and my hair was long. The stuff I'd washed was getting dirty again. I looked like a man who needed a job.

We left the next morning. We split up because we knew we would have next to no chance of getting a ride together. He stood across from the ss *Klondike*, and I walked down the road out of town for about half a mile. Each, we had agreed, would try to get his ride to pick up the other, where possible. The method was to work pretty well. I got away first, however, in a small car with a young woman and her two children and a lot of groceries. She had come to Whitehorse with her husband four years earlier, she said. They got into town without a cent and now owned a home in a subdivision about twenty miles out of town. They didn't think they'd ever want to leave. The only problem they had, she said, was bears. The day before a black bear had managed to get right inside one house in the subdivision, through a window.

I walked a long way after that solitary short ride, bothered a lot by flies, before I got my next ride at about six o'clock. There were three of them, Indians, all squeezed into the front seat, the woman in the middle. When I got in, the guy on the passenger side, whose name was John, tried to throw a scare into me. He was half joking, half drunk. I couldn't get out, he told me. The lock on the back door was broken. They were going to drive me up a side road and shoot me. Then he gave me a beer. Music was blasting from the tape deck. The driver, Dave, was the bigger of the two men. He hadn't said a word. John, the passenger, tried to put his arm around the girl, who wore glasses, and she shoved his hand away, leaning her head on Dave's shoulder instead. John was teasing her. I couldn't hear much of the conversation for the tape deck, but when she turned her head to him she had tears in her eyes. I heard her say: "But that's the last child I'll be able to have." She was very upset.

Later John said to her: "Who you going to shack up with?"

"Not you," she said.

I drank my beer and minded my own business until I saw Terry on the side of the road as we went past. We were moving fast. "That's my partner," I shouted to the driver. The driver went into a skid immediately, and we dragged along until the rear end went into the ditch. He gunned the motor violently and managed to get it out; then we went back for Terry.

"We never pass by anyone in trouble," John said, turning to look at me. "But white men never stop for us."

Terry squeezed in. He was feeling good. He'd smoked some dope and drunk some beer and played the guitar with his last ride, some kids in a van.

We got talking, and John said to us: "I can make you Indians – my blood brothers. It's legal. I have the power to do it. But we have to go to court. How much you pay me?"

"I'll work for you for a year," Terry offered solemnly. He was feeling no pain at all.

"I have nothing for you to do," the Indian laughed.

"I'll work and then pay you," Terry said.

"Naw," said John.

Drunk or not, Indian John knew the score. When we said we'd been in Whitehorse, he said: "Wouldn't give you welfare, eh?"

They drank and urged Terry and me to drink their beer, but they wouldn't accept a joint of Terry's Alaska home-grown. They didn't touch it, they said. They let us out in the driveway of an old log house where an elderly woman was visible through the front window. Before we left I asked about firefighting jobs. "Indians don't fight fire. We find a shady tree, lie down, and let it burn," John said.

We were about fifty kilometres from Teslin, and there didn't seem to be any water about, but there were two other tents and a station wagon virtually on the highway. It was a strange place to camp, so close to the road, but it turned out they were a government crew – their job was to count traffic on the highway and list the types of vehicles that passed. This they did from inside the tents while drinking beer, smoking dope, and playing board games. But they let us have some water out of a barrel they had. In the morning there was some sunshine, more black-flies, and nothing ahead but gravel.

My first ride was with a dark man in his thirties, an immigrant fourteen years before from, of all places, the south of France. He lived, by coincidence, in the same housing development outside Whitehorse as the young woman with the two children and the problem with bears. He was on his way to Teslin to pick up his wife who, with a girlfriend, had just completed a canoe trip down the Teslin River. He said he was out of work for the first time in fourteen years, the first time since he arrived in Canada. I asked him how he reconciled the differences in climate between his birthplace, to which he said he returned every couple of years for a holiday, and his adopted north. He shrugged. "When I'm here I like it; when I'm over there I like that."

This easy-going adaptability, however, did not extend to the city of Whitehorse. "It's a hole in the ground," he said. "That sterile park [in the area of the river bridge] used to be an Indian village, Whiskey Flats they called it; tall willows with shacks almost hidden in them – but with character. They cleaned it out, of course. Now there's a bandshell there nobody ever uses. I've seen a concert there once."

He was really angry about Whitehorse. "It's a town in which there is nothing to do. And it's dirty. Why the hell don't they just clean the place up, move the garbage. The town's dirty and now they're working on dirtying the landscape around it. If there's a beautiful vantage point in Whitehorse they have either put a garbage dump or an industrial site on it, or they're planning to do so."

He dropped me off at the Teslin River bridge where the two women had been waiting for him in tents on the river bank, and I watched them load the canoes and gear. It had turned into a beautiful day. I put my pack up against a traffic sign at the end of the bridge and waited in the sunshine. On the sign some weary hiker before me had scratched the mournful message: "Three days – 114 miles." It had taken him or her three days from Whitehorse.

That bridge should have been a good place to get a ride. There were gas stations on both sides of the road, a café, and a store. Almost everybody stopped for one reason or another. But it wasn't. I thumbed for an hour or more, and then Terry caught up to me in the station wagon belonging to the government group that had been counting traffic the night before.

We stood there for a while, evaluating the traffic. Terry was philosophical about the truckers who passed. "They're goddam rednecks," he said. "I know. I was one." But somehow the huge motorhomes drew from us both – and from many others I met on the road – a more deepseated resentment. It was amazing the depth of feeling these vehicles evoked in people who didn't own one. Not just hitchhikers, who were resigned to the fact that they never stopped, but other motorists, people who lived along the road, truckers, bikers, men digging ditches . . . it was as if these trundling behemoths carried the weight of all the resentment progress brings. A hitchhiker, standing on the side of the road, looking for recognition through the glass, saw the skull's head of progress. It never moved or smiled or turned as it went by, or so it seemed. I got so that I didn't want a ride in one of those babies – a childish and completely redundant emotion, since not once in thousands and thousands of kilometres did I have the opportunity to decline.

On the Teslin River bridge, however, it was beginning to look as if nobody at all would ever give us a ride. We were starting to get a little delirious. Terry would do a little dance for the truckers; we'd grin insanely and salaam at harmless old ladies in Dodge Darts.

"I'll go and get us some money," Terry said. He took his guitar and crossed the road. I thought he was going to play, either inside or outside the restaurant, for tips; but he went to the service station where the government people were getting their station wagon serviced, and I saw him hand the guitar over. He came back for me. "Let's get a coffee," he said. Just then the government crew drove off, waving to us.

"You shouldn't have done that," I said.

"I've got to have some money. I can't go around with my pockets empty," he said. They'd given him ten bucks for the guitar.

In the coffee shop I said: "Hell, we both got more than ten bucks worth of pleasure out of that thing every night." It was true.

"I'll get another one," he said.

He bought the coffee, then gave me four dollars, which I tried to refuse. I didn't want his guitar money. I was annoyed about the deal.

But he wouldn't take it back. He kept four for himself. The extra change he wanted to use to buy fishhooks, to try to catch some supper. Amazingly, they didn't sell fishhooks on either side of the road. And when we got back to our packs on the bridge Terry discovered that he had left his jacket in the station wagon. In the pockets were a knife, some cheese, and a few other odds and ends. The jacket, though, was rainproof and a big loss. The government people got a good haul for ten bucks. We thought they might come back, but they didn't.

With one thing and another I'd had enough of standing on the Teslin River bridge. We went down to a picnic area on the riverbank below, bathed, washed some clothes out, and lay in the sun. An old Indian came down for water. "It's easy once you get to Dawson Creek," he told me. "You can ride a boxcar. Just ask the conductor. As long as you got some bread and cheese you're all right. We used to do it all the time."

"How far's Dawson Creek?" I asked Terry when the old-timer left.

"About eight hundred miles," he said.

I was ready to call it a day, but just as I got my tent up on a sheltered area of the beach near a dilapidated house, a camper drove up and a red-faced character leaned out the window. "This is private property," he yelled. "We don't want no garbage here." He was about fifty yards away, and I set off for him at a dead run. Some days you've just had enough. He took off quickly back over the bridge. I wanted to stay, at first, but the prospect of being moved on by police in the middle of the night – if this really was private property – didn't appeal to either of us. So we trekked over the bridge and found a place down by the water where many other campers had obviously sought refuge. Small areas had been cleared and flattened in the bush, not by any tree-cutting process, but simply by bodies and baggage coming to rest there over the years. We could see the span of the bridge in front of us, and the road going back the way we had come, to the north. As it grew darker, the lights went on in the gas stations and in a couple of cabins on the opposite bank. We collected some raspberries and rose hips from the bushes around us and started to make a meal.

We heard the voice from the bridge before we could distinguish figures amid the dusk and the metal spars, a shouting, singing, chanting voice, and then the girl emerged on our side and yelled down to where we had a fire going.

"Any room down there?"

"Sure," we called back.

She came down the bank, a shiny-faced girl, and there was a dog behind her, a piece of dirty blond fluff. The girl carried a brown hand-bag in one hand and a rolled-up sleeping bag in the other. She said her dog had got into a fight with some huskies in the gas station while she was in the bathroom. "They're not trained at all," she complained of the huskies. "All they know is 'git' and 'mush'."

She sat down on a log and rolled the legs of her jeans up. "I shaved the hair on my legs in June and it's already an inch long," she said, as if she was talking about the weather. She wore a gold-coloured piece of wire on her head with two loops in the front, like a fairy in a panto-mime. She looked crazy to me.

Terry said politely: "I can't for the life of me understand why a woman shaves her legs. I lived with a woman once who did, and I said: 'Go sleep somewhere else. I don't want to be all scratched up.' "

"Why we do it is because we want our legs to look thinner," the crazy woman said.

"You think you're fat?" Terry asked her.

"No, I think I'm skinny after all that walking. I shave 'em once a year, actually, on my daughter's birthday. Do you gentlemen mind if I sing?"

I didn't mind. Anything to change the subject.

She threw her head back ecstatically, stretched her neck, tilted it a bit, smiled with her teeth, closed her eyes and sang. It was gross.

Ricky was her name. She was from Seattle. The dog was Tuffet and belonged to her daughter, who was still in Seattle with her grand-mother. Ricky had left Seattle with twenty-eight cents, U.S., and now, some months later, she had about the same amount, give or take a few cents, Canadian. Sometimes she slept in the cab of a truck, but often she would walk all night because she was frightened of bears. Tuffet was no help in that department. As a dog Tuffet would have made a good pair of earmuffs. Anyway, in Fairbanks, Alaska, Ricky had met a man. Now she was going down to Watson Lake to pick up some things she had left there on the way up – and then she was going to turn around and go back to Fairbanks, because there was something she had not told her man. She was going back to tell him she loved him, and then she would see what he said and did. She said she didn't know how he felt about her.

"What do you like about this guy in Fairbanks?" Terry asked.

"I don't know," she said. "He yells at me. He's disgusted with me going around hitchhiking like this. He thinks I should settle down. I've been on the road for most of the past eight years. I want somebody to take care of me."

She whirled around, slapping at the air. "I hate these mosquitoes," she said.

She said she saw colours around people, a sort of halo that denoted their mood, and she told Terry and me what our colours were. We were both in a pretty good mood, if I recall.

At one point, no doubt wondering what villains she had fallen among, she told us, quite unasked, that she "wasn't into sex or touching bodies right now."

Terry said, quietly, with considerable presence of mind: "You have nothing to worry about. We are honourable." A strange, old-fashioned thing to say, a very brave thing for a man to say who had been in Alaska, largely without women, for two years. And he said it with a surprising tenderness.

"Speak for yourself," I told him. We laughed, and then we had supper – rice with sardines, green peppers, and ketchup. This was followed by a dynamite combination we'd put together on the banks of the Yukon – yoghurt, honey, and wild raspberries – and unlimited quantities of rose-hip tea to keep the mosquitoes away.

The girl bedded down in front of the fire, with the dog inside the sleeping bag, too, squirming to get comfortable on the rocky ground. Terry and I were coming and going, cleaning up. I heard Terry say: "What the hell are they for?" and I went to look. Ricky had dug from somewhere a whole bunch of those aluminum pie plates and spread them over top of her sleeping bag, one on top of each breast, and others balanced precariously in strategic places. "Keep off the rain," she said nonchalantly, lying flat on her back with an armour of pie tins carefully balanced.

The last thing I heard before I fell asleep was a wail from outside. "Oh, shit, a rock – right in my *glutinous maximus*."

The next thing I heard was a scream and a clatter of falling pie plates and the little dog barking furiously. I started giggling like a madman. What now?

"Who's there? Who's there?" Ricky was yelling in a frightened voice.

"Who's there?" came the reply, like an echo. It was unmistakably a policeman. He flashed his flashlight and told us he was just checking the fire. (We had built it up a bit to keep Ricky warm.) There was a forest fire out of control just past Watson Lake and the hazard rating was high all over the area. Traffic was being halted on the highway, he said. He didn't know whether we would be able to get through.

My thrift-store boots were coming apart at the seams, my jeans were falling apart, my hair and beard were starting to look like kelp. And I figured that tomorrow or the next day I might finally get a job, somewhere near Watson Lake.

We left Ricky at the campsite in the morning and climbed the hill out of town. Looking back, there was a lovely pastoral view beyond Teslin. Despite our bad luck the previous day I was full of emotion for the massive land I was slowly passing through, as I had been many times since I began to hitchhike. You get to walk, or just sit, in places where nobody ever goes, except in a vehicle, and there are things you see, angles, light, shapes, that nobody else sees. When I looked back on the trip afterward the images my memory reproduced were all those of a man afoot, never those views I might have seen from vehicles.

Terry got the first ride, and they stopped to pick me up. I squeezed in the cab of the pickup, a '63 something with a big blunt nose and a lot of rattles. The driver was from Oregon. He had spent two years in Alaska and was headed home. He was going home because he, like Terry, had had enough of the north. They had been to pretty much the same places, and they talked about the land and the fishing, the availability of cocaine, and the shortage of women.

"I met a lot of nice people up there," he told us. "I got just what I expected when I set out. I expected to have a hard time getting work, I expected to be broke a lot of the time . . . and it happened."

He said: "I was dreaming about Oregon sunshine all the time I was on the boats. All I saw was rain and cold."

He dropped us at the Cassiar turnoff, about twenty miles from Watson Lake. Terry stayed at the junction, and I hiked down until another pickup stopped, and I jumped up behind with the oildrums. In Watson, I climbed out of the back, and a young guy with a packsack got out of the passenger side. He was from London, England, and as we walked through town together he told me he had waited for two whole days and nights to get a ride out of Dawson – which made me feel better about the way we'd been stuck in Teslin.

I left him at the Forestry Service workyard and garage, on the main drag. The barometer outside indicating the fire hazard was set at moderate, but the weather was broiling, the late-afternoon clouds like tons of red feathers. I went in, found somebody to talk to, and asked if they needed firefighters.

"You'll have to go down to Lower Post, just over the border," an employee told me. "The fire is in B.C., not in the Yukon." By now I'd hitchhiked about 3,000 kilometres. Chasing fires seemed to be a lot like chasing rainbows, but I was getting closer. "Persistence is good fortune to the wanderers," say the Chinese. Rather than continue, I made camp in a provincial site, to wait for Terry. If anybody had come around to collect money I wouldn't have been able to pay the toll, but nobody did.

I didn't see Terry that night, but in the morning his pack was outside the supermarket, and he was at the checkout. He'd borrowed a guitar and played for beer and a couple of dollars in a tavern the night before. He'd also lucked into a ride with a forestry official who said he'd telephone ahead and try to get us hired on at the fire. We headed out for Lower Post. The night before, just before the sun set, the sky in that direction had been black with smoke. Now there was just a low haze, a singed tapestry of smoke and sky.

# 11

*Whereat he formed his ranks, and at their head,*
*Set the example, trampling the hot ground,*
*For fear the tongues of fire might join and spread.*
 — Dante, *The Inferno*

The helicopter dropped us on a desolate clay pad in the middle of a burn. As far as the eye could see there was smoke. It was absolutely, drearily silent. And it was raining slightly. "Wait there," the pilot told us, as if we had an option. We waited, sitting on our hard-hats on the chopper pad, Terry looking around with his droopy eye as if to say he didn't ever think this firefighting business was such a great idea.

Finally, we climbed a slight ridge at the back of the pad. When we got to the top there was a man with bare feet – no shoes, no socks – scrambling in the mud, in the burn, up the other side to meet us, jabbering indistinctly. It was like stumbling on an enemy who doesn't know the war is over. A mountaintop Crusoe. He was scrambling at our feet like an animal, trying to make the last few inches to the summit of the ridge, his face a bedlam of tics. And now, finally, we could hear him, could tell what it is he was saying.

"If they don't get me some fucking boots right now I quit."

I looked at Terry. This must be the guy we'd heard about earlier, while we were waiting for the chopper. When he got to camp he found he'd packed two right boots.

"I know all there is to know about firefighting," he said, panting, wiping his muddy hands on his pants. "If they leave this to me I'll have it out in two days."

They fired him that night.

We walked and ate and slept for three days, Terry and I and a bunch of Indians. We were putting out hot spots, the small fires that kept breaking out alongside the rough cat roads in the bush. We ate massive lunches, and afterward the Indians slept with their heads together on the grass, like children. The straw boss was an Indian called Colter. Everybody knew Colter. He carried a portable radio. At last somebody missed us, wondered how we were getting along. The voice came crackling from a helicopter somewhere in the sky. It was an urgent voice, full of call signs, over and outs, Rogers, the whole shot.

"Colter, where are you?"

On his back on the grass, Colter pressed the answer button on his little black machine. "In the middle of nowhere, layin' down," he said.

We marched fairly aimlessly. It didn't matter where we went, there were always spot fires. Everything was so hot they flared up at the slightest breeze, or a hint of sunshine. They would start in the roots of burned trees, and the fire would burn deep into the earth itself, rekindling the very ash of an old burn. Trees would go up in a sudden explosion of fire. The ground had been water bombed and sprayed and ploughed, and still the heat lived, seemingly in the fibres of nature itself. Helicopters circled overhead with infra-red scanners, which picked up the hot spots. Rolls of toilet paper were dropped from the air into the trees near any area the machine indicated to help the ground crews locate the trouble spots. We moved along brown, gouged, fire-break roads like a bunch of guerillas. Trees had burned right down to the ground and then some, so that the blackened roots sprawled in all directions. The trunks lay like black poles. Occasionally, four or five trunks, still standing straight but blackened, rose together in a regular alignment amid the greenery, like some abandoned, overgrown Doric slum.

We carried four-gallon water tanks known as pisscans, shovels, and the pickaxe-like tool known as a pulaski. If it was a minor hot spot, in the roots of a tree or in a restricted area of bush, we would dig up the fire, turning over the earth, burying it – and then dig a guard around it. If a whole area was burning, we would have water barrels lowered by helicopter, from which we would fill the pisscans and spray the fire; or a skidder would be sent in carrying water.

Several times a day we stopped to sprawl in the bush and eat the food we had brought with us. Lots of food: bully beef, Spam, bread, canned salmon, oysters, milk, pop, peaches, cheese, honey . . .

Just clean-up, we had been told at first. Three or four days' work. The fire wasn't going anywhere now. But the government people, both on the scene and in Victoria, were nervous. They weren't cool like Colter. They were scared. Further down the Alaska Highway a mistake had been made. They had lost a town. They had thought the fire was out. They had pulled out men and machines. But the fire was not out. It came alive again, and it wiped out a community. A very small community, granted, and only a dog died, chained and helpless and mad with desperation to get away. The town was called, of all things, Fireside. There had been a great deal of criticism of that incident and of others, in a year that had seen many forest fires in the north. A lot of mistakes had been made. Fires that were supposed to be out flared up again. There was bad publicity. And now the government people, the fire bosses, were saying to the firefighters: "We want it out. O-U-T. Out. Cold." Our fire, the last one still posing a danger, had become a symbol. It would be handled properly. No heads would roll over this one. Before we left it would be cold.

It had started in a roadside garbage dump. The man who first spotted it, a stranger, a passing motorist said later: "It was so small I could have pissed on it and put it out." But he didn't. Neither did he turn back and report it in the nearest community. Instead he decided to keep going, report it at the next place he came to. But distances up there are vast. By the time he turned in the alarm the fire was off and running — running, in fact, like the wind, for it was so hot it made its own wind.

The base camp was on the Hyland River, in a clearing under trees bearded with moss. The Indians did not like the country in the old days. Something evil lies here, they said. Long before the first whites came, a party of hunters had met with a terrible fate at the headwaters of the Hyland. They were working their canoe through a canyon when a sudden darkness overtook them, and the evil thing rose out of the water, turned over the canoe, and dragged the hunters down.

It was a bit like that in the fire camp. Like being trapped in the maw of something ugly and powerful and dragged down and drowned.

It was, in short, a government job.

After our second full day, the fire boss, who had taken over from somebody else, was himself replaced.

And then, on our third day, another crew, not ours, found a hot spot in a swamp area, a peat bog. The whole swamp was burning. And that's when our fire really began, when it was supposed to be all over.

For these peat bogs were everywhere. And they were all burning.

We lived in four-man canvas tents. They were white, and there were about fifteen of them set up among the trees. The trees dripped moss and rain, and lying everywhere were fallen, rotted nurse trees, sprouting seeds. On a grassy bench overlooking a gravel bar in the river were two wooden log cabins, built many years earlier by gold prospectors, now headquarters for the camp boss, the cooks, and the first-aid man. There is still a great deal of gold in the Hyland River, but the flakes are very fine, and it is said to be uneconomical to go after it. This did not stop some men in camp from spending what little free time they had panning or sluicing. They could get thirty or more colours to a pan, which is a very high count. These were all white men. I never saw a native man panning for anything but washing water.

I suppose there were about fifty or sixty men there when Terry and I arrived, more Indians than whites. The natives were almost all from Lower Post, which had been an Indian settlement for many years. (Seven were shipped in one day from Telegraph Creek and mysteriously shipped out again the following day. It was part of the general confusion that prevailed.) Most of the whites were from other places. The natives knew each other. They were, in many cases, family. They didn't know the whites.

There were only white men in our tent; Terry and I and Bill – the oldest guy in camp – and a young man who was married to a Lower Post native woman and who claimed he was persecuted for it by the Indian men, beaten and hounded and discriminated against. He quit within a few days, leaving just the three of us.

Bill had been on the oil rigs and in the mines and lumber camps and big construction projects. He was at home in camp and very happy to be working on the fire. He had mouths to feed and mortgage payments to meet, and he was glad to be earning, however low the pay, when so many weren't. Dammit, he would swear, it was filthy horrible work, and there were grizzly prints down by the water where he was working a pump, alone every day, and claw marks on the trees, and fresh droppings, but he was still glad to be working.

Bill kept us entertained. Everything he said was funny. He was a big grumbling godsend. There was a naivety there when he bitched. Even though he'd seen pretty nearly everything, Bill still couldn't believe his eyes. He never would. Once somebody in another tent fed him some pot, the first he'd ever used. They must have slipped him something else, too. We could hear him coming back in the dark, tripping over things, muttering, praying. He talked in his sleep all that night: numbers, names, barnyard grunts, arguments with ghosts, gibberish . . . oh, what dreams! It was Bill's reaction to drugs that piqued Terry's interest. Terry was something of an expert, and Bill became an object of curiosity to him after that night. Bill was interested not only in drugs, now his virginity was lost, but in criminal matters of all kinds. Easy money was a consuming topic for him. He dreamed of a way to make easy money so that he would never have to work hard again. Terry showed him the little dots on currency bills that show the difference between real money and a careless forgery, and Bill was like a child who had discovered Christmas.

Bill could never get up in the morning, though. He had an alarm clock that ran down unheeded every dawn. He wouldn't hear the camp boss beating on the steel pipes, which you could have heard clear to Watson Lake. You could shake him or kick him. Nothing. In the end he was laid off because he couldn't get out of bed; but while he was there, the subject of easy money occupied his waking hours. And that being made on the fire itself did not escape his attention.

There was an aristocracy on the fireline. Skidder operators averaged $500 a day; the tab for a helicopter was $500 an hour. A tanker sat high atop a ridge supplying water to the firefighters in the burn area below. The driver spent most of his time sleeping. He slept for four hours, until the water ran out, then filled up the tanker again at the river and slept for another four hours. He got $75 an hour.

The economic impact of the fire was felt far more widely than the camp, though. If a firefighter wanted anything, from toothpaste to rain gear to new boots, he had to order it through the commissary. All these orders went to a single Watson Lake retailer. And businesses in the area supplied everything from pumps to rental trucks to food.

It was said that all of the food, not only for our camp but for the men working other fires in the area, was being supplied by one small campground store that had previously catered to tourists on a modest scale. Nickels and dimes. Somebody said that at the height of the various Alaska Highway forest fires, the woman who owned this store had told him: "The only thing I don't like is owing my suppliers four hundred and fifty thousand dollars at a time." No more nickels and dimes. She trucked in food, she flew in food. And we ate it. Steaks and more steaks. Bacon, hams, roasts, salmon, oysters, ice cream, fruit of all kinds, thousands and thousands of cans of pop. Enough food to sink a ship. In the morning we'd fill garbage bags full of food for lunch. There was incredible waste. There must be a thousand dollars worth of unopened canned food in the bush out there and a thousand dollars more that had been fresh, abandoned, rotting. Where the fire was, there was no recession.

After the discovery of the burning swamp the focus of our work changed. Other swamps were discovered, red-hot, burning like fuel. They had shown themselves hitherto as little more than wisps of smoke and had been ignored while flame was devouring trees and jumping highways. But now, with the major fires out, these areas of peat burned on, pushing ever outward to devour new ground, igniting bush and bringing down trees; not as glamorous as a sheet of flame, but more uncompromising. To stop this new threat we would need cat guards right down to bedrock around each of the fires, a massive, perhaps impossible job, even if we had the time.

Freddy, an Indian who had fought the same type of swamp fire in the same area back in '58, said it took a long, long time to put them out. Freddy was a quiet man, given to spitting in the dirt and speaking in understatement, when he spoke at all. When he said a long time he meant the duration.

Freddy was highly respected by the other natives. If not a head man, he was certainly a man of consequence. He could have been thirty-five or fifty, but he had done everything there was to be done in that country. He'd run most of the rivers on rafts he'd built and loaded with the carcasses of moose he'd shot. He could guide, or buck wood, or ride wild horses. He was completely at home in the bush, strong, without any fat on him, a man who did everything properly. He was also a legendary drinker, but he was on the wagon at the time.

Not knowing any of this I got off to a bad start with Freddy.

The first morning in camp it was grey, still half dark when we stumbled out of the tent. I was half asleep and weary from the day before when this Indian spat through his teeth into the dirt and said to me: "Pack the lunches." I didn't know him from Cochise. "Pack your own goddam lunch," I told him automatically.

"One guy packs all the lunches for a crew," he said slowly, surprised, but only for an instant. He looked right at me with his buffalo-hunter's eyes. Neither of us moved. People stopped what they were doing. Whatever had been there fizzled out. I didn't pack lunch that day, but I was uneasy for the next few days after that brush with Freddy. His quietness seemed deadly, made more so by his reputation for proficiency with everything from a power saw to a knife. When Freddy went hunting nothing was wasted, they said. Nothing.

Freddy was very patient with me, as it happens, and weeks later, the first time I got out of that hell hole of a camp and needed a drink it was Freddy who, unasked, pushed a ten-dollar bill, all the money he had, into my hand for a bottle. Even though he wouldn't take a snort himself.

At the start there were other tensions, too. Terry and Colter weren't getting on too well, either, but the blame for that lay with whoever was in charge at the time. I was there when Terry was asked to act as straw boss for a crew. We had just arrived and didn't know which end was up, and we wound up with Colter's crew. Now, on Colter's crew, Colter was the boss. There were no two ways about that. He had a lot of personality, brilliant eyes, and knew his way around. The result was a certain amount of disarray. It didn't last long, and when we got to know the other guys on the crew and Terry repeated what he had been told, Colter said: "So that's why you haven't been taking any notice of me." He said it with a sort of awe that made me think he had been on the edge of doing something drastic to remedy the situation.

Colter was special – charismatic, you'd have to say. Later, I saw a perfectly sane, quiet kind of girl ask him, within two minutes of meeting him, whether he was married.

"What's your first name, Colter?" I asked him when we first met.

"Colter," he said. I never did know his second name.

Minor discords were ameliorated somewhat by Terry's performance each night around the fire. He played a borrowed guitar, and at the sound of the music and his voice people would come out of their tents and sit and listen. It was a harmonizing sound, his music, especially along with the soporific noise of the river. Still, we were on probation, no doubt about it.

On about our fifth or sixth day we were still on Colter's crew when the fire boss, a new one, told Terry and me, by radio, to get to the nearest chopper pad quickly, to be ferried to a new area. This was about nine-thirty in the morning. The lunches we had brought were a long way distant at a bush camp we had set up, and we had no time to go get them.

From the air it was a graceful land, pleated with valleys. All I had really known about the country before the fire was that there were hot springs with temperatures as high as a hundred degrees Fahrenheit in a number of places in the region, most notably a resort on the Liard River. Incredible rumours of lush, hidden, tropical valleys, with ba-nana and orange trees, monkeys, parrots, even dinosaurs, had per-sisted for many years, right through the thirties. The chopper dropped us not in paradise, however, but in the most desolate of swamps. Rupert Brooke once talked of the unseizable virginity of the Canadian woods. But the fire had seized and whored its way through this virgin. Even the sun was turned back upon itself by the pall of smoke. The pilot put us down, with shovels, pulaskis, and pisscans, on a flat area of tufted grass – the only landing pad possible, for the rest of the valley bottom was strewn with blackened stumps, the stunted remnants of the fire. We got out, laden with gear, and were immediately up over our boots in swamp water. We had to leap and wade our way to the slightly higher ground where the earth was burning. Before slamming the door on us, the fire chief said he would have the chopper come back with some lunch and a radio.

He never came.

There was no drinking water in this swamp, so we were hungry and thirsty. Because we didn't have a radio, we were completely out of touch, which is not supposed to happen in the middle of a forest fire.

The whole area was criss-crossed with the burned skeletons of fallen trees. The swamp where the peat was still burning was about the size of a football field. When we threw the water from the pisscans on the burning ash, it first blew ash and sparks into the air, then bubbled like soup, subsided into paste, and finally turned back to ash, which smoul-dered and spread, exactly as it had before. It was like trying to put out a volcano. Much of the fire burned in subterranean caves eaten away in the banks of the perimeter of the ever-enlarging football field.

We continued to work in that vast burning mould of peat because there was nothing else for it – though we did spend some time examin-ing the antlers of moose that had been trapped in the fire – but, as the dismal day wore on, we became increasingly incensed. We had to make a reservoir in the swamp from which to fill our water cans, but the ground was simply too hot to be quelled by two men pouring cans of water on it. Cavern after cavern of red-hot ash . . . it looked like the pits of the moon in that valley. We were wet, hungry, and thirsty. As if to remind us of our vulnerability, a tree would occasionally go up somewhere on the valley slopes in a flash of fire. Terry was ready, when we were eventually picked up, to break bones and tear limbs. I said we should take a more restrained line. We needed the money.

It was six or so in the evening before the chopper came back. The fire boss was in it. We sat in the back and put the headsets on.

"No lunch?" he said.

"No lunch, no water, nothing," Terry said.

He apologized, said he had had to use the chopper somewhere else, and that was that. Until the following day.

Again we were initially sent out with Colter's crew, and again the fire boss called for us to meet the chopper at the pad. This time he was not in the helicopter. The pilot had orders to drop us back in the same peat bog. Again he said he would drop us lunch and a radio. I guess we just couldn't believe they would do it to us twice in a row, so we climbed in. Lambs to the slaughter. Another ten hours in the swamp. No food, no communication, and, as far as anyone else knew, no water (though we did find a stream that day). We were almost frantic with anger. It rained all day. To find shelter we had to travel to the slope of the valley. We stayed reasonably dry only because we had stuffed in our pockets a pair of garbage bags. We cut holes for our heads and arms, and the bags made adequate rain gear. We had worn them before for this purpose, and other firefighters wore them too. Terry's rain jacket had been left in the station wagon in Teslin and mine, a cheap plastic affair, was in tatters. Rain gear was not provided on the fire, so we had to do the best we could – and that was a garbage bag.

Terry could barely trust himself to speak when we got back to camp that second day. I forestalled him by saying to the fire chief: "No food, no water, no radio – no swamp."

"Okay," he said. "Christ, I'm sorry. From now on you guys are a crew. Fix yourselves up with whatever you need. I'll see you get a radio. Two radios. There won't be any more mix-ups."

We were told next morning that there were no garbage bags left in camp – that we would not have even that meagre, makeshift shelter should it pour again – and Terry exploded. Right outside the cookhouse he had a wild fist-fight with the man – a giant, well over six feet tall – who had roughly denied Terry the bags he thought we needed.

They came together like two moose, Terry driving the Indian back into the wall of the cabin, where the cans of pop were stacked, buckling his knees. But he dragged Terry with him, and they clattered together against the racks of canned juice. The Indian had Terry in an armlock around the throat, and Terry's straining grey face was directed for a moment, pop-eyed, unseeing, toward those of us who were around the fire. Nobody moved for a minute as they thrashed in front of the cabin, and then we broke it up, and that was that.

Later, back at the fire, one of the Indians said: "Doesn't your buddy know that's the camp boss he was fighting with?"

"I guess he didn't stop to think about it," I said lamely.

It had all been such a jumble of new faces, and we worked such long hours each day, that we had not sorted out titles or identities much beyond the crews we worked with. And Andy, who was now revealed as the camp boss, had been a particularly quiet sort, taciturn to those who didn't know him, though I never had any problem with him, before or after that day.

That day nothing else happened except that we were back in the peat, which was torture enough, for it was a day on which the thunder boomed and the rain came down in sheets, in spears. We had garbage bags, for a supply had quickly appeared after the fight, but this was a drenching rain there was no escaping, and we were soon soaked to the skin. The sky was heavy as a slab of marble. We headed for the trees on the valley slope, made a rough shelter from a couple of garbage bags, and prepared to sit it out as best we could. In an area hot and steaming as the aftermath of an air raid we had an uncomfortable amount of trouble starting a fire. The pits of ash, though they extended into the live trees, were not as hot there or as extensive. And the fuel was sodden. We had food, but what we needed was something hot, and when, eventually, we were able to get a fire going we collected rainwater in the garbage bags, boiled it, and made tea.

I was in worse shape than Terry. One of my boots leaked now like a sieve, the stitching torn beyond repair. It was not only uncomfortable but dangerous, for if I stepped into the ash pits I could suffer bad burns. The ash was like snowdrifts and frequently came up to our knees. It was like stepping into a cloud of steam. All you could do was lift up your feet and blunder out rapidly. If you stayed in there a second too long the heat burned the way frostbite does. One man on another crew had already suffered bad leg burns.

We sat there under a too-small, makeshift shelter that dripped a fringe of water around and often on top of us, trying to keep warm, but having to plunge out frequently to cut wood for the fire, which we did with Terry's machete, a big, black-handled scimitar of a weapon. (We had no power saw, for one was not generally needed in that area.) The machete had proved useful in many ways, from opening cans of food to splitting wood.

I had that deep-seated, malarial, shivering sensation through and through that signals hypothermia. It was no joke. I guess I've had worse days than that one, but offhand I can't recall any.

We had been given a radio, as promised. We had tested it when we got out of the helicopter, and it had worked then, but it didn't work any more. So that day we did not get to use our call name, our handle. It had been given us by the fire boss, and it expressed our plight and our surroundings perfectly. We were Swamp Portable. How better to suggest our alienation amid that smouldering morass that day. Swamp Portable.

The chopper came early, about mid-afternoon. He toured the area twice before spotting us, then used a P.A. system to call us out of the bush. But we were already on our way, out of the trees and across the charred, saturated, steaming hellscape to the swampy, makeshift pad.

That night, the one following the fight, was awkward. The guitar Terry had played was not available to him now – no coincidence – so there was no music to relieve the tension. He hit the sack early, and I dried my stuff around the stove in one of the cabins. Wet clothing hung from lines across the roof. It was the first time a halt had been called early, and there was to be only one other such time. That was how bad a day it was.

The following day was much better. We had food, water, and a radio that worked. We poured water on the burn all day, labouring with our shirts off and actually making some progress. But when we got back to camp the machete had been stolen from the tent. We had left it behind because in the better weather we wouldn't need a fire, and because it was difficult to carry along with all the other stuff we had to pack. Nothing else was missing, just the machete. The loss was serious, we agreed. It deprived us of the only real weapon we had and armed somebody else in camp. It sounds melodramatic in retrospect, but in that isolated camp full of men who had reason to resent us, our fears did not seem at all far-fetched. We searched, but with no success.

In the ensuing days Terry, with no musical outlet, foul working conditions, and long hours in the swamp, brooded, holding onto himself tightly. In fact he was ready to hit the road. I urged him to stay, to get together a stake so he could buy both a decent guitar and some time to play it, wherever he wound up. After a week in camp I had seen enough confusion to be able to predict we would be there for quite a while if we wanted to be. And I was interested in seeing how things turned out. At this stage we were only getting firefighters' wages of $6.80 an hour, the lowest rate; but shortly afterward I was promoted to straw boss, which paid $8 an hour, and I then put Terry on a pump, which paid him $7.40 an hour. We were working twelve, thirteen, and sometimes fourteen hours a day. And apart from the $6 a day for food – a real bargain – there were no deductions. Firefighters do not pay tax in British Columbia – though they did in the Yukon a mile or two further north.

We had now been assigned a larger, slightly more congenial peat bog, beneath an escarpment, with a cat road to it that trailed down precipitous cliffs. We could pump our water from two small ponds. Sometimes the smoke would combine with a morning mist in this valley to make a suffocating fog, and there was a lot of hose to lay from the ponds to the burn, but generally we were much happier. We had a crew now – there were five or six of us – and we no longer needed to carry water on our backs. When we hit the peat with the powerful spray all the colours of fall could be seen in the awakened earth. Beautiful reds, oranges, and greys kaleidoscoped with gushers of hot ash and the explosions of pent-up gases in a sort of light and sound show. The gases would release with a whoof and a peat-reek that drove us back.

This area burned in a huge semi-circle, fanning for a mile around our water source, and the kilns of burning peat were spreading right in among the trees. Occasionally the relentless heat in the ground would ignite a tree, and it would go up like a sulphur match or a flame-thrower, silver and red.

The peat was fascinating stuff. Whole vast areas of it had been found now, threatening to ignite the forests once more. It burned in pits, some as small as bathtubs, some bigger than swimming pools, but all expanding relentlessly, creeping out of the swampy areas into the trees.

There are extensive peatlands in northern Canada and, for that matter, in central Russia – areas that are underlain by permafrost and where the decay of plant remains is checked because there is a limited period in which the temperatures will allow it. The potential heat energy, originally derived by green plants from light energy, is stored in peat for long cycles. Large deposits of plant remains accumulate in swamp areas, forming organic litter that becomes peat. This soil – the "auld sod" – is very rich in organic matter, sometimes over 70 per cent. It can reach a depth of fifty feet or more. It is incredibly rich in gases, sour with them, and its reddish-brown to black fibres contain the whole range of chemical reactions. Our present coal deposits were once deep deposits of peat, and the soil itself is still used extensively in Europe as fuel. Peat is hot stuff.

I was as sick as I've ever been during this period, probably as a result of our earlier soaking. My throat was so hoarse and constricted I could barely speak. I was perpetually sneezing, and had alternating chills and sweats. I was feverish and aching. Band Aid, the first-aid man, gave me some pills and lozenges.

At camp a small bear had been trashing tents, and the only other excitement was gold fever among the whites. Band Aid, with little to do during the day, was slowly filling a vial with gold flakes he had panned, and a couple of others had built a wooden sluice box into which they shovelled sandy soil from the banks of the Hyland, pumping water through a hose from the river.

There was a tradition of gold-seeking here. A few miles up the Liard River was Watson's Bar, where the man after whom Watson Lake is named installed a wonderful home-made placer-mining water wheel in the old days. It was held together by sinew and straps of moosehide, and water was raised by an arrangement of old jam tins as the paddles were turned by the current of the river. From this it is said Watson took $400 every fall, right through the Depression.

Our men took flour gold. Not once did we see those flakes the size of a grain of wheat that are the placer miner's dream.

One of the incomprehensible things about the camp was that there was no shower of any kind. Fifty filthy men would have to do the best they could. You could either bathe in the river, which was already yearning toward winter, or get permission to go into Lower Post where there was a shower in the community centre. The fire bosses did not like people going to town, though, because they figured once the men got out of camp they might get drunk and stay out, which did happen – to Colter among others. "I couldn't stick it any longer," he told me when I met up with him later. To give Colter his due, he had been fighting forest fires a long time that summer before he went AWOL, but even for people who had been in camp a much shorter time there was a pervasive, trapped feeling. The filth, the lack of facilities (the only toilet was an old wooden two-holer left by the prospectors who put up the cabins), the constant tramping in the rain, the wet hoses, the belching dragon-pits of peat, the whirling devils of ash and cinders took their toll. When we got in after work we were stove black with a viscous coating, as if charcoal had been pounded into grease and painted on us. A mould of peat and ash was in our hair and on our teeth. It seemed inconceivable that the various government men in charge at one time or another had not thought to put in some kind of shower for the firefighters. It seemed less inconceivable when you remembered that not one of them lived in the camp. They looked after business from the office in Lower Post, or from helicopters in the air, making the odd appearance, work gloves dangling from their pockets with the deliberateness of a foulard. They went home every night to wives and baths and liquor cabinets and washers and dryers and central heating and hot, hot showers. In all my wanderings, when I brushed up against government there was almost always this constant – the dumb inability of people in positions of authority, however meagre, to project themselves into the world of the men and women on the other side of the fence. A failure of the imagination, and a savage, all-pervasive one. One standard for them ("Why are you late for your appointment?"), and one for you ("I'm busy, you'll have to stew here indefinitely"). Finally, near the end, we did get a small pump and ran a hoseline from the river to a spot where we hooked up a shower. But the water was icy cold by then, and the set-up required a man to trek fifty yards to the river to start the pump, go back and take his shower, and then trek back again to switch it off. Mostly we were too tired for such elaborate stratagems. Mostly we wanted to sit around the fire where the slow talk was of hunting, trapping, mining.

We sat around, filthy, like a bunch of sluice robbers, and talked a lot about gold.

Conversation was conducted in a desultory fashion. There'd be long silences and somebody, maybe fuelled by the good hash oil, would put in a sentence, which, more often than not, would be accepted for what it was and allowed to die. But sometimes themes would be pursued, and the strangest patterns would emerge, as in the fire. Gold was one of these themes. I had imagined gold mining to be a fairly sophisticated business in the Yukon in the 1980s – company mining anyway – but stories were told of young girls, clerks, driving station wagons full of ten-pound bricks of gold to town, alone, over hundreds of miles of desolate road; of labourers scooping coffee cups full of partially refined gold from unguarded bins; of teenagers left in charge of the gold room who got quietly rich from their systematic thieving; of the lowliest employees chipping away discreetly at the sediment left in gutters where the pure gold had been melted into bars.

A man who had worked as an assayer at various mines confirmed this laxity for me. He said he had a stash worth thousands of dollars near a mine he had worked recently. A large multinational corporation with expertise in other minerals but not hitherto in gold had bought the mine and hired him. They knew very little about gold. The enterprise was chaotic and doomed to failure. Instead of bringing the assayer small samples to evaluate – in vials, perhaps – they would bring it in buckets. The assayer did not correct this procedure. Instead, he painstakingly worked overtime, doing his job, of course, but also stashing sediment containing a high quantity of the riches. The mine was now closed, and when the formal pull-out process was completed he would go and pick up his stash.

I saw only two girls working the fire line, and they both lasted only a short time. The only women we spoke to were the cooks. On the radio we could hear the voices of the girls in the office at Lower Post, but we never saw them. When the fire was over I did meet the owner of one of those voices. She had originally been hired on fire watch in a lookout post on top of a mountain, she said. Before that she had been living, penniless, in an abandoned airplane hangar near Watson Lake. It was a motley crew, to be sure.

If gold was always a topic that absorbed the whites, drugs were the equivalent conversational topic among the Indians. In the north, drug use is rampant from the fishing boats of Alaska to the bars of Fort St. John; there's a psychedelic haze over the land, a blitzkreig of magic.

I heard one firegazer, glumly contemplating another day on the fire line, say thoughtfully: "Five or six grams of coke and a guy could project an image to work."

"Yeah," somebody else chimed in. "You'd be schizoid all right. Send one of you to work, one stay here."

A marvellous thought.

One guy who should have stayed in camp was Mike, who was more than a mite crazy. He would laugh insanely for absolutely no reason, or fix you with an unblinking stare for five minutes at a time. If he thought you were teasing him he could be quite frightening. He looked as if he was about ready to slit your throat. This wouldn't have been too bad if some genius hadn't hired him as a power-saw man. On any other job he couldn't have done too much harm; but it was as a power-saw man he had been hired, he was getting power-saw rates, and he wanted to work the power saw. A lot of the time power-saw men cut a trail for the hose lay. Mike cut figure eights and trails to nowhere. It was quite something to see the guys scatter when Mike was cutting. If they had to go past they would give him a berth of about a hundred yards. Often this didn't take them out of their way, for Mike was frequently scything away in entirely the wrong direction, in a world of his own. He had gone through most of the other crews by the time he got to mine, and always his stay had ended in acrimony, if not in violence. He was a huge, droopy-lipped, blond character, an anthropoid, big-boned, well-muscled, and a danger – though mainly to himself.

After the first day I took him aside and said to him: "Mike, you're getting power-saw wages, right?"

"Right," he said. He was very proud of his job. He had his own saw, and any attempt to get him to do another job failed because he saw it as a demotion that would cost him money.

"As long as you're with me you'll get power-saw money, okay?"

"Okay."

"Now I want you to go sit by the fire and keep Terry company at the pump there; just sit down and take it easy."

He and Terry had been through an initial spat before Mike was on our crew, when the big man had tried to take some of our food. Ever since the incident in the swamp where we went hungry for two days,

Terry had watched the food situation like a lion guarding a cub. Mike didn't get far when he tried to heist a few cans. But after that Terry had developed an interest in Mike, talking to him and trying to help him.

So Mike sat there and cleaned his saw, and after a while I got him to lay some hose. Over the next couple of days, though, he got restless, and I knew he wanted to get back to using the saw. Then a fire boss from headquarters in Dease Lake got me on the radio and asked me if I had a man to spare. This happened to be the very man who had hired Mike. I figured he should get to know him better. I sent Mike to meet him.

Next day the boss came over to me like a broken man. "I figured you'd done that on purpose," he said accusingly. "Christ, I never had a ride like that one in my life. He stared at me for a half hour while I drove the truck, then he starts to giggle for no reason. I'm in the middle of saying something, and he goes to talk about something completely different . . ."

"Yes," I said. "He's going to hurt himself."

I thought he would surely get the message and put Mike to some other work, maybe in camp. At least Mike didn't come back to us, but two days later, on the radio, we heard an urgent plea for Band Aid. Mike had hurt himself with his saw. In our burning valley, ten miles from anywhere, we listened for a long time to the calls going back and forth. Power-saw accidents don't tend to be minor; however, this one fortunately was. A cut between the fingers. Mike was laid off with an extra week's pay from compensation, which was the best possible conclusion.

One day we went crazy, all of us. The clearest case of swamp fever ever seen. I probably started it.

The night before, Wes, the only skidder operator remaining, had brought a couple of bottles of whiskey to the tent. Wes liked to have a couple of drinks at night in Watson Lake. He was on contract, so as long as he was there in the morning to work what he did was his business. He was good at his job and well-liked.

Heavy-equipment operators in the backwoods are a special breed, an elite. They almost all seem to be huge men, as if to complement the bulk of their earth-scouring machines. Some of them are prima donnas who look disparagingly down at the chaos of earth and men around them. Their machines, however, they tend fussily. They have big payments to make usually, and can brook no breakdowns or work stoppages. The whole earth, to them, is something to be moved. It is their business.

We drank and talked the night away. Terry and Bill had a few drinks, then went to sleep. Another man who was with us went back to his own tent. But I was stir crazy. I wanted to drink, but I needed the conversation more, the word from outside the filthy world of Swamp Portable.

Wes told stories of his debut in the firefighting business, which had come earlier in the year, down in Houston where he lived.

Skidders, which are normally employed in getting felled timber out of the bush, are machines made for hauling in heavy terrain. But there was little or no logging any more, and the men who owned machines foresaw a summer of big payments and no work. Suddenly, a whole new career opened up, a job that inflicted almost no wear and tear on the machines, paid good money, and racked up long hours. A government job. They rushed to it like flies to honey, big yellow machines grinding in from every direction to get close to the twinkling yellow gold – the fire. It was an army on the march, an army where every soldier wanted to be a waterboy, for that was what they were needed for – to carry water to the flames.

When the fire broke in Houston, Wes said, every skidder operator for miles around shipped in. But they had only the scantiest idea of what to do or how to do it. This was a new ball game. They knew they were supposed to haul water – but how? In what? The minds of these men, not normally an imaginative breed, raced with images. They went away to return again with all manner of strange barrels, cans and boxes, bolted, welded and chained to the backs of their machines. Many of the containers leaked; others fell off under the weight of the water. Their owners tore their hair, learned from the more successful ones, and went away to repair the damage and make ready for a glorious return.

Wes, whose machine, with the addition of a 500-gallon silver-painted barrel, had passed the first test, mused and fretted. He could not rest on his laurels, for there were many competitors for the few jobs and more coming, and he knew that only the strong and the cunning would survive. The first night he extricated himself and his skidder from the chaos of falling, leaking barrels, cursing men, and water slopping all over hell's half acre and made a round of the junk yards, knocking up junk men. Then he yanked a welder out of a bar, thrust at him two bicycle wheels, a modest drum affair, and some other weird odds and ends, and gave him a commission . . .

Next day, Wes's bicycle wheels were the wonder of the woods. Between gleaming spokes wound neatly on the drum, was a length of firehose. Wes could not only deliver water to the fireline, he could also, if the need arose, pump it from his own skidder. He was King of the Waterboys.

The next day twenty other skidders sported exactly the same set up.

Wes sat there, cross-legged in the tent and contemplated with a certain amount of drunken wonder the money he was making in a summer when he had looked forward to nothing but grief, when he should have been behind the eight ball; and he praised to the skies, through the canvas, the awe-inspiring miracle of fire. We toasted fire, enshrined it; but we did not dream about it, for we got no sleep. About dawn, Wes said, without a hint of frivolity, fervently, religiously: "Man, they're going to have to shoot me to get me off this job."

And that morning I was, so help me, still drunk when I commandeered the radio waves for a gonzo party. Like Colter, I couldn't stick it any longer. By mid-morning everybody was grabbing for the portable radios. Over that far-flung, burned-out bush, in miserable swamps, the crews were tuned to a portable party, gonzo radio. It was spontaneous combustion, as powerful as the fire, a geyser of jokes, hillbilly music, and pointed references to women and fire bosses – a wild trade in unpent hysteria. It was said the ladies at the office in Lower Post, who could hear every word on their own radio, walked off the job in disgust. It was the only time, apart from the day of the vicious rainstorm, that we were picked up early.

Getting bushed like that is a phenomenon known to thousands of men who have worked in these camps. You can take it for so long, and suddenly you can't take it any more without some release.

Around the same time Terry went berserk, and that could have been much more serious.

He was down, I knew that. I had the sense that when he'd crossed the border from Alaska, penniless as he was, he'd had his heart set on something big, something creative, without working out the details or considering that he would have to earn some money. This is common in transient men and women. They are, many of them, dreamers.

Instead he had found himself in a sort of hell, week after week, and in the end he just cracked wide open.

He was driving the truck one morning to an area where we were working. There were five or six of us in the four-wheel drive. There was a particularly bad stretch of mud, and to avoid getting stuck you had to take a real run at it. We had laid some corduroy, but short of rebuilding it every time we went through, there wasn't much to be done. The truck would go right up on its side, really lean and lurch for a spell, but it would usually make it all right. Terry was a fine driver, and he had been through it many times. Only this time he kept his foot down hard when he shot out of the mud. These roads bore no resemblance to real roads or even to logging roads. They were just bulldozed out of the bush, barely wide enough for two thin vehicles to pass. The trees and bush were right there.

Terry just kept the hammer down. I've never seen anything remotely like that ride, even in the movies. I had no doubt he would kill us. Whatever was holding him together had bust. Freddy knew it. I was in the back seat, and I could see Freddy on the front passenger side. I could imagine him saying to himself, "I try to hold my peace with stupid white men and this is where it gets me; he's going to crash my head against a tree and kill me stone dead." His fists were clenched on the dashboard. His knuckles were brown and hard as prune stones.

But nobody said anything. Nobody screamed or shouted. There wasn't enough breath in any of us. We were in the bush, hitting trees – thump, thump, thump – knocking smaller ones over and taking grinding, gouging hits from others. The vehicle seemed to be screaming as the wheels tried to obey the dictates of Terry's sandbag foot. It would careen out of the bush back onto the road and then smash into the bush again. Nobody could have held it on the road at that speed – there were too many curves – and Terry wouldn't let up on the gas. I was holding on to the seat in front, trying to keep my head down, but I couldn't control it. It was jerking back and forward as if it had worked loose.

Finally, it stopped. Nobody said anything, then or later. Perhaps a weary "Jesus Christ," but nothing else. There was nothing to be said. We knew the beast when we saw it. We just kept our mouths shut.

Freddy was beautiful to work with. We'd get to some desolate, steaming swamp, and in ten minutes he had a fire going, a canvas tarp overhead to keep the rain off, a flat place to sleep, seats he'd chain-sawed, and the coffee on. It was like the goddam western White House. You'd sit in one of Freddy's camps in the middle of bush where no man had trodden before, and you'd wonder why the mailman hadn't been yet.

All the Indians were thinking ahead. We'd have the first frost soon. About the third frost, the big moose would start rutting. And then the hunting. They saw all the new roads, which would provide easy access, the chopper pads from which they could scan the land, and the new luscious green shoots – dream food for moose – already pushing through in the burn. They couldn't wait. They dreamed about the hunting there would be. One night around the fire in camp we heard two shots from over the big ridge across the river. "That's Melvyn, got himself a moose," one of the Indian kids said. It was, and he had. He came in a couple of days later to tell us about it.

Melvyn had been a straw boss, another who went to town one night and never came back. He was cheerful and popular, and he knew what he was doing. It was Melvyn who early on warned the fire bosses not to bring in the expensive water truck, but instead to lay hose from the river. That was the first time he flew over the fire. "You're going to have to lay hose in the end," he predicted. And just about the time he was getting his moose that's exactly what we were doing – laying all that hose, the longest hose lay anybody had ever heard of, a record. This was weeks after Melvyn had suggested it, hundreds of hours of tanker time at $75 an hour, not to mention the time lost while the men waited for the tanker to be driven to the river, refilled, and driven back again.

I'd got to be straw boss by default. With Colter and Melvyn gone there were gaps in the ranks. But I did use the position in a way that left even the hard-to-impress Indians admiring my initiative. My feat was to claim longer hours for myself and my men, and thus bigger pay, while starting and finishing work at exactly the same time as the other crews.

Lunch was the highlight of the day in the bush. Work would stop, and we'd eat and then sleep or talk. We were paid for this hour of idleness. We were paid, in fact, from the time we left camp – seven or seven-thirty in the morning – to the time we got back at night.

One morning I got on the radio to Terry, who was on the other end of the long hose lay, running the pump from a creek, and told him to keep the water running over lunch. This posed no problem for him. If the Mark III broke down he had to fix it, but otherwise he had nothing much to do. He could just as soon leave the pump running as turn it off. It wouldn't interfere with his lunch, except for the noise maybe – and he didn't really have to be anywhere near the pump as long as he could hear it faintly and know it was still running. Terry, in fact, was happy to keep it going. He wouldn't have to stop it or start it up again, which were sometimes his only chores of the day. (He'd got hold of some thin rope with which he made hammocks a lot of the time, using his net-mending technique. A firefighter who had been a fisherman told me it was some of the finest net-work he had ever seen.)

I put the nozzle of the hose down in a particularly stubborn burn, a pit of ash that would have to be filled with water like a bathtub to drown out the fire, and then we broke for lunch. After half an hour I got up and moved the hose to another area, then went back to sleep.

That day we left at seven-thirty in the morning and got back at seven-thirty at night. I put the name of my men on the time sheet and credited them each with thirteen hours.

I was waiting for supper when the fire boss called me over. He was by the fire, but a little bit away from the other men.

"You put down thirteen hours," he said. He lifted his watch and looked at it significantly, in dumb show.

"We had a bad patch," I said soberly. "We had to get it out today. I kept the water running over lunch."

He looked at me. He had a kind of lopsided, quizzical look. "Okay," he said.

And each day after that I put in thirteen or thirteen-and-a-half hours, even fourteen, whatever I could get with the extra hour for lunch.

It took a week for the other crews to catch on to the lunch-hour scam. When they did, and water was pumping away more or less uselessly all over the land, the fire boss rightly called a halt.

There were differing views of the value of our efforts. We heard that our own immediate bosses, the on-site people, had recommended that we pull out, that the fire wasn't going anywhere. But from Victoria had come the word: "Stay there until it's out. We don't want to take any chances. We want it cold."

The last fire boss we had, Pat, told me: "This stuff [the peat moss] is so hot it will burn through the winter. It will burn right through sixty-five below. And it will still be there in the spring. It's dynamite waiting for next year. Next year it will just fuck off again if we don't get it out."

Still, we were winding down. We had all the bad area if not cold then pretty well damped down. And we were into September. Even the food was going downhill. The cook, the last of three, produced a huge ham one night after we'd had a long wet day, tried to cut it, and found it was still frozen solid. She put it back in the oven and we had to wait a couple of hours for it to defrost.

The end came in an abrupt, perplexing manner. When we were called in, I asked Pat: "Is it pretty well out all over now?"

"No," he said. "We found a new swamp burning. A big one."

On a final reconnaissance flight the new burn had been discovered, an area around which guards would have to be bulldozed, to which hose would have to be laid. People and equipment would have to be recalled. And that's why the work stopped. Not because the fire was cold, but for the opposite reason, because a new hot spot had been found. It would be too expensive to begin to tackle this new fire, it was said. "We can't afford it. Shut her down."

Weird and wonderful convolutions of logic, but no different from those we had been getting throughout. Following them had been a little like tracing the life cycle of the silkworm. But this final twist bothered nobody. We'd had enough.

# 12

*Blood will be spilt in front of the people.*
*—The Prophecies of Nostradamus*

We were now, the handful of men who remained, encamped in the middle of Lower Post, on forestry property. There were a dozen of us. We rolled hoses, loaded and transported empty fuel barrels, burned garbage, that sort of thing – wrapping up the loose ends.

We were camped on a treed area adjacent to the forestry buildings. There was a dirt road directly in front of us and across it a central grassy area fronting the community centre, a big building with a gymnasium and, heavens above, a shower.

All the food had been shipped down with us and put in a big tent. It was stacked floor to ceiling – enough to feed the whole of Lower Post. The powers that be didn't know what else to do with it. There was no refrigeration, no running water, no cook. The meat became tainted, the bread went stale, the garbage and dirty dishes piled up. The place stank. Dogs got into the tent.

I never saw one permanent employee of forestry go near that place after the food was dumped. The waste was so stupid, so conspicuous. Presumably somebody cleaned the maggoty mess up eventually.

Some time during this period Terry's missing machete mysteriously reappeared in the new camp, and he was able to reclaim it.

From where we were camped we could see pretty much the whole of Lower Post. Up to the 1930s it had stood in the middle of nowhere. To the west and northwest lay the sources of the Liard River, to the north and northeast the unexplored Mackenzie Mountains and the country of the South Nahanni River.

First it was an Indian settlement; then from 1888 a Hudson's Bay Company fur-trading outpost – one of the most isolated of all such posts, in one of the most remote areas in Canada south of the Arctic Circle.

The explorer Warburton Pike described a visit he made in 1892: "A small store, a log hut for the man in charge, and a few rough buildings belonging to the Indians who make up the last outpost of civilization in this direction."

That situation existed until an airstrip was built in Watson Lake in the 1930s, and a town began to grow there. These were Lower Post's busiest years, for equipment was freighted two miles from Dease Lake, down the Dease by scow and stern-wheeler – a route the Tlingits had once taken in dugouts – and unloaded at Lower Post. From there, a twenty-six-mile road was bulldozed through the bush to Watson Lake. Later, with the war, came the Alaska Highway, bending past the settlement as it does today.

There was a vicious dogfight one day, in the dust of the road. A huge black dog owned by Pat, the fire boss, which had ridden, completely docile, in the back of his pickup for the duration of the fire, abruptly bore down on a small animal, the pet of a native villager. Powerful teeth crunched into the smaller dog's neck. We hit the big dog, kicked it, threw water on it, but it had become a killer and would not loose its hold.

Suddenly, out of the dust, came a vehicle, an old black car, which ran right over the dogs. There were screams from some of the onlookers. Under the wheels there was still a suggestion of vicious, frantic action, as if even now the dogs had not been separated. The driver, an Indian kid, flung the car in reverse, hit the gas, and ran over the dogs again, ending up in the ditch. We recognized him now as the owner of the small dog. Pat angrily raced over to the car and banged on the window with his fist, dragging at the door handle with his other hand, but the car raced away.

When it was over we found the tiny dog dead, the big one unhurt. It was just another of the human flare-ups this forest fire had indirectly spawned.

It was turning cold. The air had always been thin, but one of the firefighters, a South African, shivered all morning the day he left and said it was the coldest day he had ever known in his life.

The arrangement had been that we would get no money until we quit, but Terry got a six-hundred-dollar advance cheque and spent it all in one night at the Lower Post Hotel. The next day he got up around noon. Our fire boss Pat and I were in front of the warehouse loading a truck when Terry came over to us.

"Six hundred dollars," Pat said. "That's a whole week in the swamp, Terry. Seven days."

I'll never forget the reply, half-anguished, half ecstatic, replete with self-knowledge and self-revelation, part moan, part cry for help, part laughter.

"I know," he said. "And I'll probably spend the rest of my life in the swamp."

That day I took Terry into Watson Lake. I had to take a one-ton truck and trailer loaded with stuff we no longer needed to Dease Lake. I said I'd pick him up on the way back, but when I returned to Watson I couldn't find him.

Next day he phoned me to ask if I'd pack up his tent and the rest of his stuff and send it into town, to the hotel room he'd rented. The driver who took it in said he was lying on top of the bed, naked, with the door wide open, just ripped.

I wasn't able to get Terry to leave with me, but I was able to do one thing for him. He didn't know, until I told him at the hotel, that he still had almost five hundred dollars in pay coming. He thought he'd picked up the whole thing. I was able to get it delivered to him. Out of my own money I bought him a plane ticket to Vancouver and left it under the telephone.

# 13

Vancouver. Ten beggars to the block.

"Got any spare change, brother?"

"Anybody got a toke?"

"Buy a bottle of wine for a brother from Alberta?"

"Spare fifty cents for dinner?"

"You wouldn't be interested in buying ten milligrams of valium right now?"

The metropolis. Perfectly logical extension of those two-thousand-million-year-old fossils they found in Lake Superior.

There's a rock band downstairs, mice scrabbling in the walls, a guy sobbing across the hall. Without the light on, the room is dark as a kennel, even in the daytime. I got out for something to eat. Outside my hotel, among the lit-up faces, a drunken fall to the sidewalk has the same trancelike sense of oblivious distance as a trajectory to the moon.

I sit down in a Chinese place across the street. A guy with a long grey beard, a rag-wrapped tramp with a tramp's lined, grey face, is trying to get out without paying. The Chinaman is confronting him near the door.

"I got cigarettes this morning and coffee," the tramp whines.

The proprietor is dumbfounded. He can't believe what he's hearing. He stamps his foot. "This morning is this morning, now is now," he shouts.

The old man is backtracking to the door with his hands out in front

149

of him. "I paid cash. This morning," he keeps repeating, as if he can't fathom how such a misunderstanding can have arisen. "I paid cash."

The proprietor shrieks at him. "Then was then. Now is now. You just drink two coffees. *Now*."

The tramp is already outside. He raises a trembling arm through the window and shakes his head slightly. How did such a misunderstanding come about? It's beyond him. He's completely mystified. Then he's gone, flopping along on heelless shoes, shaking his head.

Back in my room, my next-door neighbour erupts once in a while in a loud growl, like the sound of a downshifting truck, and starts banging the drawers in his dresser. Maybe he's got mice too. I know what it's like. Mine get in the drawers leaving little black specks of shit. Once I opened my door and there was a little brown mouse right there at my feet, like a welcoming committee. It was spooked and didn't know which way to run; then it slid right around the baseboard and vanished behind the radiator. Everywhere in the building are little cardboard fast-food cartons full of poison seed. The mice eat it like cereal. They thrive.

Men go down the corridor to the toilet, which is next to my room, on the other side from the growler. Spitting and sweating, teary half-blind relics, sperm and sap dried up, blood corrupted, teeth rotten. They all smoke all the time. Here a clean white cigarette is prettier than a bride.

The rock band's beat goes on, and there's no sleep until it stops. I can hear it as if it's right in the room. It's a quarter to three in the morning. Sunday is the only day there is no music. Then the band rehearses.

All night you can hear hooting tugs, switching trains. At six in the morning the pile driver starts on the construction site next door. Saws and drills whine through the braying of heavy equipment. The gulls squeal. In the hallway two men are bickering, still drunk. Somewhere somebody is playing a harmonica, sadly, badly.

In these stale rooms, amid bladdery pods of dried paint, are men with every known disability. Victims of knife fights and fishing boat accidents, men whose lungs have been collapsed and whose brains have been scrambled, men with glass eyes and plastic legs, men with broken hearts, addicts – the halt, the lame, the blind, the jobless.

They wash down out of the engine of a labouring world to these rooms, like tailings from a mine. This is the sink. A garbage dump for humans. Nature's revenge. Skid Row.

# 14

*Hard it is to understand:*
*By giving away food we get more strength,*
*by bestowing clothes on others*
*we gain more beauty, by donating*
*abodes of purity and truth*
*we acquire great treasures.*
—Buddha

There were hundreds of us, standing shoulder to shoulder, back to back, head to head, at rows and rows of long tables, eating stew and dry bread. The predominant sound was a swampy gurgling and squelching, but the misery was thicker than the stew.

They used to be known, these men and women, as "rice Christians" – the name originally given by white people on the China coast to the hordes of "converts" with which missionaries padded their church membership lists. They were often broken-down opium addicts who got two bowls of rice a day to attend service.

Now it's stew.

I was in the Salvation Army's Harbour Light facility on Cordova Street, the downtown east side. From up and down the sloping street they came, hawking, spitting, coughing like seals, until every brown pew in the big church was taken, and extra seats, gaudy plastic chairs, ran up and down the aisles. There must have been four hundred men and women, maybe more.

Some went to sleep with their heads on their arms, resting on the back of the pew ahead. Some sniffed glue. Some read. A fat, uniformed officer tapped the microphone, which didn't appear to be working. "Well, if I have to shout this will be a short service," he said. At this there was applause – and cheers – from the congregation.

The platform was designed a bit like a ship, with a wheel in the centre, two lifebelts on either side with the words "Jesus Saves" on them, and, flanking them, port and starboard lights, one red, one green. On the back wall, above the heads of the platform party, were the words, in big gold letters: "CHRIST IS THE ANSWER TO EVERY NEED." The platform was full of men, most of them rough men of the streets who had been born again. There was only one woman, the brigadier's wife, in uniform.

The fat preacher urged the men to put their faith not in friends, in the welfare system, or in government, but in the Lord. He said they should give the confusion of their lives to the Lord and he would smooth it out.

It was a desultory service. Very few members of the huge congregation joined in the hymn-singing. Many openly read paperbacks or newspapers. There was the riffling of a deck of cards, and the coughing, like a bank of Vegas slots. A young man in front of me talked to his seat-mate about "taking a dive" – pretending to have got religion – so he could get into Miracle Valley, the Salvation Army's dryout centre for alcoholics and addicts. Collection plates were proffered but few people contributed. These were paupers. It was why they were there.

The highlight of the service was the testimony of a former drunk, a squat man who many in the congregation obviously knew from the streets. They sat in encouraging silence as the man, now driving a truck for the Salvation Army, talked about his past frankly and plainly and in terms they could understand. He had been a horrendous drunk, he said, a man with no past and no future, an embryo in a bottle. But things had changed for him. There was loud, heartwarming applause when he finished. Even an outsider had to be touched by the implications of that heartfelt applause, coming as it did from the doomed to the saved. It was as if the men wanted to hoist him up even further out of their own pit with their emotions.

When the service ended, the church emptied row by row, from the front to the back, and the men filed into the back room where the food was served.

There was a long counter staffed by some of the men who were on the platform during the service, including the man who gave his testimony. As each man reached it he was given a tray with a plate onto which some stew was ladled, a spoon, and some bread and buns.

"I'll be nigger rich again on Monday," one man – expecting a cheque – called to another.

"And you'll be back here on Tuesday," was the retort.

At the end of the serving counter, plastic bags were offered to those who might want to take the bread or buns away to eat later. Most had brought their own bags, however, and as I looked at the line from the back I saw them poking out of pockets.

Each person found a place at one of the waist-high tables. There were no chairs, nor was there room for any. The place was packed with standing bodies. I could see individuals more clearly now, as they stood and ate. Here I saw in people what Van Gogh saw and painted. The stricken multitude. Skins stretched over rearranged bones, like faces distorted when seen through bottle glass. In profile some seemed to have chunks missing from their heads. Such faces are not seen outside of Skid Row. Smashed and twisted, with shattered cheekbones or noses not just broken but half-severed, as if by an axe-blade. Some so swollen they looked as if stung by the deadly man-of-war jellyfish, or like a sculpture smashed by a hammer. Faces that were a twin to the chewed leather of the shoes their bearers wore; faces like the brown smears left at the bottom of a roasting pan; mad eagle eyes; names like Chicken, Goofball, Cowboy, Moonshine . . .

There were a number of elderly men with occasional bizarre hearkenings to a distant respectability: ties so old they were rotted down to a shoestring, high button boots, dirty straw hats, even filthy spats.

There was not much talk, only the sound of the breaking of bread into stew. Still they filed in. The brigadier greeted each one, shook hands, smiled, said God bless you. This was a Sunday ritual, this greeting, like the collection plate. There were services each day, but only on Sunday were the hands shaken and the plate offered.

The stew was watery, with little meat, but the diners fell on it like horses eating hay. Some had brought salt, or salt and pepper mixed in shakers or in the little plastic containers with the flap top in which breath mints are sold.

Some offered their bread or buns to others. Most took away some of the bread and buns in the bags they had brought. One or two even spooned their stew into plastic containers to take with them. Others waited for seconds.

I went back many times to the Harbour Light during the recession's worst hardship. Every meal was stew, with sometimes a mixture of tuna fish or macaroni added to the same old vegetable base. Sometimes there were seconds, once or twice a dessert of prunes.

The church was open at noon on weekdays, as well as in the evening.

At midday there would be no service, though, just a short prayer, a one-liner giving thanks for the sunshine or the food. In the evenings there was always a service with hymns, lasting half or three-quarters of an hour, usually conducted by the brigadier. Always the church was packed. One old man, sitting next to me told me one day: "I'm going to stop coming. Too many people. I'm going to budget, and that's that." As he spoke a man wandered around aimlessly at the front of the chapel, stoned. When he tried to sit down, a tramp with long grey hair pushed him away so that he fell against the mercy seat. "I know the Lord," he harangued. "You get away. I know the Lord." In the pew in front of mine a young man had pulled his coat right over his head, sleeping, or, more likely, sniffing something. An old man across the aisle clutched a browning head of lettuce in one hand, as he waited for the service to begin.

Another time I had a homely conversation with a neighbour about mice. "Where there's mice you won't find any cockroaches," he told me. "They eat 'em. I got all sorts of cockroaches. Cockroaches like warmth. I found a bunch of 'em living in the back of my clock radio. Warmth . . ."

Occasionally, someone would respond to exhortations from the preacher and walk, shaky-legged, to the mercy seat at the front to kneel, fly open, shoes holed, and pray for the Lord to accept his sins. The brigadier or someone else from the platform would pray with him, arms around his shoulders.

There was a special place up at the front on the left, by the door that led into the lunch room, for the handicapped, those walking with canes or crutches. They were always at the front of the stew line. Once a man seated there had a seizure.

Only a small proportion of the congregation were women. Sometimes you would have to look hard to find any at all. A couple were bag ladies. One of these, a big woman with cheeks rouged like a doll's, was truly amazing, with four or five bulging garbage bags and other smaller shopping bags clutched in her hands, hanging from her shoulders, affixed to a string at her waist where her skirt was gathered and bunched, giving her a duck shape. The bags seemed to be light, full of rags, or, perhaps, other bags. When she walked she held the bags high in her fists, like charms to ward off bad luck, and she was haughty, repelling anyone who got close to her, ignoring anyone who spoke: a low-life Lucretia. In the street she would push her bags in a shopping cart. Another poor creature of this type I'd seen frequently on the streets in Victoria, a woman with a stringy beard, a hermaphrodite who wore a brown scarf, the tail of which was generally thrown over the straggling hairs on her chin. With the way she walked, and the scarf across her face, she was like a snake with its tail in its mouth. Over her hunched shoulders and on her back she carried her ensemble of plastic bags. One time I passed her and she bared her teeth at me, incanting and trembling with her own hideousness, peeking like a graveyard ghost, with her head on one side. She was a spectre, a sibyl, and the moan she left behind was that of an animal in a slaughterhouse.

On Remembrance Day, in the evening, there was a guest speaker, a Dutchman. He said, in a heavy accent, that he had been a drunk and a sinner until four years previously. He said that even after he was born again he was not wholly convinced; he could not pursuade himself that the Lord had forgiven all his sins. Then, one night, he said, he had a dream. He prefaced the story of his dream by saying that after World War Two, as soon as he was old enough, he had joined the Royal Dutch Navy. Even the Japanese had surrendered by then, but there was still some scattered fighting in Indonesia and on various islands, and he was part of it. In the dream he was lying on a beach full of dead soldiers, hundreds or perhaps thousands of them. He became aware that a landing craft was coming in to pick up those still alive. He tried to get up to go to the craft but couldn't. There was a heavy weight on his back. He struggled but could not move. Finally an officer arrived and lifted off the heavy pack under which he was trapped. That was the dream, the preacher said, and he woke knowing absolutely that, as the pack had been lifted from his back, so his sins had been lifted from him, forgiven for ever.

One night, instead of a service, the lights were turned out and a half-hour film, *Not a Sparrow Falls*, was shown. It was a sort of docu-drama, made in Chicago, supposed to illustrate the role of the Salvation Army. It is worth digressing to give the plot, for it illustrates the Army's view of itself and its clients – and this is an organization that deals, at one time or another, with virtually all transients.

In the opening sequence, a drunk is found in an alley, slumped in a doorway, covered in snow. It is the middle of winter. The man is spotted by a grey-haired Salvation Army officer who lifts him up, dusts him off, and half carries him to the Harbour Light, where he is given a bed and dried out, and where, as he lies amid clean sheets, he remembers, by way of flashbacks, his earlier life. He pictures his wife, an attractive woman, playing the piano in the living room of an attractive home.

Later, when the delirium tremens have passed, he eats with the other men, and afterward attends a church service. Then, late at night, we see him returning to the darkened and empty chapel to play the piano alone, again recapturing a bit of his more graceful past. As he does so, the brigadier and another soldier, hidden in the doorway, listen, smiling.

The Salvation Army assists the man in getting temporary work. His job is to help put up Christmas decorations in a fine house. As he is doing this the lady of the house asks him to look after her sleeping child while she goes to a neighbour's. Shaken and wild-eyed at this request, the man opens a bedroom door to find a cute blond boy asleep in a bed. In a panic the man rushes from the house, past the startled mother, and reels out into the street. In another flashback it is made clear that this man had a son. One morning as he was leaving for work in the family car he had accidentally backed over the boy, killing him. This is the source of his agony and his drinking.

Now we see the man getting drunk again in a bar and then staggering out into the snow with a bottle of whiskey. He is attacked, beaten up, and left on the sidewalk, where he freezes to death, within a couple of blocks of the Harbour Light. In the final scene the brigadier writes a letter to the man's wife, breaking the news of his death. As he leaves the building after completing this sad task he finds yet another drunk half-covered by snow, and so the work continues.

It was maudlin and romanticized. The men watched in silence. The movie was meant to be a warning, they knew. Just a couple of days earlier the Vancouver police chief had been quoted in the newspapers as saying drunks were going to die in the streets because of a reduction in funding to the city detox centre. Detox, it should be said, is a real turning point for many men. Detox staffs are often revered by the men on the street – and some of the more dedicated are regarded almost as saints.

Luckily the winter of 1982 was to be a mild one on the West Coast, once again justifying the annual migration of the hordes of homeless from the east. About this time, a wire-service photograph in the papers attracted a lot of attention on Skid Row. It showed a solitary transient in snowbound Quebec reaching to warm himself at a hot-air vent on the side of a building. Up until the picture appeared, it had been easy to see the men among whom I was living as the most desolate of creatures. Now the still harsher reality of winter in the east impinged and provoked pity from the pitiful. That single true picture was far more salutary than the Salvation Army movie.

George Orwell once said: "A man receiving charity practically always hates his benefactors – it is a fixed characteristic of human nature – and when he has fifty or a hundred others to back him he will show it."

I don't necessarily believe that is true. I've seen men eat day after day in places where the food is given without any strings attached, without any prayers offered, without any undue waiting to be endured. I've seen an honest rapport between giver and taker. It is the price the Salvation Army insists on extracting – the hymn-singing, the prayers, the sermonizing, the simple-minded movies – that causes many men to harden their hearts toward the organization. A man does not put himself through all that for a meagre meal of watery stew unless he is in need.

When you're hungry you want to spit all the time, your stool is pale, you're dizzy. But the biggest torture of all – far worse than hunger itself – is the thought of that hunger. You cannot stop thinking about it. The thought of it frightens and demoralizes. To make rice Christians out of such men and women, to treat them as mission stiffs, is to manufacture hatred. This is an old complaint, and I will not dwell on it except to say that surely there is a gentler, finer, more generous way to distribute the funds with which the Salvation Army is entrusted for the poor.

Still, the seething resentment that Orwell and many others have pictured among the recipients of charity is a somewhat superficial exaggeration. These characters are not exactly country-simple. When you have been hauled off the tailgate of a paddy wagon a few times by your feet, so that your head slaps down onto an alley, it either kills you or broadens your imagination. The men and women of Skid Row understand power and powerlessness. If they started to despise deeply every individual and organization by whom they are repeatedly exploited and debased, they would throw a fit, be dead in a week. Some, indeed, do become absolutely paranoid and have to be locked away, but most develop a measure of stoicism, as self-protective and natural as nature's camouflage.

More unforgivable than the way hunger is used, I believe, is the unimaginative, paternalistic, parrot-like nature of the services themselves at most Salvation Army centres. The sermons are badly prepared and delivered. The point is invariably lost. They are embarrassing performances. A social worker once said to me, of the people on Skid Row. "They are not there because they are stupid." That is true. They are far from stupid, most of them. But the Salvation Army insists on treating the members of its congregation as if they are dumb as cattle. If it does not inspire outright hatred, this certainly leaves the Army with little leverage.

One night, as winter deepened, there was an announcement as the men waited in their seats for the service to begin. The proceedings would be filmed in their entirety by a television crew. Nothing could be calculated to embarrass the hungry more. Nothing could show less compassion. Many left, of course, and went hungry that night so that comfortable, full-bellied viewers could go slumming from their armchairs.

The wildest scene I saw at the Harbour Light came when a guest speaker began giving away dollar bills.

First he held up a single dollar note. "Who wants it?" he asked. It took a second to register, and then a guy in front of me, an Irishman, scuttled up the front and returned with the dollar. "I needed a dollar," I heard him tell his buddy.

When the congregation, as one, realized the speaker was still holding a roll of bills it was like the storming of the Bastille. The Pope in a crowd never received such homage, so many upraised, supplicating hands. The outreaching arms were as dense as vines as a hundred men rushed to the front to fight for some of the money.

The man peeled off dollar bills and thrust them out as if feeding performing seals. He was a sharply dressed, born-again character. He said he had been in detox in such bad shape that he literally could not remember his own name. Later he had gone to prison, to Oakalla, for five years. Now he had his own business. He said his gesture was not meant to illustrate how easy it is to get money if you commit yourself to changing your life, but rather how easily, if you reach out to God, you would receive a whole lot more than a dollar.

"Everything I have I owe to the Lord," he said. He told the congregation: "You're not thinking of God. You're thinking of the next drink, the next mark. I did, too. But then I got sick and tired of being a loser."

The congregation seemed to be increasing now almost daily. One rainy noon I got there fifteen minutes before the service was to begin. The doors were locked, and there were twenty or thirty men on the sidewalk outside. The chapel was packed to capacity; they could not squeeze another body inside. They gave us tickets and we waited in the rain until the people inside began to file into the lunch room. We stood around waiting, trying to digest this new state of the street. "It's okay, we'll get the bottom of the pot where all the meat is," one guy joked. It was a good joke. There was never much meat in those pots.

That evening there was a disturbance. There was always a disturbance of one kind or another. Tonight it was a big man in a brown coat punching a seated member of the congregation in the head. You could hear the smack. There is no sound quite like that of one man punching another.

"You bastard," the assailant said. "You and your fucking partners. Come outside." This was happening in the middle of the church. An usher took the big man away to the back where he stood rubbing his knuckles in the palm of his other hand. He seemed sober, but he was very angry. A few minutes later there was another smacking sound. Everybody turned to look. The man in the brown coat was again standing alongside the aisle pew where his victim was sitting. The victim's face was red, and he had red, drinker's eyes. He wore a blue shirt. His hair was brushed straight back from his forehead. He looked straight ahead. Once he raised his hand to brush the side of his face where he had been hit.

His assailant could not restrain himself. He ignored the usher, who was again pulling on his arm. "You and your three partners," he sneered. And he hit the seated man again, a good knuckle punch right to the side of the head. Then the usher dragged him away.

"I'll be waiting outside," the big man shouted.

Outside.

My abiding memory, though, will not be of the sermons or the fights or the feeding, but of the men leaving by the back door, walking down that dripping valley in the wet dark through smashed glass and sooted walls running with rain, each man carrying a bag containing a few slices of bread in one hand, like looters stealing away in a wartime blackout.

# 15

*What use are laws where money is king,*
*Where poverty's helpless and can't fix a thing.*
— Petronius

My neighbour across the hall had a habit of crying like a baby. He sobbed, groaned, caterwauled, and flung himself about his room, stamping his feet in flurries, just like a child. They were unearthly sounds, and while they continued there was complete silence elsewhere on the floor, as if by consensus. Nobody complained. Sometimes he would throw open his door and continue to weep unashamedly in the hallway. He would sob and babble unintelligibly, frantically, in a high-pitched voice. The mechanism that normally holds in grief was completely broken in this person. I assumed he was a young boy, but I had never seen him. I did not want to come face to face with so much grief.

My room was generally warm, and sometimes very hot indeed. It had been painted fairly recently, an off-white colour, and it was fairly clean. It cost $180 a month. I still had not been able to discover where the mice were getting in, but I stuffed a couple of small holes in the plaster with paper. The room was tiny, perhaps ten by ten – a perfect box. A bed, a dresser, a washstand, and a small desk and chair were all the furniture, but they took up practically all the space there was, leaving a tiny L-shaped piece of open ground as you entered the room. There was also a small recessed closet to hang clothes. No stove, no fridge. There were two windows, one over the radiator at the foot of the bed, and one up high over the bed. Out of either could be seen only other walls and windows, at a distance of about two feet. The rooms were so boxed in by other rooms, other windows, that the weather remained an unknown factor until I hit the street, unless it was raining hard. Through one window I could see a slice of my neighbour's room. On his dresser were some salt, jam, margarine, peanut butter, and a can of black shoe polish. Across his roof, like mine, ran the ubiquitous pipes that grace all these rooming houses and serve to hang washing and, occasionally, people.

Once, while moving the dresser I found a card tucked in the back of the mirror. If it had been the Holiday Inn or the Hilton it might have been a salesman's card, or a doctor's or lawyer's. But this was Skid Row, and the card was inscribed, in smartly marching capitals: "BAIL SUPERVISION PROJECT. DEPARTMENT OF THE ATTORNEY GENERAL, CORRECTIONS BRANCH, 193 EAST HASTINGS STREET, VANCOUVER, B.C."

There was a place for the bail supervisor's signature, but he had not signed it. Instead, his name and address were written on the back of the card. Presumably, my predecessor in this room was no longer on bail, or had skipped, or was back in the joint. Perhaps he'd preferred the joint to this room.

Many of the men on Skid Row now were good workers, recently laid off. Initially, they had brought a confidence that they would be back at work soon; but as time went on with no sign of a recall, they seemed to develop an incapacity for considering consequences, an undirected recklessness. As their initial Cossack mentality toward work disappeared, they became more like serfs in their drunkenness, their suspicions, their crafty obsequiousness.

I renewed a few old acquaintances, people I had met on my travels, most noticeably an incredible scavenger I had worked construction with on the island some time before. This was Buchanan, a cadaverous Ahab character, seemingly completely unself-conscious. He always looked starved. He had hips you could hang a hat on. "You're so skinny you have to stand sideways to throw a shadow," one crony had mocked. But Buchanan looked after himself better than anybody I met. He was a magpie, an unprincipled scavenger who would work furiously at filling his own small camper truck with good lumber – two-by-fours, studs, shiplap – ignoring the job for which he had been hired. He would take anything: carpeting, insulation, tools, wiring. One time when it had been a bad day for Buchanan – his truck was still empty – he gave me a ride and said he had to make a stop on the way. We sat for a few minutes outside a big lumber yard until the shift changed. Buchanan strolled into the yard, hopped onto a forklift, and began to shovel lumber into his truck. I sat in the cab, stunned. Just as we were about to pull away, a foreman stood in front of the truck. "I want twenty dollars a load. You've been doing this for at least a week," he yelled. "Fuck off," Buchanan said. "If this lumber isn't free I don't want it." And he drove away – with the lumber.

In his spare time Buchanan made burl tables, which he sold at flea markets. Once we were working right next door to a dead tree full of beautiful burls. Buchanan knocked on the door of the house and asked the owner: "Do you want that tree?" The top was lopped off, but there must have been ten burls on the trunk.

"Somebody already paid me $300 for it," the man said.

"I'll give you a righteous price," said Buchanan, who rarely offered to pay for anything, but the homeowner declined to haggle.

"When's he coming for it?" Buchanan asked.

"Saturday," the guy said. "I'm going to be away until then, so he's coming Saturday."

As he walked back to me Buchanan said: "Well, I like to try and make a deal, but if that tree isn't gone Friday night it won't be there Saturday morning."

He always had some dirty little angle. On the other hand he could be tremendously patient with people who were disadvantaged. Once we worked with a Vietnamese guy, one of the boat people. He didn't understand anything that was going on. Buchanan tried to explain that he should shovel one inch of sand off the site of a carport so that concrete could be poured to the right depth. The Vietnamese labourer didn't understand and was throwing sand all over everywhere. The boss had already given up on him, but Buchanan was still trying everything he could think of to impress upon the immigrant that only one inch of sand need be removed. He was fascinated by the problem of communication. At last he decided the only thing they had in common was a bit of a knowledge about oriental food. He spread two fingers about an inch apart. "One egg roll," he said. "One egg roll."

"Ah, egg roll," the Vietnamese said, and by some miracle he understood. He was all smiles and completed the job very quickly. After that he stuck with Buchanan. They next had to dig a deep hole. The drain tile, which was buried under backfill, was leaking and had to be dug out. The three of us went over to the site. Buchanan thought deeply for a moment. Then he turned to the Vietnamese, looked him in the eye, and said: "Fifteen thousand egg rolls."

When he first left home as a youth, Buchanan told me, he had stolen such a large quantity of fruit and vegetables from the jobbers in Toronto's Kensington Market that there were wanted posters up for him in the shop windows, featuring an artist's impression of his unmistakable features – sunken cheeks, and burning eyes, his nose flattened and grooved like a seashell even then.

He still had one of the posters, and he showed it to me. He was living then over a plumbing store, and he also fished out a hand-lettered sign that said in red ink: "Industrial accident. Cheated out of compensation. International Year of the Disabled. Give generously."

He said he had rented a wheelchair and made $200 on a good day begging from it outside the Bay. I could imagine him, his long bony legs twisted, his workboots undone and the laces dangling, his bearded head thrown back like a suffering Jesus. This type of fraud didn't bother his conscience in the least. He believed, as many do who have been on the streets for any length of time, that it was every man for himself, and that no scruples or morality should interfere with his survival. But time ran out on that scam. Many others had the same idea, and there were mutterings in the newspapers about the inordinate number of disabled veterans outside department stores. Their wheelchairs were blocking the sidewalk, their crutches were getting tangled in the feet of passers-by. . . . The phonies were eventually moved on by police.

Once I saw a contractor confront Buchanan about his thieving. "Why don't you take the walls?" he demanded superciliously. "Why don't you stick around and take the plumbing, the wiring, the appliances. Eh?"

Buchanan stood up and stretched. He looked as tall as first-growth timber. He waved his hand toward his camper, already jammed with stolen material. "You can't get a hundred pounds of oats in a fifty-pound bag," he explained gently.

He appeared to have no scruples. One ghoulish coup he was very proud of was the winter he spent digging bodies out of snowdrifts in Cleveland. It had been a terrible winter, and people got stuck in their cars and buried. The recovery crews were supposed to take the bodies to the morgue. Buchanan used to rob the corpses first.

When I ran into him again he was living in a hotel on the Skid Row strip waiting for warmer weather. He had an idea, he said, to go after some gold an old prospector was supposed to have buried in a boot by a river somewhere up-country. The prospector had gone to hospital with a serious illness, but before he died he'd given a map to the local newspaper showing where the gold-filled boot was buried – near a certain grove of trees by the river. Before the story could be investigated, however, there was a flood. The river overflowed its banks and changed its course, and the landmarks on the map were no longer identifiable. That was twenty years ago. Since then, hundreds of people had tried to find the gold. The river bank was now reputed to be like a giant molehill from all the digging. But Buchanan thought he could find it.

"Easier to go after the gold in the rivers up north," I said, remembering the Hyland.

Buchanan hunched forward, interested. He became deadly serious when money was being discussed so that every conversation with him had the atmosphere of a thieves' kitchen. "I know two things about gold an Indian once told me," he said. "It was in a gas station, and I give this Indian a ride. He said to me, always remember two things about gold. The rounder the pebbles and the darker the sand. Two things to remember and that's where you find gold." He repeated it for emphasis. "The rounder the pebbles and the darker the sand – the more gold there is."

Meanwhile, Buchanan and a partner were making money in the following manner: A customer in a store pays for a purchase with a twenty-dollar bill and receives his change at the checkout. This is the accomplice. Buchanan is the next customer in line and he pays with, say, a five-dollar bill. When he gets his change he complains about it, alleging that he had, in fact, paid with a twenty.

"No," says the teller. "It was a five."

"I can prove it was a twenty," says Buchanan. "Bring the manager."

To the manager he says: "I won the twenty in a card game. It has my name on it. If the top twenty in the till has my name on it and some numbers I scribbled, that's proof."

"Fair enough," says the manager.

The accomplice's bill is produced from the till, of course matches the description, and Buchanan pockets the change from a twenty, making fifteen bucks for five minutes' work.

"We can do it twenty times a day," he said, rolling a cigarette without spilling so much as a curl of tobacco.

# 16

*God loveth a cheerful giver.*
— St. Paul, 2 Corinthians, 9:7

"I know a guy, he's got nothing to do. He's going crazy from boredom so he gets everything he can from welfare. It's a game. He wrings every penny and every service he can from them. He's got twenty-nine different diseases. He has to have special food, so he gets extra money for that. His doctor wrote him a prescription for a special coat to keep him warm. It cost two hundred bucks, but he had to have this coat. 'Prone to pneumonia,' the doctor wrote.

"Another guy took his jaywalking tickets to welfare. He couldn't pay them. He didn't hear anything back. I guess they paid.

"Last June I said I had a job interview, needed a suit. I got a Christian Brothers suit, a beautiful suit. They paid. Nobody ever asked me if I got the job."

The man speaking to me was in a line-up for a welfare cheque. It was November 24, 1982. The line-up was a thing to behold, the real yardstick of the recession. The cheques would be given out at 8:30 A.M. By the time I got there, before eight, hundreds and hundreds of men were waiting on the street. The Human Resources office was on Seymour Street near the heart of the city of Vancouver, on a corner. The line-up, two or three abreast, extended a full block on Seymour and then disappeared around a corner in one direction. The payout was conducted in two different locations, however, and the recipients were split into two camps, alphabetically by surname, so another army of the unfortunate, equal in size, wrapped itself around the building in the other direction, flanking the whole side of the long office on Nelson, and curving into the alley that backed it. I was just not prepared for this early-morning aberration. My mind at first endowed it with a movie-set quality. Rather than depression at the sight there was an initial thrill akin to that provoked by the gathering of many people in an epic of the screen. It was preposterous.

And this was just one of several downtown-area welfare offices where the cheques were not mailed out, but distributed.

People with jobs, on their way to work, on buses and in cars, stared and then looked away. Those who waited, indifferent to this attention, were hunched like wolves. They appeared drained of strength, perhaps because many had already been waiting for hours.

The vast majority were single men, unskilled workers. True marginal men. Men left over when the bookkeepers moved us from primary, resource-based industries to more skilled trades, from blanket stiffs to the biggest per-capita purchasers of life insurance in the world.

And then the recession came, like a million wetbacks, and the margin got so wide it wasn't a margin any longer but a whole fresh page in history.

It was almost 8:40 A.M. when the doors were finally opened and we shuffled forward. At the front a security guard allowed in six at a time, so we shuffled and stopped, shuffled and stopped. It would take the men at the back of the line two hours to reach the door.

One man up ahead held, incongruously, a bunch of flowers.

"For your old lady?" someone finally asked.

"For my worker," the gallant one replied sheepishly. The flowers, he explained, were an attempt at bribery. He was not able to produce the rent receipt she had demanded.

My companion said: "Sometimes I just pay a week's rent – in case something comes up." He laughed. "Usually nothing comes up."

If nothing came up this month, he and a lot of others were in for a miserable Christmas, for the money they got that day would have to last until December 29, which was the next cheque day – thirty-five full days away. On top of his rent (maximum allowable rent was $200 a month) a single man would receive $175 for food, plus, this month only, a $20 Christmas bonus. Less than $6 a day for food, clothing, and such luxuries as drink, soap, a newspaper, bus fares, laundry, a haircut, toothpaste, razor blades, deodorant, smokes. And Christmas.

"They don't know how we can live on it," my companion said. "Even the welfare people can't understand how we do it. I've talked to them about it."

It was a wry observation, not a complaint. I never did hear complaints from welfare recipients about the amount of money they received. The overriding concern, right through the recession, was with jobs. And this day in the welfare queue was no exception.

"There's going to be ten thousand new jobs, government's goin' to make 'em."

"Government's going broke. How they goin' to make ten thousand new jobs?"

"A war'd do it."

"You'll still be in this line six months from now, I'll bet you."

"No way. I'll take a course if I have to."

"There isn't one course, for anything, that has less than a six-month waiting time. Not for anything you can name."

So it went. Predictable, naive even, but still reflecting in miniature the essentials of the national debate. Things were so bad and the shock of the recession still so acute that originality, like cash-flow, seemed to have been stifled – except perhaps in the case of one letter writer who suggested that the proliferating and protected ducks and geese in Stanley Park could be killed off for the tables of the unemployed. Less exotic ploys occupied the men and women edging toward a welfare cheque. They did not whine, but they reserved the right to protect themselves, and they knew a few angles. Clothing money was available from welfare for those who needed it; welfare would pay a security deposit on a shared apartment, or buy a bed for a person with a bad back. There were food banks, soup lines, provision for free swimming and ice-skating for the needy; there were the Salvation Army, the St. Vincent de Paul, thrift shops. Some churches still gave alms. For entertainment there was the provincial court. But the grind of it all. To live. Just to live. And every month more were having to learn the ropes.

Finally we made it to the door. The security guard, an elderly man, said to me: "I don't know why they can't mail the cheques. It could have been raining hard, or snowing."

The process by which I got in that line-up began many days earlier when I filled in an application for welfare upstairs at that same Seymour Street office. That day I was given no money, but received meal tickets to tide me over until the date of my interview a week later. (I was fortunate. Many applicants had to wait ten days for an interview because of the tremendous pressure on the system. Usually during this period, if they were homeless, they were bedded down at Dunsmuir House, the downtown hostel for men.)

Although it was not a cheque day, the office was full of people, also applying for the first time, or waiting for interviews, or meal tickets, or money. There were many stories on the street about burn-out among employees in welfare offices, and the stories were not hard to believe. The girls on the desk were incessantly busy, and there was an air of tension in the office – a patent fear emanating from the nervous poor – that added to the strain. People were afraid that they might be overlooked or rejected, or that they might make some minor mistake on a form or in an interview that would doom them. One man was told to return when he was sober. Others had physical or mental disabilities.

I was to get a first-hand indication of how harassed the clerks in these places can become under pressure.

I was furnished with enough meal tickets – the value of $5.50 a day – to last me until my interview date. Each day's supply consisted of one voucher for $2.50, one for $1.75, and one for $1.25. I left the desk with these and got in the elevator to go down to the street. There was another man in there, and as we went down he asked me if I knew where I could use the vouchers. It was a thing I had completely overlooked. I had no idea which restaurants would honour the vouchers. The man said they had typed lists at the desk. Back upstairs I went. I went directly to the front of the line and asked for a list.

"We don't have any," the girl said. "You'll have to find out for yourself."

Now the places that accept welfare vouchers are not signposted, they're not in the tourist guides, you won't find them in the fine-dining ads. I hesitated, and from the line waiting behind me someone pushed a crumpled but current list into my hand. At the same time the clerk, realizing her error, located some more of the lists. I mention it not as a criticism – the wonder to me was always how well most of the people in these welfare offices functioned – but as an example of the impatience produced by pressure that taints all bureaucracies in the eyes of the public. Hundreds of little problems like mine cutting across larger problems, breeding strain.

Here is perhaps a good place to give a personal view of these welfare offices, which suddenly became so important to so many. The hardest decision I had to make in researching this story was to take welfare – just as it was the hardest decision of a lifetime for so many others as the recession took its toll. Welfare has become a threshold, as the work-house was once a threshold. You cannot understand it without crossing it, which is why so much rubbish is written about poverty.

For the most part, as I have indicated, I was impressed with the people who staff these offices. The system is doomed, though. We cannot afford it. It will have to be replaced by a far more energetic job-finding program, incorporating retraining and new educational opportunities – a movement that has already – belatedly – begun.

I quote one authority – one of the few empiricists to be found amid hordes of theorists. He was a man called Henry Paul who for ten years through the thirties, rode freights, went on the bum, and lived in restless flophouses. At the end of that terrible decade he wrote an article – "I Am a Transient" – that was published in May 1939 in *The Canadian Forum*. In it he said that any effective program for the transient must aim at his absorption into normal and useful industry. He advocated work-training schools and a federal program of constructive public works, with jobs at union rates.

"Work and wages [are] what these men need," he said then. "Moreover, the hours and nature of the work must be adjusted to the endurance of their weakened bodies, and the wages must be high enough so that they can build up physical and moral and mental stamina once more."

He said some other things, too. "What is really noteworthy is that these young fellows, like myself, have stayed on the road. I have met them repeatedly in past years, in freights, on the highway, in flophouses. In fact I may say here that I have never met or even heard of anyone who has lived this life for any considerable period of time and been able to rehabilitate himself completely.

"There may be persons of sufficient strength of character to live through the combination of filth, misery and beggary that I have described, without becoming to some extent demoralized, but I have never met them."

And before Henry Paul there was Rousseau, who said the same thing somewhat differently. The habit of work, he said, is undone by " . . . discontent with oneself, the burden of idleness, the neglect of simple and natural tastes."

In many ways welfare is a remarkably generous program. All of the money dispensed goes immediately back into the economy, but still it is generous. There's something almost existential about it. One wonders how it will be viewed a hundred years from now. Certainly as a contentious blip on some computer screen. Perhaps as the biggest revolution of them all.

With my food vouchers I went to eat. Menu selection, I quickly learned, is important. The restaurants that accept these meal tickets do not give any change, so that if you go for lunch and it costs, say, $3.10, you have to hand over a ticket worth $2.50 plus a ticket worth $1.25. You will have paid sixty-five cents more than the meal is worth – sixty-five cents that you, of all people, can ill afford. It is money down the drain. And you are left with $2.50 for supper. Needless to say, you cannot get three meals in a restaurant for $5.50. Now, having wasted the sixty-five cents, you'll be lucky to get two meals. But you learn quickly to make the best possible use of your tickets. Any man you spot in your local greasy spoon who is banging his fist against his temple, counting on his fingers, and cursing is on meal tickets. Give him fifty cents, you'll do him a big favour. Most of you won't meet him, though, unless you eat on Skid Row, where most of the restaurants that accept the tickets are located. These are places where sometimes you get only a fork to eat with – no knife. That's to avoid the possibility of a stabbing. It's those sort of places that take meal tickets.

I eked out the vouchers until the day of my interview. It was the morning after a major economic speech in Ottawa, a speech amounting, in fact, to a new budget. In it the Minister of Finance announced slight increases in unemployment insurance benefits. The woman who sat across the desk from me, my welfare worker, said: "What I hoped they would do instead of increasing benefits was to lengthen the amount of time people can remain on unemployment insurance. For people who have worked all their lives, whose insurance is running out, welfare is an awful thing."

She was concerned, efficient, and sensible. I got a cheque for $360: $185 for rent, $175 for food.

Each month now, as the cheques were being distributed from the Seymour Street office – and the line of men and women, supplemented by late risers, seemed destined never to be reduced – another logjam was building up a few blocks away, outside the bank. One branch of the Royal Bank on Granville opened at nine and bore the brunt of the welfare-cheque business. There, another incredible line snaked from the sidewalk through the building to the tellers' cages, draining the cash reserves – a demanding, expanding tributary to the free society. Inevitably, there were problems. Imagine the frustration of one man who had endured both line-ups only to be refused service by the teller because the printed amount on his cheque did not agree with the dollar numbers – a computer or typing error. He became a madman, plunging back to the welfare office, through the queue, up to the desk, to rant and rave and threaten, to be told nobody could help him, a new cheque would have to be issued, he would have to return later. Finally, by dint of volume and fervour, he wrested from them a new cheque and once again joined the tail of the snake outside the bank. Another man lined up all morning only to be told his cheque had somehow got to a Burnaby office and would have to be retrieved. He chose to go out to Burnaby, borrowing the bus fare to get there and returning by cab to the city, just to make sure of getting the cheque, to grasp that feeling of temporary security.

The stress of incidents like these cannot be adequately understood by an outsider. There was an enormous psychic build-up to this day each month, a more suffocating count-down than any ever heard at Cape Canaveral. When a man or woman is thwarted, a fury like that of a hungry child deprived of milk is unleashed. An absolute internal panic sets in, a frenzy of desperation, self-pity, and hatred. Physical hunger is an ache, the thought of hunger is a crazy fever.

In a milder form, though more frequently, this frustration can be seen at any employment centre. These places are far worse in my view than welfare offices – prime examples of a huge sodden bureaucracy. In my experience and, I think, that of many, many others, the domain of Employment and Immigration Canada is a gleaming wasteland of partitions and partitioned minds. Here the computer rules, and if anyone ever had any doubts about the cowed slavery to which that machine can subject human beings – or the hate it can engender – it is with this branch of government that he or she should become acquainted. The staff here are reduced to useless puppets; they are to be pitied. This is the Nightmare.

A man has changed his address. He wants to know why he has not had a cheque since he moved into his new place weeks ago. The following is a verbatim transcript.

"It takes eight weeks."

"It takes eight weeks to get a file sent from one office to another?"

"No, it takes two weeks."

"Oh."

"But you have to wait eight weeks. That's the system. It's computerized. Then you'll get all your back benefits."

"Then I'll be rich," the man says, permitting himself a modicum of satire. The rent is overdue, he can't make his car payments, he has no food in the house . . . and what's worse – far, far worse – is that he and thousands of others have learned there is little point in fighting this vacuum, this contemptible horde of button-pushers. They are beyond redemption.

I quote from a pamphlet, put out by a fringe organization, only because it expresses in print what I heard so many times as I shared the lives of the unemployed.

Anyone who has ever made application for benefits or just gone to make enquiry at [an employment centre] knows the delays and constant excuses that are thrown at the workers by this arrogant bureaucracy. "I don't know" – "I don't have the time" – "You'll have to wait" – "I'm sorry but we don't have anyone who can find this out for you" – and so on . . . These are the daily stock-in-trade comments from these offices. In some centres waits of an hour just to ask a question are not uncommon, and persons enquiring are given numbers, like lining up for meat purchases in a supermarket . . .

. . . Unemployment Insurance benefits are not like going out to plan a trip to the Caribbean, or lining up to see a movie. UI benefit cheques are the desperately needed dollars to pay rent and feed and clothe a worker and his family. For a man to have to wait two or three months for his first cheque after being dumped on the street by a layoff means possible ruin. His landlord does not accept "UIC backlog" as an excuse. His loans' officer is not interested in some story . . .

These Canada Employment offices commit hundreds of petty crimes daily against the workers, which they pass off as errors when confronted. But these "errors", interestingly, always work against the applicants and cause delays and untold hassles for those who desperately need the money.

Hysterical propaganda? Well, it may sound that way to anyone who has not run afoul of the system, but there are thousands who can relate to that type of criticism. I have absolutely no axe to grind here. I knew little or nothing about Employment and Immigration Canada before I became acquainted with its victims and witnessed for myself the inhuman procedures to which rightful claimants – whether for cheques or jobs – are subjected.

The differing reactions toward authority to be seen at welfare and at an employment centre are striking. When a man is thwarted at welfare he is likely to scream and shout until something is done. At the employment centres the "clients" quibble and then retreat, for somehow they know they have stepped beyond free will into a land of slavery. As for the staff – if they ever are faced with genuine anger, with boldness, with right and common sense they retreat – with the same frightened lonely impulse that makes some immigrants to North America exaggerate their "national" characteristics – into the land of the microchip.

# 17

*Have another toke,*
*And a little drink,*
*To drown your sorrows.*
*— A street singer*

They call it Mardi Gras. Welfare Day. It's a drunken celebration in all our inner cities. Rightly or wrongly, an amazing proportion of the welfare cash that goes to single people who live in the core areas is spent immediately on drink. It would take an ostrich mentality to deny it. And Mardi Gras is one of the things about welfare that makes a lot of taxpayers very angry. But it is more a tribal rite than a premeditated rip-off, more sad than scandalous. In the end it is always very sordid indeed. Sordid and often violent. But in the beginning Mardi Gras is all talk, the language of the streets.

"Two beer?"

"I'll have two shots of morphine my dear, and a couple of liberals to beat the shit out of."

"Would you believe I used to weigh one hundred eighty, one hundred ninety pounds? Something happened serious. I'm a walking miracle for thirty years by the grace of God the Saviour, the Master, and the Holy Bible."

"I can't dance, I'm too fat to fly, I'm goin' to have a smoke."

"I had a good job fuelling airplanes, but you couldn't smoke all day. I couldn't handle that, not smoking all day. Then I had a good job spraying rock with water for compaction. We used pumps and fire hoses and we just sprayed that rock all day. That's all we did. I got $2,200 clear a month for that, but it was so damn wet I got athlete's foot. Can you believe that? Athlete's foot! So I quit."

"Oh, yes, I was married. One day she said to me: 'I don't turn you on. What can I do to turn you on?' I said: 'Get a tattoo.' I read about it somewhere. So she got a tattoo, just a little thing up on her leg right here. That was all right for a week, then I said 'Why don't you get another tattoo, you know, turn me on.' So she did. Soon she's covered in tattoos, an' one day she says to me: 'You don't turn *me* on, I'm leaving you.' "

"My dad? Last I heard he'd sold fifty gallons of home-made booze. Forty-eight-and-a-half gallons were water, the rest was whiskey. I don't know what he asked for it, but he got eighteen months."

"I was boogyin' last night and I lost my socks. Boogyin' so hard I lost my socks."

"I was workin'. Teamsters shut the job down because a labourer drove a pickup truck. I was workin' for nuthin' anyway. It all come off the wife's welfare cheque."

"God will not forsake me. God did not make me a pervert."

"I got married on VE day. Finished one war, started another."

Mardi Gras. The Overdose Show.

An old woman stares darkly at an old man across the tavern table. "Thank God I have the Bible," she says fiercely. Then she gets up and begins to dance a lone quadrille, making grossly emphatic gestures with her hips. She has on a dress that goes down almost to the floor. Only her socks can be seen, rolled down on top of her shoes. Her gums are bared. She has no teeth in. "I see a poor sinner repented," she suddenly screams, pointing at the tramp who has been sharing her table, bumming drinks. The tramp looks around, frightened.

"Fall on your knees," she screams. She stands with one saddlebag hip out. Her finger quivers.

"I don't know nuthin' 'bout prayin'," the tramp says sheepishly.

"I know that, you heathen fool. Get down there."

The tramp kneels on the barroom floor.

The madness is beginning, and around it the talk goes on and on.

These people talk like prisoners, or dog soldiers, or shipwrecked sailors. There are strippers or a band, for this is a big money day for the bars in this part of town, the biggest. Some don't talk at all. They sit there like carved monkeys, rotting in booze, so sodden they might have been drunk from the time the monks invented the cork, from the time the sap of the palm tree was used to make wine. In eighteenth-century England, liquor sellers used to provide basements strewn with straw where those who had become insensible were dragged to lie until they were fit to drink some more. No such respite is allowed now – not on Mardi Gras. It is Mardi Gras in the bars, and later it will be Mardi Gras on the worm-eaten, bird-pecked benches, or in alleys, or on gravestones. Amid lights and music and then amid dessicated sputum, blood, and garbage.

Already the street lights are on, highlighting a particular slouch, a flailing hand brandishing a bottle, the convulsive strain of a drunken laugh. Two drunks stack up a third against a wall, as if he is a plank. They remove their hands slowly, carefully. Their friend pitches to the sidewalk.

"I just like to sit there and watch everybody get totally blasted," my companion in the welfare line-up had said earlier.

A young blind woman, drunk, runs her fingers over a parking meter, over and over again. A haunting image. It is clear she cannot figure out what she is touching. A madman walks in a tight circle nearby, shadow-boxing.

"Why do they have to go crazy like that?" people ask. "Why can't they budget their money?" To them this orgy is as incomprehensible as a jungle rite.

Oscar Wilde wrote: "To recommend thrift to the poor is both grotesque and insulting. It is like advising a man who is starving to eat less."

And so it is.

They have been picking the crumbs of Sally Ann soda crackers out of their bedding for the past few days, or begging, or living off soup lines. Very few have had any cash money for at least a week before today. So now they overcompensate. Cash is anonymous, the equalizer, and for this one day, for Mardi Gras, they will be more equal. They will pay and pay. The paying is as intoxicating as anything the money buys. Every panhandler and cab driver knows welfare day is the best time to work the streets.

But other factors, more concrete, also militate against thrift.

Most of the rooms available at welfare prices are sleeping rooms, as mine was – rooms without a fridge or stove. You can buy a plug-in frypan or a crockpot, but without a fridge you have to go shopping virtually every day or the food goes bad. As any housewife knows, this is a most uneconomical way to shop. Budgeting becomes a day-to-day thing, a daily battle against temptation that the men and women on welfare are destined to lose, month after month. It would take a far stronger person than I to handle it. I lived for the last two weeks of that month on twenty dollars, and it was no fun at all. The following month was even worse: my budgeting went completely awry; I had no money; I got sick; and I realized much better the vulnerability of the people who populate downtown rooming houses and hotels. I came to understand why some hotels check the rooms each day for deaths.

That first month I was new to it, though. I did not know that the psyche must be budgeted, even if the money is not. Especially if the money is not. I began to be frightened. I was so desperate for money I took some paperbacks I had accumulated to a bookseller. I needed the couple of bucks they would bring. An employee was minding the store, and he had no authority to buy books, so I left them there for the owner to price when he arrived. I went back a couple of times, but the owner did not show up. These delays gave my need an extra urgency out of all proportion to the circumstances. I became almost frantic to get the money, a condition I had seen other men in and wondered at, one that could impel a murderous rage over the slightest trifle. I would have sworn it would never happen to me, but it had. The same impulse that drove people to go for their welfare cheques early each month instead of waiting until the line-up had dwindled sent me to haunt the bookstore. The effects of poverty on the nerves are cumulative indeed.

But poverty is no problem on Mardi Gras. Drugs are given away as grandly and openly as hashish was distributed in eighteenth-century India; rounds are bought for whole tables, groups of tables, for the bar. These are the most generous of consumers. Today they will tip the waiter a dollar a round, two dollars a round. Next week they'll be a couple of bums fighting over empties, over enough pennies to get starched on Lysol, or hairspray and wine, because it's the best high they can afford. After that they'll be going through the change slots in telephone booths, through the garbage . . .

Now, though, they live with an abandon like that which is said to exist in a leper colony or a city stricken with plague. The coin in the pocket is devalued on receipt by the urgency with which it has been required. Spend, spend, spend. Even though every penny spent today brings a curse down on tomorrow.

The volume is up now. The band is playing. There is a huge fat woman right in front of the bandstand, and she's here to have a time.

"Eat my shorts," she tells the singer.

"Cook 'em first, I like 'em well done," he sneers.

"Don't look at me with love in your eyes, lust in your heart, and nuthin' in your pants." She's up on her feet now. And she's stung him.

"I got plenty in my pants, lady."

"Well, if you go to bed with me you'll never go back to women." She looks at her buddies, preening and wobbling. They stamp their feet, clap their hands, yell her on . . .

The singer, who doesn't know when he's beaten, says: "You sure got a big body, lady."

"It's big, but a road map comes with it."

Outside, nests of lights illuminate the streets polished by rain. The concrete looks a bit sticky, like candle wax. It is populated by insubstantial phantoms seeking frivolity in a place where nothing is proscribed. From one bar to the next they go. Up above, windows are propped open with beer cans or soy-sauce bottles, for those who remain inside, the thrifty, the born-again, the party goers, the abstainers . . . They don't want to miss Mardi Gras either. Over all is a Rosicrucian, a gaslight aura. Occasionally, a bottle is thrown from a window to smash in the street, drawing eyes up to those lighted chambers, which attack the spirit anew, as much in the occasional signs of an effort at orderliness to be seen there as in the overwhelming seediness.

Hastings Street feeds off its own misery. The sullen, bullying waiters, the timid novitiate air of the slummers, the police patrols, the chairwarmers in hotel lobbies, the prurient social workers trying to squeeze from all this an essence with which they are comfortable, which can be explained. And the pathetic walkabouts by politicians and press – people from another planet – when yet another household-cleaning product is dramatically exposed as a popular intoxicant. "What do they think goes on down here," one guy asks, "polo?"

On Skid Row the reality is four rubbies spending an afternoon pouring down a mixture of hairspray and alcohol. They drink it down, screaming and beating the air with their fists, and when it is gone they look around for something else to drink, anything. They pick up a bottle they find lying in the grass. It is bitter and they stop drinking it; then, one by one, they fall down. One tries to get up and falls down again flat on his ass. Three of the four men die. At the inquest it is said that the substance in the bottle is strychnine, a poison used to kill gophers and other pests.

The reality is the way this Mardi Gras would end for two young men with six grams of black hash. They would do the hash and then they would break the top half off a Coke bottle, spray Pam cooking spray into the bottom half of the bottle, and breathe it in. They would go to hospital. One of them would die.

Lysol disinfectant spray had long been attracting attention and a measure of outrage. Skid Row shopkeepers had been selling tons of the stuff, which had a 68 per cent alcohol content, to wasted remnants of men . . . killing them. But there are many such alternatives to liquor, more than any sober imagination could conjure up.

I met men, alcoholics, so sick of booze, so heartsick, and yet so helpless to stop drinking, that they got rid of their money immediately and deliberately in one binge, so as not to have to worry about temptation the rest of the month – to be forced on the wagon. Once the money was gone, the theory went, they would be far more peaceful. Now they would be able to say, as Henry Miller put it: "The only thing that stands between me and a future is a meal. Another meal."

After Mardi Gras comes the abyss, the counting of pennies. Thirty dollars into twenty days, ten dollars into fifteen days. Nothing into a week and a half. You buy a carton of milk, fifty cents, and when you get it home you find it is sour. Your anger is unimaginable.

If you didn't pay your room rent before you got drunk you walk up and down looking for a place to flop, by the week, or maybe by the night. Maybe something will turn up. But it never does. You end up on the street.

Dammit, you have to get out of this cycle, hit the road. . . . Somewhere there will be an exit, a job, a woman. But this drinking. It's killing you.

# 18

*The unhappiest person in the world*
*is the chronic alcoholic*
*who has an insistent yearning*
*to enjoy life as he once knew it,*
*but cannot picture life*
*without alcohol. He has a*
*heartbreaking obsession that by*
*some miracle of control*
*he will be able to do so.*
— From an Alcoholics Anonymous booklet.

The closest branch of AA held its meetings in an old brick building just across the parking lot from my hotel. In a bizarre didactic, a drunk was actually sick right in the doorway as I approached. Protest or accident? Who knows. I had to step over the watery vomit to get inside. Up a flight of stairs in a large plain room the meeting had already begun. The chairman was calling for members to give testimony. Each one walked to the front and began in the traditional way: "Hi, my name is _____. (first name only) I'm an alcoholic."

The room was full of people, mainly men, largely a Skid Row crowd. One man, better-dressed than most, said: "I should have been a doctor now. I'm a disgrace to my family."

He said he had slipped off the wagon three times since joining AA, each time after periods of sobriety lasting around three or four months. On the final occasion he had come around in a hotel, sick and crying. He opened the window to jump out, he said (he was on the seventh floor), but something held him back. Now after six months of sobriety he claimed he was starting to see results – some "spiritual and emotional development" as he put it. He gave thanks for his family, who had stuck by him, and for AA.

"I love you and I need your fellowship," he told the meeting, completely openly and earnestly, in conclusion.

He was obviously an educated man, dressed in a white sweater and slacks, with gold jewellery around his wrists and neck. He was overdressed, in fact, for the group. Beyond the rudiments of cleanliness and some attempt at neatness the others seemed largely unconcerned with their appearance.

A woman rose next and walked to the lectern, which was situated at the front of the room under a list of the twelve steps – the key to the program.

She said she had been a drinking housewife. She was drinking a gallon of wine and twenty-four beers in a day. One night her husband, at his wits' end, tricked her into getting into the car and drove her to a psychiatric clinic. They put her in a group session. When it was her turn to speak she said she did not know what she was doing there. "I just drink socially," she had said. "But I was puffy-faced and perspiring," she now told the AA members. "I was obviously a drunk."

The speaker who followed her at the group session, she went on, looked directly at her and said: "I am an alcoholic and I fell off the wagon. That's why I am here."

His honesty, the woman said, shamed her into being honest with herself and with others for the first time. From the group therapy she had gone on to join AA. Ebulliently, she praised God and AA. Almost never is the AA dissociated from God in the minds of its members. It is sometimes as if the fellowship *is* their God.

One young woman, obviously a newcomer, was asked by the chairman to offer her testimony. Embarrassed, she said she had come in support of her boyfriend, who was seated next to her. Then, quickly, she added: "But I know it could happen to me. I had an alcoholic father and have been surrounded by alcoholics all my life." Her boyfriend did not speak then, but later he got up and said simply: "My name is _____. I am an alcoholic." He sat down without giving any further testimony, but knowing he had taken that first vital step.

Another man, more typical of the group, said he kept getting drunk and then fighting. He said he knew that if he kept drinking "somebody will blow my head off."

There was a desperateness in the way he spoke that held the attention of the group. He told them he had to go into hospital soon and might have to have his arm amputated. This crippling injury had been sustained while he was drunk. He finished his testimony by saying: "Hell, if I had any money I'd probably be out there drinkin' and fightin' right now, Mr. Chairman. So next time don't ask me to talk, okay? I'll just listen and I might finally learn something."

All this was delivered with an anger at himself and a hopelessness that made it the most moving testimony of the night.

Alcoholics Anonymous was started in 1935 by a New York stockbroker and an Ohio surgeon, both considered hopeless drunks. The heartfelt confessions have been part of the program ever since. Nowhere are they more fascinating – or more important – than among the Skid Row community. For these are not just reformed or reforming drunks. They are men practically back from the dead. Most of them have been through detox, prison, mental institutions – not once but many times. They have been poisoned, robbed, beaten, stomach pumped, pistol whipped, force fed, starved, and frozen. But their testimonies, whether given at AA or during Salvation Army services, are revealing not so much for what they say as for the response they get. Then one realizes just how conscious of their position the men and women on Skid Row are. The applause, the calls of congratulation for a brother or a sister who has made it without booze through another day, or another week, are so heartfelt it makes the skin crawl. No paperbacks or newspapers are read during these confessions. There is not a sound, usually, or a smile, unless it is on cue, in support of a quip. There is unadulterated respect and, I think, love, of a kind I have never seen before in a communal situation. Respect and love from people without the will for the battle (in the case of the Salvation Army congregation) for the individual who is fighting back. These are people who know from their own experience that there is no battle with higher stakes.

On another level these testimonies, patently truthful, confirm what I had found in private conversation – that there are inescapable common factors uniting most of the men and women who become transients and who end up on Skid Row. Inescapable and mundane. Bad relationships with parents (especially the father), poor attendance and performance in school, lack of will power in pursuing conventional goals (though not in all things), and essentially romantic natures, addiction to the sense of freedom produced by constant change and movement.

# 19

*Once I loved to roam, but now I stay at home.*
*All you punchers, take my advice;*
*Sell your bridle and your saddle,*
*quit your roaming and your travel,*
*and tie onto a cross-eyed wife.*
— Old cowboy song

The sobbing boy, who had been silent for several nights, started up again early one morning. It was the most awful sound. On a horror-movie soundtrack it would have silenced an audience for as long as it played. Racking sobs, as if over a fresh grave. Utter, unrestrained despair. The little room could not contain his grief, and he flung open his door and burst out into the hallway. He went to the other end of the building somewhere so that his cries became fainter. Then he rushed back.

These outbursts would be preceded by a diatribe in which he worked himself up. He would talk to himself, in his room or in the hallway, as if he had a companion who was listening. Always it seemed to be about money. "Run up five thousand dollars' worth of debt, just like that," he would say. Or: "Ten thousand dollars. He's crazy. Cra-zee."

I had never clapped eyes on him at this point, and I had never heard anyone else talk to him. There was an unspoken conspiracy to leave the corridor to him when he unleashed his despair. It has been said that we are always fearful of the level of society below us. My neighbours, humble though they were, obviously were given pause by this man.

I dwell on him because he was more typical than I would ever have believed. There were many, many sick people living in our inner cities, and especially in the Skid Row areas. My Victoria friend, Ricketts, once told me about a neighbour he had had. Long before dawn the sweeping would begin in the hallway – a retarded kid sweeping the corridor every morning for more than a week, walking up and down with a broom, hour after hour. Ricketts went out to confront him.

Under the bare bulb hanging in the hallway the boy continued to push the broom. The door to his room was open, and in the doorway clothing was piled neatly.

"Stop that," Ricketts said. "People are trying to sleep."

The boy stood stock still and then began to tremble as if nerves were flashing throughout his body. Then he began to hiss with his lips drawn back from his gums.

"Do you know what it's like to have a piece of your brain missing? Do you?" His eyes stood out, he stamped his right foot, and the thin veins bulged on his forehead.

At the hostel in Victoria I met a young man who told me a long story about how he had been kidnapped and taken to a morgue, where a doctor removed his brain. He was in such bad shape, his habits so untamed, that he had been given the use of two bunks. He slept in the lower and the mattress from the upper was draped down to obscure him from view, as if he were a wild animal.

I could give ten more such examples. People not eccentric but sick, receiving no apparent help or support, except that offered by the low-life community around them.

A guy who worked in the hotel said, about my neighbour: "He's loony tunes. But we can't get him out. We've got to give three months' notice, and then the government wants to know why the eviction – we have to have witnesses. We've stopped trying to evict these people. Let the other tenants complain."

"Go to the desk and complain," he told me.

"Look, if I do that and he's out on the street where's he going to get another room?"

"So you lose your sleep," he said.

One evening I was trying to read, and the wailing, the berserk rage of frustration from the hallway, was so bad I went out to confront my neighbour.

I swung open my door. He was at the end of the hall, out on the fire escape, an old wooden stairway with a platform that flanked his room. His back was to me, and he had no shirt on. He was huge, a good middleweight build, with big muscles and a broad back covered in hair. I had expected a much smaller person. He turned when he heard me. His face was crumpled, like a crushed beer can, like the face of a newborn, the eyes slitted from crying. He turned away, weeping, but more quietly, and I closed my door. Later he began wailing loudly once more. By now I had made up my mind to confront him, but I thought it would be pointless to do so while he was in the throes of one of these spasms. He had disturbed my sleep, and I decided to disturb his. At about 2:30 A.M. I rapped on his door. Then I tried the doorknob, and the door opened. "Anybody in?" I called into the darkened room.

There was no reply, but when my eyes got used to the dark I made out his shape in bed at the back of the room. "You awake?" I said, and I repeated it until the head moved on the pillow and he said, very quietly, "Yes."

"I live across the hall, and you've got to make less noise," I said. "I'm not going to hurt you, and I'll help you if I can, but you have to keep the noise down so I can sleep. Understand?"

"Yes," he said. And I shut his door.

I was not optimistic, but in fact my visit had a remarkable effect. There were no further disturbances for a long time, indicating, I suppose, that he did have some control over his behaviour.

The hotel employee who had advised me to complain about my neighbour had also told me there were many men living in the hotel now who spent most of their lives in the bush. They were going crazy in their rooms, he said. They had nothing to do, no money, and no prospect of work for the first time in their lives. They were living like rats.

Despite the occasional electronic sounds — TV and the music from the bar – there was generally a stifling muteness to the place. One guy upstairs, above me, used to unburden himself by banging on the steam pipes, the way prisoners communicate from cell to cell. As time went on, though, my own reaction was the opposite. My room seemed to impel a monasticism from which these intrusions detracted. I began to resent any noise at all, even the faint pipe-screech of taps turned on and off.

My next-door neighbour, whom I had heard banging his furniture around when I first moved in, was truly lonely, I think. He, too, would talk to himself in his room or in the hallway, quietly, but with dramatic fluctuations in tone interspersed with half-throttled cries. "God damn it!" he would sometimes shout desperately, but whether at a recent annoyance or some long-nursed grievance it was impossible to tell.

I'd spoken to him a couple of times, and he had always withdrawn in awkward shyness. He was going on for fifty, with an economical build and light hair. I had him pegged for a camp cook, or perhaps a guy who had worked in the mines years ago. I swear he was so lonely he would walk down the hall and flush the toilet for something to do, to get a response. Yet his shyness prevented him from talking to others. His clothes hung off him untidily. He had so little shape he was like a walking sack, feet splayed, shoulders stooped, irresolute, like a pathetic, silent-screen funnyman.

I heard him talking in the hallway once, with a woman.

"You're lost," the woman's voice said. "You're missing somebody." She sounded like an older woman, left over from the night before, kicked out of somebody's room. Lost herself, probably.

"Oh, well . . . " my neighbour said.

"I've been married three times, but all my husbands are dead. How many times you been married?"

"Oh, I never . . . " he stuttered. When he talked to himself his speech was unimpaired, but when he talked to anyone else he had a stutter.

"Been in love?" she asked. She hissed the question, like spit on a stove. I could picture my neighbour, transfixed by this spotlight-glare of sudden interest.

"You want to be looked after," the woman announced.

"Government's been good to me as far as that is concerned," he hedged.

The woman gave him an address. "I live there. They'll look after you there," she said.

Then she got tired of him. She wanted a cab. She lived three blocks away.

"You can walk," he said.

"No, I want a cab," she told him. And I heard him go down the stairs to find her a cab.

Once a different woman visited him in his room, a loud, domineering woman who berated him in a fishwife screech for several hours. Perhaps she was his ex-wife, perhaps his sister.

There is misery inside the rooms and outside on the street, but you might think that at least from the air this area of the city looks like any other. It doesn't. It is a human garbage dump on the ground and an actual garbage dump if you climb up a few stories. There are huge, rotting dumps of garbage on the roofs of all but the highest buildings on Skid Row. For decades people in upper-storey rooms have simply tossed their garbage out of their windows onto the adjoining roofs. If you take a light plane or a chopper over the city you fly first over a world of imbricated roof shakes, from cedar to tarpaper, mixed in with the flat tops of highrises and stores, and then you reach it. And you know it when you see it. Skid Row. Like a signpost, the rotting heaps, cans, bottles – the detritus from a thousand meals – loom below. I could see it outside my own room, right outside the window. It fell from above onto the ledge between my own window and that of my neighbour. Cigarette packages, matchbooks, spent matches, bread crusts, bits of onion, cellophane wrapping, toilet paper . . .

What would seem to be inexcusable, animal behaviour on the part of individuals, however, is largely part of an institutionalized degradation imposed by slum landlords who don't collect garbage or provide basic facilities. It is such an old story, people say. It has been going on so long. Why doesn't somebody force these people to clean up their act? There are fire hazards, buildings that should be condemned, people living with rats and fear. Why can't we do something about it?

Let's take an example – not an entirely hypothetical one. As I heard it, it happened pretty much this way . . .

A partnership owned a slummy hovel, a rooming house. It had borrowed, say, $200,000 at one time or another from a certain contact. To repay him the partners leased the building to him for a nominal sum, and he collected the rents from the rooming house in repayment of the debt. Repairs or renovations were his responsibility, so he put in a caretaker to look after things. There was a fire, which killed several people, followed by a public scandal. There were no fire alarms in the building, no sprinklers, extinguishers, or exit doors.

At the inquest a spokesman for the partnership said: "I knew we had leased some property to Mr. X, but I was never inside this particular property before the fire. Mr. X was supposed to keep the place up, though we had no written agreement to that effect."

Mr. X said: "I was never inside the property. Nobody told me any repairs were needed. I had a man who collected rents, and he was supposed to fix the place up."

The man who collected rents was a recent immigrant, a ship-jumper who spoke no English. Through an interpreter he said he had no money to make repairs. He simply delivered the rents to a certain real-estate office each month in return for a free room. He did not know the law. He had never seen Mr. X personally.

What had seemed at the outset a cut-and-dried matter, a scandal, thus became a matter of "mere" neglect, of a badly run business. Perhaps there was a lack of liaison, a pass-the-buck attitude, but who can be blamed for that . . . ?

Inspectors were dispatched in the wake of the inquest to check all rooming houses in a crack-down greeted with a great deal of fanfare by the press. But it was hopeless. There were too few inspectors with too small a budget and too little power.

Reforming interest fizzled, not to be revived till the next tragedy.

There were no jobs during this period. At the downtown employment centre, over a period of weeks, I came across only one unskilled job that could possibly be filled by the unemployed transients now adrift in the city – and then only by the fittest of them. It was sorting and cleaning bricks – rummaging in demolition debris to find whole bricks, chipping off the cement, and cleaning them. The pay depended on the number of bricks processed, but to make four dollars an hour a man had to sort and clean 1,200 in a working day. More than 150 bricks an hour, two or three a minute, in the depths of a wet winter. Filthy, freezing work.

The following appeared in the want ads around this time: "Well-groomed people who enjoy working with the public are required for hostess/host and reception. Laid-off nurses, flight attendants, models, waitress-waiters with good dispositions would be ideal for the above. Willing to train. No experience necessary. Please apply to Bosun's Locker, Hotel Vancouver, Monday at 5 P.M."

I could hear the hubbub from outside the hotel. Inside, the lobby was awash with people and perfume. The line-up of well-groomed jobless, four deep, curled back from the elevator banks right down the centre of the wide foyer – cutting off the well-groomed with jobs from their rooms. Hundreds of men and women, mostly young, all out of work. Several times I encountered these massive turnouts when jobs did surface. It brought home both the severity of the recession and the speed with which it had developed. Two years earlier, when I set off, there would have been no such turnout. Now there seemed no end to the hardship. The mingled perfumes in the Hotel Vancouver lobby that day gave off a stifling odour, but it was nothing to the odour of recession, one that seemed now to be entrenched.

I went to work in a phone room, selling carpet cleaning. There are always jobs for commission salesmen. I had been initiated early in my journey. Now these were practically the only jobs.

It was a typical phone room, bare except for the desks and telephones and the big blackboard where sales were recorded. There was just one poster on the wall, one of those irritating exhortations without which no office is judged complete: "Without dreams there is no need to work. Without work there is no need to dream."

The salespeople, almost all high-school students, worked one of two shifts – four or five hours either in the morning or evening. They made hundreds of telephone calls each shift from various telephone directories to homes, offering to clean the living room, dining room, and hallway for $29.95. It was a good deal, and it wasn't hard to sell if you kept at it. But the work was wearing in its boredom, the parrot-like repetition of a simple pitch. I'd taken the work only to prove I could get a job if I had to – but I would end my shifts stiff-jawed, tight-stomached, and dry-mouthed. And it proved nothing much. These sales jobs are not for the vast majority of the unemployed, who are used to working with their muscles and would be even less prepared for the inactivity and silly glibness.

While this type of work provided for some young people, many others were stalking the streets as if their inner compasses had gone wild. They had gone through the school system and, at the end of it, they had been told that their job prospects were zero. Some of them, now on welfare, watched television in hotel lobbies with middle-aged men who no longer expected much either. It was interesting to see them, sitting in front of the TV screen, trying to make sense of what a politician or civil servant was saying about them and their future.

I would look at the older men in the audience, the spittoon philosophers – such faces, such scarred characters, such lives they had led – and then at the screen. Two different worlds. The people who governed did not have the faces of the men who found gold or logged the woods; they did not look like the descendants of fur men or railroad builders. They didn't look like anything much. The men who watched were like the moraine deposited by an old, old glacier. The end of a time.

In the early days their predecessors spiked railroad ties, harvested wheat, cut lumber, at different times of the year, in different places. Blanket stiffs they were called, because they carried around the blankets in which they slept. Unskilled itinerant workers. The rootlessness and volatility of these men has been acknowledged by historians. They covered greater distances than the Bedouin nomads. They were unparalleled as drifters. Until after the Depression they were inhibited by no border, for it was easy to get itinerant work in the States. We needed them, and we used them. They suffered criminal conditions on railroad construction and in lumber camps, in coal and hard-rock mines. In a courageous battle early in this century the Industrial Workers of the World tried to organize them and fight for them. They told the wandering stiffs: "You have produced too much and have allowed it to fall into the hands of a bunch of parasites who do no work."

But the IWW was killed off by other unions who wanted a piece of the action, by the establishment who hated and feared them, and by the great Depression, when mounted policemen spurred down this same Hastings Street where the unemployed now watched television, clobbering demonstrators, the displaced who had moved west, as they have always done when pursued by bad times.

The men who build a country, who do the really hard, filthy groundwork, are no good for much once that part is done. Nobody is whining about that, least of all the spittoon philosophers, who know it better than anybody. At least we've got a bed, they'd say if you asked them. For tonight. The blanket stiffs were gone. This was their posterity. And all these men could think about was a seat in front of the tube, a bed, and a meal.

If then, in this environment, a man got lucky, got a job, there was a deliriousness to it. On New Year's Eve, in the bar beneath my room, I met the happiest man I'd seen in all my travels. He was an ironworker in his fifties who had just that day landed a job in Sarnia, Ontario. He was leaving on a bus at midnight for Calgary, and from there he would take a plane. He had been out of work for two years.

Now this man beamed. Everyone who came within his orbit was infected. He was completely sober and utterly happy. He said he had been calling the union hall every couple of days all the time he had been out of work. He had called just the day before and been told to call back after the holidays. But something made him call New Year's Eve and the job was there.

It was only one man, one job, but in that chilling climate it was infectious.

What battles that man must have fought in two years. What crow he must have choked on, what a distance he must have travelled into hopelessness before the lifeline was thrown to him. Constantly we underestimate the problems of the unemployed, the disadvantaged, the poor, the sick.

Skid Row serves as an example. We can rationalize it. The city started here with a saloon, and so what if there are now ten saloons, twenty saloons? That's progress. If we could leap the gap for a moment we would see what an appalling place it is, a monstrous perversion of our system, stripped of any hint of morality or Christianity. The extension of Skid Row is a concentration camp where everything, including gold teeth, is ripped away and the bodies are tossed in heaps. Nothing that is clean survives there. Literally. During my sojourn there was no laundromat on Vancouver's Skid Row, or anywhere near it. All those rooms, all those people whose struggle to hold onto a shred of pride, a feeling of cleanliness, is already a terrible one – and not a washing machine on the horizon. When I first moved in I couldn't believe it. I asked a mailman. "I don't know of one within thirteen blocks," he told me. "I guess they figure the equipment will be wrecked."*

And so it is made that much easier for people who already have problems to fall totally into a state of neglect.

Skid Rows are dominated by dirty businesses. They are places to shake a man down, or set him up: hotels where rooms are mere cribs in which to sleep drinkers until the money is gone; grocery stores whose staples will always include large quantities of anything cheap and poisonous that can be sniffed, snorted, eaten, or drunk; rooms like filthy lairs; pawn shops. Every type of human misery squeezed into one area to propagate. Because of that gap between what we know and what we do black can be made into white. Perhaps black becomes such a deep stain we are forced to distort it. In other neighbourhoods the number of bars is restricted for all sorts of petty, aesthetic reasons. On Skid Row, where booze kills people, where the arc of the bottle is actually that of the Reaper, there are six to a block, all illustrating the truth of

*AUTHOR'S NOTE: Since this was written a laundromat has opened in the heart of Vancouver's Skid Row district.

191

the old English adage: "Where there's muck, there's money," the adage that put small children to work in the coal pits.

We are not talking about charity, about helping people who can't help themselves. We are not talking about saving drunks from themselves – none of the people in my book are habitual drunks. We are talking about putting tools back in the hands of people who know how to use them, or who could learn. About recreating a future we, through neglect and indolence, have let slip away from our children.

There are greatness and great evil side by side in the shadows beneath the gold windows of our office towers. But the future is on those dingy street corners, too. Not just the future of the destitute and homeless, but all our futures. Something must be done . . .

This is not the end of the journey. We'll take you out into the fields for a breath of fresh air in a minute. We'll manage to find hell, it is true, even among the flowers. And then back to the city for a last look. But here is an appropriate place for some reflection. Perhaps the reader who has come this far might want to throw back his head, close his eyes, and consider the weight of the life to which he has been introduced.

If there was a war tomorrow, the men and women in these pages and their counterparts all over the land would line up in their thousands to be slaughtered. Not out of bravery, though they are extraordinarily brave, far braver than you or me, but out of wisdom, impelled by the same old cry – death or liberty. For the very poor have no liberty, make no mistake. And we would cheer them as heroes out of a hypocrisy as deep and dark and endless as a jungle.

The challenge inherent in the system we have chosen in this country is maintaining reasonable equilibrium between the riches it will produce for some and the poverty and hidden suffering it will inevitably bring to others, if unchecked. We are failing.

Parts of our major cities are ghettoized by people with no jobs and no money. The alleys behind luxurious high rise apartments have been infiltrated by an army of men and women, with shopping carts or shopping bags, who live off our garbage. The streets are full of runaway children, like the legendary gamins of the streets of Paris in the early nineteenth century, of whom Victor Hugo wrote: "They are at once a national emblem and a disease."

Where can these people go, what can they do? There are no jobs for them, there is no longer any accessible land from which they can feed themselves. All doors have been closed except the one that leads to the depths. Continue to make of these people, as we are doing, a race of desperadoes who want everything around them in ashes, and the future will be a terrible one. If we want to wait until the sight of the misery of the poor makes us sick we will not wait long.

Who will flood this underworld with light? The politicians won't do it. Just look at them. The weight of the belly has deadened the heart and mind. And they don't want to do it. Poverty has always been the bloodstained dipstick they use to show the rest of us how well we're doing. Never, of course, to be blatantly waved, but never to be wiped clean either. The press? They feed, as never before, at the same trough. Laws have never protected the poor. The church is often exploitive. No, it will take many, many decent people carrying small torches to bring this abyss into the light of day . . . holding the torches to the heels of those in power, forcing them to deal with this single, all-important issue.

And it is a single issue, even though it is jobs and housing we are basically talking about. The issue is the horror of this life so many are forced to live.

Jobs and housing, then. Why not just make a start, for God's sake? Force city governments to do what they should have done long ago and tear down the rotten rooming houses and slum hotels whose landlords have, for years, scoffed at every standard for decent housing. These places are firetraps, sinkholes, garbage dumps, prisons, lunatic asylums. They are sitting there in the heart of every city. Tear them down and employ the unemployed tenants and others from poor neighbourhoods to build new, decent, housing. Appeal to industry to donate heavy equipment, lumber, concrete, nails, tools, free expertise where it is not available within the community. How could they refuse? What a simple thing to do. Start with one building, in Toronto or Winnipeg or wherever. The Brotherhood of Labour will surely not object to such a project. Meanwhile their membership must be put back to work, financed, at least in part, by pension-fund money or dues. The unions must initiate, far more aggressively, projects, however small or experimental, that will put tools back in the hands of their membership. For it is a very small step from the union hall to Skid Row, as more and more men and women are discovering. Perhaps, when they lose their homes and apartments, some of these people can be housed on the broadloom in our air-conditioned employment centres until society can accommodate them. Then watch the speed with which the moribund staff get to work. It'll be like watching a volcano, long considered dead, blow itself to smithereens.

Churches and community centres can provide meeting and hiring halls for these projects. Individuals can contribute money. Allow those who can only work a couple of hours because of their physical condition to work only two hours; let women work alongside men; and let volunteers look after the children. The light, once introduced, will spread. But we must force some action. No more studies, no more speeches. Nails to be hammered, trees to be planted, lumber to be sawn and hauled, people to be saved. If the politicians tell you they can't create jobs laugh in their faces. Force your church or charity organization or government to end the degrading line-ups that give this book its title. Deliver the food or clothing yourself, if you have to – and you will have to. Ordinary people, understandably cowed and enslaved by massive waste, insanity, cynicism, greed, and ridiculous rules and prejudices must demand that this one problem – acute, visible, disgusting poverty – be tackled, in this richest and newest of lands.

The contemplative reader will have a hundred ideas for my one. They will fill his head so that he cannot sleep. And we must not sleep without taking one small step toward making one of those ideas come to pass.

# Epilogue

Hour after hour the women stood at the long wooden tables amid mountains of flowers, eternally separating blooms from buds, daffodils from narcissuses. Chinese, Japanese, East Indian women, they stood on scraps of sacking or cardboard so that their feet would not freeze on the concrete floor. With fast hands and elastic bands they tied the flowers into bundles of ten. The pay was $3.65 an hour. It was the annual daffodil harvest on the island.

Out in the fields it was raining, had been for days. Cutting daffodils is backbreaking labour at the best of times. When the fields are wet it is coolie work of the harshest kind. But hundreds of pickers slogged through the mud for the minimum wage – for this year it was the only work to be had. Some quit after a few hours, handing in the numbered badges that identified them and the cheap knives with which they had cut the stems of the flowers. But for every one who quit there were five or ten to take his place, people desperate for a job – any job.

I had escaped the fields through luck – the trucks had already left with the fieldworkers on the morning I hired on. So I was put inside, to tie.

When I first entered the tying shed it was like being transported, in a dream, to some previous life.

There were more than a hundred people tying, almost all women, only half a dozen of them whites. The noise level was high as a variety of tongues competed. Dozens of times a day an abusive forewoman harangued the workers. "It's tie time, not talk time," was her unchanging slogan whenever she felt that the fluting conversation was interfering with the work. "You can't talk and count," she announced, threatening to send the loudest out to the fields or fire them outright. Most of the women neither spoke nor understood English, but the staccato noise faded for a while after each rebuke, to return again as inevitably as a tide.

We started work at 7:00 A.M. and continued until 5:00 or 5:30 P.M. In all the intervening time we tied flowers into bundles of ten. The women worked with dexterity and energy. There was a fifteen-minute break in the morning, and one in the afternoon, and a half an hour for lunch. The women ate lunch out of thermoses with chopsticks, or nibbled on chapatis and exotic sweetmeats. During lunch the unchained babble of languages was deafening, and the yellow and brown faces flashed in the dingy recesses of the boiler room where we ate, bundled against the cold. We sat on the floor or on a couple of benches, or, more pleasantly, in an adjoining hothouse planted with tulips. The washrooms, just off the tying shed, were tiny and filthy, swimming in dirty water and rubbish, the sinks and toilets blocked and useless.

It was a long day, and several of the women were quite old, but they all remained cheerful and unflagging. When they ran out of flowers they would shout, in pidgin accents, "Flower, flower," and it became my job to dump another box of blooms in front of them. They would break out in great tinkling exclamations over the state of the flowers, the position in which I had dropped them, the sticky wetness of the stems, or any one of a dozen other things that remained a mystery to me. Though they were packed in the shed like battery hens there were no quarrels – just the bewildering concert of rapid fingers and even faster tongues.

There were a few white people in the shed, including two older women, a pair who had, strangely, reached the same place in quite different ways, and whose stories spoke, in a simplified way, of the fascinating dilemma of transience *versus* security that had, in large part, prompted my journey.

One, a genteel, grey-haired woman, an unlikely figure in that turbulent room, was trying to earn enough money to go to Oregon to visit with her guru. In late life she had become a disciple of a sect that advocated pleasure, an uninhibited joyful lifestyle. She told me she had lived very conventionally until she got cancer of the cervix in mid-life. She tried every possible cure, orthodox and otherwise, but it was only when she lost her guilt feelings and, believing she was about to die, began to do things she had always dreamed of doing that the cancer cleared up, she claimed. She travelled, slept on beaches, got rid of almost all her possessions, and worked when she could – and she was still doing it. In fact, this surprising woman, at least sixty years old, was the most exuberant proponent of the transient life I had met.

The other, though a grandmother, was younger and quite different.

She must have had her children at an early age, for she couldn't have been much more than forty-five herself. She said she had never had a vacation in her life. Not once. She had always been too busy or too broke. She wanted to travel now, she said, but she would always want a home, a place to go back to. She was working to earn enough to visit her daughter and grandchildren in Calgary.

The work was over quickly. The daffodils would be in the stores for Easter. Everybody was paid off on the same day, field hands and inside workers. Somebody said there were fifteen hundred of us. We lined up for hours, since the company had only one woman paying out cash through one window. Like a villain strayed from the pages of *The Grapes of Wrath*, the company clung to the ignorant, exploitive role to the end.

In *Country Life* magazine, B.C. Federation of Agriculture President George Aylard said: "Farmers have few choices. Our ability to provide workers' benefits is limited [by] the price we receive for our products. No one is prepared to pay more for food, and consequently we cannot afford a lot of additional benefits."

So filthy toilets overflow, as they have in these places for decades, workers are underpaid, exploited, abused, herded like cattle, and treated like thieves when they try to collect their pay. Mr. Aylard's special pleading notwithstanding, the limits are imposed, as they were when Steinbeck wrote, by greed and monumental ignorance.

I stayed during this period, as I had almost two years before when the recession was first beginning, at the hostel. I had come full circle; and so, it seemed, had the hostel – there was a new director and a completely new staff. Nothing else had changed, however. The problems were the same – there were just more of them now.

One morning there was an old man in the director's office. A very old man. His dirty grey hair was down his back. His coat was held together with safety pins. The director was trying to get him out of the hostel. The door was open, and from the corridor I could hear the conversation.

"You don't understand," the old man was saying. "You've got a job. You just take –"

"Why don't you take your money and get a place?" the director interjected.

"That's what they told me at welfare. It's not so easy. They want so much for these places. I can't sleep in the cemetery."

There was a minute of silence, and then the old man said: "I have a hernia, too. I had an operation, but it's not right."

Suddenly he lost all restraint. He began to whine. "I'm eighty-six," he said. "I'm desperate. I'm near suicide. You people don't understand . . . it's a terrible time. I'm sick. I should be in the hospital."

"You can't be sick," the director said. "The hospital wouldn't have sent you here."

And on it went. I thought, as I had thought a hundred times before in the past couple of years: Why doesn't somebody do something? Why doesn't the director, or welfare, or somebody, go out and help this eighty-six-year-old man with a hernia find somewhere to live? Why don't they get off their butts and do it? Why don't I?

Instead the problems of individuals seemed to go round and round like birds, always coming back to roost. So many rules and regulations, so many departments and budgets, and nobody to show an eighty-six-year-old man with a hernia to a room where he could live in some peace.

The thoughts, probably naive, are recorded as they came, and demonstrate my increased anger and agitation as my exposure to the havoc around me increased. What began as a fairly objective odyssey had embittered me, as the recession was embittering so many others.

A group was marching the length of the island to protest unemployment. Meanwhile, hundreds lined up for hours outside the Victoria employment centre because they had heard they could apply for jobs in a new company – only to have their hopes dashed when the centre's doors opened. They were only taking names and addresses today so that job application forms could be mailed out. There would be no interviews. There had been no need to queue. There were, as yet, no jobs. Oops, sorry folks. Just another little gaffe.

Back in 1932, in "The Experiences of a Depression Hobo," an anonymous writer said: "My spirit is by no means broken. I just feel angry, and the more Canada kicks me the more I'll retaliate . . .

"Until such time as I get a decent job I intend to live well, dress respectably, eat all that's good for me, keep myself clean and have clean clothes. Canada generally will pay for this. I will obtain what I need by bumming and other comparatively honest methods. If such

ways and means should fail, I shall resort to thieving and other criminal ways . . ."

In the spring of 1983 I walked the waterfront through the night with a
homeless transient who told me he had already robbed one bank during the recession and was planning to rob another.

"I want to work," he said. "I don't like stealing. But I'll take it any
way I can. I'm not going to be a bum."

In the dawn we saw men going to work on the fishing boats, getting
the boats in shape for the season. Working for nothing, in the hopes of
landing a deckhand job.

One way or another, the survival instinct showed itself, as it had not
done since the thirties.

To eat was the prime concern, and Victoria churches had rallied to
aid the unemployed in a far more vigorous way than their counterparts
in Vancouver. In the mornings there was bread and soup in the basement of St. Andrews Cathedral. They called it the 9-10 Club. Three
nights a week there was a soup line at another downtown church. This
was in addition to the Upper Room (where I had once eaten Christmas
dinner with the Frenchman, Jean), the Mustard Seed street church,
which now ran a food bank, and the St. Vincent de Paul Society, which
was also giving away bags of groceries.

Every soup kitchen was full every day, and the volunteers who
staffed them did a sensitive job. No religion was forced on the jobless
here – only food.

Nothing was moving now out of the once-busy labour pool. The
men spoke of weeks between temporary jobs. After I finished on the
daffodil farm I sat in the pool every morning for a week. It was now
housed in a much smaller building. I started off with priority number 38
and barely moved. After a week I just gave up. Many others did so, too.
The better weather was coming. People were talking about riding
freights.

Back in my room in Vancouver, the rain on the window had become
indistinguishable from the scratching of the mice. Acoustic vibrations
grated through the room like a braking boxcar. The plaster ceiling had
collapsed in the hallway, and the rain dripped through into a garbage
pail. I was coming apart. I'd flown at the sick kid, the screamer, and I'd
berated my next-door neighbour, the older man. Increasingly, I felt my

dark side overcoming my charitable one, like mould forming on good, clean cheese.

The evening before I'd heard somebody calling me as I passed some dive on Granville, and I had kept going. What would I find if I stopped? Krishna chanter, pool shark, Ku Klux Klanner, drughead, tramp, hype, freak, born-again prophet, second cook from a fishing camp, rag-picker, panhandler? I didn't need it.

I checked out of the hotel. I left the few things I had accumulated – pots and pans, books – on the table at the head of the stairs for anybody who wanted them.

Outside, a bum with hair all over his face, like a man sprung from seaweed, pranced lasciviously in front of a leaping, snarling, half-crazed dog that was chained to a lamppost.

I went across the street to a greasy spoon. Through the window I saw a young man go by, a Christer, carrying a wooden cross bigger than himself. He was on the streets all the time with the six-foot cross on his shoulder. To the base of the cross, where it would have dragged on the ground, he had affixed a tiny, white wheel, so that it glided across the sidewalk.

I ordered something. As I ate I could see the hotel where I had lived. Two men came out of the tavern and turned into the restaurant. One was French, volubly drunk, the other a fat guy in a squashed cowboy hat held on with a string underneath his chin. He had the look and sound of a man worn out by drinking, worn almost sober.

"Something stopped me in the tavern," he said in a drugged voice. "I've been going down the drain but I'll pick myself up."

"I'll help you," the Frenchman said.

"No, you won't," the cowboy said wearily, but with a smile. "Today, yes, but not tomorrow. You can let me have ten dollars, though. If you give me fifteen I'll take it."

"You want fifteen dollars right now?" the Frenchman said fiercely, reaching for his pocket.

"No."

"I give you fifteen dollars right now."

After a minute the cowboy said in his tired voice: "We'll get a place. We'll live in the same house, and we'll play cards."

"Yes," said his buddy.

"I've been sick, but I'll pick myself up," the cowboy said.

The waitress came toward me with the check. I could see her sizing me up. Faded torn jeans, sweatshirt, work boots, beard, long hair.

"Cash or meal ticket?" she said.

"Cash."

ABOUT THE AUTHOR

Alan Mettrick is a journalist who became, in the course of researching and writing this book, a great many other things ... ditch-digger, fruit picker, straw boss, welfare bum. For almost two years on the road he struggled to survive with the worst victims of poverty and unemployment.

Mettrick has worked with major daily newspapers across Canada as a writer and editor, and has freelanced for magazines here and in the United States. He co-authored a highly praised book, *Thrasher ... Skid Road Eskimo*, about the violent, doomed struggle of a Northern native to survive in the city. His work has also been published in *Playback*, an anthology of the best Canadian non-fiction.

Alan Mettrick now lives in the Cariboo country of British Columbia. He has a son and a daughter.